German Universities.

CONTRIBUTIONS

TO THE

HISTORY AND IMPROVEMENT

OF THE

GERMAN UNIVERSITIES.

BY KARL VON RAUMER.

Reprinted from the American Journal of Education.

EDITED BY HENRY BARNARD, LL.D.,

Chancellor of the University of Wisconsin.

NEW YORK:

PUBLISHED BY F. C. BROWNELL,

NO. 12 APPLETON'S BUILDING.

1859.

INTRODUCTION.

The following Contributions to the History and Improvement of "*The German Universities*" constitutes the fourth volume of Prof. Raumer's "*History of Pedagogics*," and was translated from the last German edition, for the "*American Journal of Education*," by the Associate Editor, Mr. Frederic B. Perkins, Librarian of the Connecticut Historical Society. Prof. Raumer introduces his work with the following quotation, on the title-page, from Savigny's "*History of the Civil Law*."

"The Universities have come down to us as a noble inheritance of former times; and we are bound in honor to leave them to future generations with their condition improved as far as possible, and injured as little as possible."

The work is dedicated by the German author

TO THE

STUDENTS OF THE PAST AND PRESENT,

WHO HAVE BEEN MY COMPANIONS FROM 1811 TO 1854,

I DEDICATE THIS BOOK,

IN TRUE AND HEARTFELT LOVE.

The Preface is as follows:—

The reader here receives the conclusion of my work.

It is a contribution to the history of the universities. When I commenced it, I hoped confidently to be able to make it greater; but in proportion as I gained an insight into the difficulty of the enterprise of writing a complete history of the German universities, my courage failed. Many of the difficulties which the historian of the German people has to overcome, are here also found in the way, and in much increased dimensions.

If all the German universities possessed the same features, if the characteristics of one of them—important modifications excepted—would stand for all, then the task of their historian would, apparently, be quite simple. But how different, and how radically different, are the universities from each other!

Even the multiplicity of the German nationalities, governments, and sects had much to do in distinguishing them. To compare, for instance, the universities of Göttingen and Jena, as they were at the beginning of the present century; what a contrast appears between them! And how much greater is the difference between these two Protestant universities and the Catholic one of Vienna!

Further than this, each single university undergoes such changes in the course of time, that it appears, as it were, different from itself. To instance the University of Heidelberg: Catholic in the beginning, it became Lutheran in 1556, Reformed in 1560, Lutheran in 1576, Reformed again in 1583; afterward came under the management of the Jesuits; and, at the destruction of their order, returned to Protestantism.

To these difficulties, in the way of the historian of all the German universities, is added this one: that the most important sources of information fail him; as we have, namely, but few competent histories of single universities—such, for example, as Klüpfel's valuable "*History of the University of Tubingen.*"

These considerations will sufficiently excuse me for publishing only contributions to a history of the German universities, which will sooner or later appear.

What I have added under the name of "Academical Treatises," is also a contribution to history; for the reason that these treatises will, of necessity, not be worthless for some future historian of the present condition of our universities.

In conclusion, I desire gratefully to acknowledge the goodness of Chief Librarian Hoeck, for books furnished me from the Göttingen library. Mr. Stenglein, librarian at Bamberg, also most willingly furnished me with books from it. The use of the Royal Library at Berlin was also afforded me, with distinguished friendliness and kindness; for which I would once more most heartily thank Privy Councilor and Chief Librarian Pertz, and Librarians Dr. Pinder and Dr. Friedlander.

ERLANGEN, *9th April*, 1854. KARL VON RAUMER.

NOTE BY THE AMERICAN EDITOR.

In order to a full understanding of the basis upon which the university system of Germany rests, and to furnish the data for a comparison between our American colleges and professional schools, and the corresponding institutions of higher learning and special scientific instruction in Europe, there are from time to time published in the "*American Journal of Education*," accounts of the Gymnasia, Latin Schools, Lycea, and other institutions of secondary education, and also of the Polytechnic Institutions, Schools of Arts, Science, Agriculture, &c., of the principal states of Europe.

In this place we can merely remind the reader that, in order justly to estimate the absolute and relative excellence and value of the German universities, and their systems, as compared with our American colleges, he must always bear in mind the great differences between the states of society in which the two classes of institutions exist, the different ages of their undergraduates, the different classes of avocations into which their graduates enter, and the different tests of attainment which are applied to these graduates before their entrance into actual life.

UNIVERSITY OF WISCONSIN,
MADISON, *June 4th*, 1859.

CONTENTS.

PAGE.

I. HISTORY OF THE GERMAN UNIVERSITIES.

I. THE GERMAN UNIVERSITIES.

(Translated from the German of Karl von Raumer for this Journal.)

I. Introduction.

The foundation of the earliest German universities took place at a time when both Italy and France had long possessed them. Tacitus' saying of the youth of Germany, "*Sera juvenum pubertas,*" is equally applicable to the development of her intellect.

Among the oldest universities of the middle ages,* we may here remark upon three—Salerno, Bologna, and Paris.

The school of Salerno was an extremely ancient school of medicine; a sort of isolated medical faculty, which had no special influence upon subsequent universities.

At the University of Bologna, law was the leading study. The origin of the university is obscure. At the diet of Roncaglia, in 1158, it received from Frederic Barbarossa a grant of privileges which has often been referred to on occasion of the issue of charters to later German universities.†

The organization of the University of Bologna was materially different from that of all the later German universities. This appears from the fact, that in it only the foreign students (*advenæ forenses*) had at Bologna, complete rights of membership. They chose the rector, and their assembly, summoned by the rector, was the proper university. In this assembly the teachers and professors had no voice, but were wholly dependent upon the rector and the university.‡ This single fact shows clearly enough, that Bologna was not the model of the German universities. Paris served in that capacity, especially for the earliest; such as Prague, Vienna, Heidelberg, &c.

The University of Paris differed from that of Bologna chiefly in that theology was its prominent study,§ and also in respect to its organization. At Paris, the authority was exclusively in the hands of the teachers, the scholars having no part whatever in it. As a rule, only actual professional instructors could be members of the governing assembly, and other graduates only on extraordinary occasions.

* The following brief sketch I gather chiefly from the clear and thorough account of Savigny. (*History of the Roman Jurisprudence in the Middle Ages*, vol. ii. 2d ed. 1834.)

† Compare, further on, the charters of Archduke Rudolph and of Albert of Austria, to the University of Vienna.

‡ For later extensions and changes in the university, see Savigny, l. c.

§ In Paris, however, only the canon law, proceeding from the Church, could be read,—not the civil law; and this prohibition was not removed until 1679.

Both teachers and scholars were divided into four nations: French, English or German, Picard, and Norman. Each nation had a procurator at its head; as their subsequent derivatives, the four faculties, had each a dean.

The rector was chosen only from the faculty of arts (of philosophy), and, indeed, only from masters in that faculty.

To the university belonged colleges, some of which were foundations for the poor, and others pension (boarding) institutions for those in good circumstances. One of these colleges was the Sorbonne, founded in the year 1250.

In discussing the German universities, especially the oldest, we shall repeatedly refer to the organization of the University of Paris. We have no complete body of statutes of this university, but can arrive at a near approximation to them, from various sources. For some of the German university statutes, as for instance those of Vienna, repeatedly declare that they wholly follow the organization of the Paris university; so that we may consider them, in substance at least, as representing those which formed there, in fact if not in statutory form, a common law.

II. List of the German Universities in the Order of their Foundation.

The universities of Germany were founded in the following order:

a. In the 14th Century.

1. Prague, 1348.
2. Vienna, 1365.
3. Heidelberg, 1386.
4. Cologne, 1388.
5. Erfurt, 1392.

b. In the 15th Century.

6. Leipzig, 1409.
7. Rostock, 1419.
8. Greifswald, 1456.
9. Freiburg, 1457.
10. Ingolstadt, 1472; transferred to Landshut in 1802, and in 1826 to Munich.
11. Tübingen, 1477.
12. Mentz, 1477.

c. In the 16th Century.

13. Wittenberg, 1502; removed to Halle in 1817.
14. Frankfurt, 1506; removed to Breslau in 1811.
15. Marburg, 1527.
16. Königsberg, 1544.
17. Dillingen, 1549.
18. Jena, 1558.
19. Helmstädt, 1576; dissolved 1809.
20. Altorf, 1578; dissolved.
21. Olmütz, 1581.
22. Wurzburg, 1582.
23. Grätz, 1586.

d. In the 17th Century.

24. Giessen, 1607.
25. Paderborn, 1615.
26. Rinteln, 1621; dissolved in 1809.
27. Salzburg, 1623.
28. Osnabrück, 1630.
29. Linz, 1636.
30. Bamberg, 1638.
31. Herborn, 1654.
32. Duisburg, 1655; dissolved.
33. Kiel, 1665.
34. Inspruck, 1672.
35. Halle, 1694.

e. In the 18th Century.

36. Breslau, 1702.
37. Göttingen, 1737.
38. Erlangen, 1743.

f. In the 19th Century.

39. Berlin, 1809.
40. Bonn, 1818.
41. Munich, 1826.

III. The German Universities of the 14th and 15th Centuries.

A.—CHARTERS.

The origin of the universities of Bologna and Paris is uncertain, as is that of the two English universities of Oxford and Cambridge.

The origin of every German university, however, is known. German princes, either temporal or spiritual, founded them, except a few, such as Erfurt, Altorf, Strasburg, and Cologne, which were founded by honored town magistrates. The memory of these founders has been acknowledged by naming the universities after them.*

That such a grateful memory is well deserved, appears from the charters which they gave to the universities; which show clearly the sincere benevolence, and noble princely conscientiousness, with which they cared for the temporal and eternal well-being of their subjects, as well as their real respect for learning, and recognition of its value to men.

These characteristics are to be discovered even in the decree issued by the Emperor Frederic Barbarossa at the Diet of Roncaglia, A. D. 1158, in favor of the teachers and students of Bologna; and which has furnished a precedent for many charters given to universities by later princes. In this decree the emperor promises his protection to the students and professors during their journeys to and from the university city, and their sojourn there. "For," he says, "we hold it proper, if all those who do well deserve in all ways our approbation and protection, that we should protect with special affection against all injury, those through whose learning the whole earth will become enlightened, and our subjects will learn to be obedient to God, and to us, his servant." For, the decree continues, who will not sympathize with those who, when they have left their native land and exposed themselves to poverty and peril for the love of learning, often suffer misuse from the vilest of men, without reason? And the emperor threatens all, even the authorities, with fines and other penalties, if they shall disobey the decree.

From all the charters of foundation of the German universities, from the most ancient time down to the present, it would be difficult to select one better than another by way of example. All of them, so far as I know, display the same noble benevolence.

Archduke Rudolph IV. of Austria, in his charter† to the University of Vienna, founded by him in 1365, declares, "that as God has placed

* As, Albertina, Julia, Ruperta, &c. Sometimes a university has a double name: for the founder and for a restorer or some important benefactor. Thus, the University of Erlangen is named Frederico-Alexandrina, from the first founder, Margrave Frederic, and the restorer, Margrave Frederic Alexander.

† Schlikenrieder, 10.

him in authority over important territories, he owes thanks to him, and all benefits to his people. A profound obligation, therefore, rests upon him, to make such ordinances in the territory under his government, as shall cause the grace of the Creator to be praised, the true faith to be spread abroad, the simple instructed, the justice of the law maintained, the human understanding enlightened, the public good promoted, and the hearts of men prepared to be illuminated by the Holy Ghost. And if the darkness of ignorance and of error were dispelled, then would men, applying themselves to divine wisdom, which enters into no wicked soul, bring forth from their treasuries things new and old, and bear much fruit on earth. In order, therefore, to do something, though but a little, in token of gratitude to God, and to his honor and praise, and for the benefit of the human race, he has determined, upon ripe consideration, to found in his city of Vienna a university (*studium generale*)." In this university, continues the decree, shall be read, taught, and studied, that sacred science which we call theology, the natural, moral, and polite arts and sciences, canon and civil law, medicine, and other approved studies.

Similar terms are used by Rudolph's brother in the charter which he granted to the University of Vienna in 1387.* It is his sense of Christian obligation that causes him, in return for the princely station intrusted to him by God, to thank the Giver, and to exercise conscientious care for the temporal and eternal good of his subjects; and the university lies near his heart, because these good objects will be promoted by it.

Duke Ludwig of Bavaria expresses similar sentiments in the charter of foundation of the University of Ingolstadt, granted by him in the year 1472.† Among the blessings, he says, which the grace of God permits to men in this transitory world, learning is of the first. For by it the way to a good and holy life is taught, the human reason enlightened in right knowledge, and trained to good habits and morals, the Christian faith promoted, and justice and the common good established. "And as," he continues, "we are mindful that the divine mercy has for a long time maintained our predecessors and ourselves in princely honor and glory, and has in a sensible manner guided our people and our kingdom, we recognize it as our duty to give thanks for this goodness, and to exert our earnest and assiduous industry that learning shall be instilled into men's minds, that their senses and reason may be enlightened, the Christian faith extended, and justice, good morals, and good conduct promoted. And, therefore, to the praise of

* Schlikenrieder, 93.

† Mederer, iv. 42.

Almighty God, the strengthening of Christendom, the good of all believing men, the common profit, and the promotion of justice, we have founded a university in our city of Ingolstadt."

Five years later, in the charter of foundation of the University of Tübingen, in 1477, Count Eberhard* says that "he has often had it under consideration how he might best set about undertaking some enterprise well pleasing to the Creator, and useful for the common good and for his own subjects. He had arrived at the conclusion that he could begin nothing better and more pleasing to the eternal God, than to prepare means for the instruction of good and well-intentioned youths in the liberal arts, and in learning, so that they may be enabled to recognize, fear, and obey God. In this good belief, he has determined to found a school for human and divine learning."

Many like examples of the God-fearing spirit of the German princes, temporal and spiritual, could be adduced, testifying to their pure and noble objects in founding universities. In reading these testimonies, the belief is necessary, that God's blessing must rest upon institutions so evidently founded for his glory and the benefit of men.

And that these pious expressions were not mere empty or hypocritical ones, not corresponding with the truth, appears from the many proofs of real love which the princes have bestowed on the universities, as well at their first foundation as in succeeding times; such as gifts, immunities, protections, honors, &c.†

As peace and quiet are necessary to students, Duke Rudolph of Austria gave to the University of Vienna a large and retired tract of land, with all its houses, gardens, &c. He promised to all its teachers and scholars coming thither, and to their servants and goods, his safe conduct, which they were to obtain from the authorities whenever they should enter his territories; and the same promise was made for their return. If they suffer any damage, it is to be made good to them. Neither are they to pay any toll for their property or goods.‡ All the officers of the university, even including the beadles, he freed from all assessments and imposts. To these prerogatives Rudolph added this: that members of the university, even in criminal cases, should be almost or quite altogether under the jurisdiction of the Rector's Court.

---

* Klüpfel, p. 2.

† It is not my design to give full accounts of the endowments, immunities, &c., of single universities, particularly as Meiners, Dieterici, Koch, &c., have written upon them. I shall cite only a few items in relation to them, especially such as have most connection with the intellectual history of these institutions.

‡ "And if any one shall presume to receive any toll or custom for passing such goods, let him know that he shall incur our heavy indignation."

The endowments of the different universities were derived not from the single source of gifts by the princes who founded them—each university has a financial history of its own. The Popes,* in particular, gave much assistance to them, by granting them various sorts of income from the property of the Church—benefices, tithes, &c. After the Reformation, the property of many convents was given to the universities; and at the dissolution of the Society of Jesuits, in 1773, their estates were distributed, even to Catholic universities.†

B.—THE POPE AND THE GERMAN UNIVERSITIES.

In early times, when the German princes desired to found a university, they commonly made previous application to the Pope, to issue a bull for granting the foundation and its privileges. Thus, Clement VI., in 1347, issued a bull for founding the University of Prague; Urban V., in 1365, for that of Vienna; Alexander V., in 1409, for that of Leipzig; Pius II., in 1459, for that of Ingolstadt. In like manner, in 1389, Urban VI. granted to the city of Erfurt permission to found a university.

The contents of these bulls were in substance always the same. The Pope, as head of all the faithful, declared it his duty to do all in his power to promote the prosperity of learning, by which the glory of God is spread abroad, and the true faith, law and justice, and human happiness, are promoted. Therefore he willingly authorizes the foundation of a university (*studium generale*), as prayed for, and grants it all the privileges of universities already existing, which are commonly cited by name. In particular, he grants to the four faculties the right to teach, and to promote the scholars, according to rule, by gradations, to be bachelors, licentiates, and masters; and he authorizes those so promoted to teach everywhere. It was this permission especially, which, according to the early doctrine, the Pope only could grant, as standing at the head of all Christendom. From this circumstance also, it may be, the name *studium generale* is derived; not from the fact that the institution includes all four of the faculties, but because the graduates of a university founded by the Pope, were recognized as such by all the Christian universities of Europe, and so had the privilege of teaching everywhere.‡

---

* See Meiners, *History of Universities*, &c., 2, 8, &c.

† That of Prague, for instance. Tomek, *History of the University of Prague*, 340.

‡ Urban V., in his bull of 1365, constituted the University of Vienna of three faculties, but without a theological one. This omission was supplied by Urban VI., by his bull of 1384, in which he granted the request of Duke Albert: "We have deigned, out of our apostolical benignity, to grant that in the same university lectures on sacred theology may be publicly read, and that the honors and degrees of bachelor, licentiate, and master, in the said theology, may

The bull usually complimented the city in which the university was to be established. Thus, Ingolstadt is praised for its pure air, and its abundance of the necessaries of life; and it is observed that there is no other university within a circuit of a hundred and fifty Italian miles. Frankfurt, in like manner, is praised for its healthy air, its wealth in the means of life, and its abundance of proper lodgings for students; and Leipzig, not only for the productiveness of its vicinity and its favorable climate, but because the citizens are polite and of good morals.*

The Pope's bull designated some high ecclesiastic as chancellor of the university, one of whose duties was to be, to see that degrees were orderly conferred. At Prague, for instance, the Archbishop of Prague was made chancellor; at Vienna, the Provost of the Church of All Saints; at Frankfurt, the Bishop of Leubus, &c.†

C.—THE EMPERORS AND THE UNIVERSITIES.

According to what has been said, the Pope's bull sufficed to give the university standing and currency in the religious world; but the inquiry remains, whether they did not need a grant of privileges also from the emperor, who was also King of Rome? Charles IV. authorized, as King of Rome, the charter of foundation which he had given to the University of Prague the year before (1348), as King of Bohemia;‡ but no imperial grant is mentioned as having accompanied the Papal one at the foundation of those of Vienna, Heidelberg, Cologne, Erfurt, Leipzig, and Ingolstadt.§

It was only from the time of Maximilian I. that the emperors seem to have treated the founding and assistance of universities as an official privilege of their own, which they were bound in conscience to assume. That emperor, in 1495, at the Diet of Worms, even made

---

be conferred in order as is accustomed to be done in the universities of Bologna or Paris, or Cambridge or Oxford. . . . And we have further ordained that, in the said town there shall be a university (*studium generale*) in theology." The theological teachers are to possess the same privileges as in Bologna and Paris; especially that of orderly creating bachelors, licentiates, and masters; who being so promoted, shall thereafter, "without any other examination or approbation, have full and free authority to govern and to teach, as well in the aforesaid town as in any other universities whatever, in which they may choose."

* Gretschel. The University of Leipzig, p. 18.

† As an example of the bulls for founding universities, I have inserted (Appendix I.) the bull of Pius II., of 1459, for the foundation of the University of Ingolstadt, already mentioned. The oath contained in it to be taken by each scholar, of faithfulness and obedience to the Pope, is worthy of attention.

‡ Tomek, 4.

§ I found no imperial grant for Vienna in Schlikenrieder's *Chronologia Diplomatica*. May the reason have been Duke Rudolph's enmity to his father-in-law, Charles IV.? But Mederer's very full *Annales* give no imperial charter for Ingolstadt; and as to Leipzig, Gretschel remarks (p. 18) that this university never received any imperial confirmation. Neither does Motschmann give any for Erfurt.

the proposition that each elector should found a university in his own territories; which proposal may, perhaps, have occasioned the establishment of the universities of Wittenberg and Frankfurt.

All those universities founded after Maximilian's time, down to the end of the German Empire, were required to have an imperial grant; as Halle, in 1693, Göttingen, in 1737. The last Protestant university founded by the emperor, was Erlangen, in 1743. But what was the relation between the imperial and papal grants? Did the emperor define the temporal, and the Pope the spiritual, privileges of the institution, and was the Pope's authorization required before that of the emperor? These questions would be difficult to answer.

The Emperor Maximilian, in 1502, granted a charter for founding the University of Wittenberg. In this he declares himself bound, as emperor, to care for the promotion of learning in his realm. He grants the request of the Elector Frederick, for the foundation of a university* at Wittenberg, and the appointment of teachers in the four faculties. He grants further, the power of creating, after a fair and strict examination, bachelors, masters, licentiates, and doctors in all the faculties; who may thereafter possess all the rights and privileges which the doctors of the universities of Bologna, Paris, and Leipzig possess, in all places and countries of the Roman Empire, and in all other places.† And he also grants to the university the privilege of making its own statutes and choosing its own rector.

This imperial grant was recognized by Cardinal Raymundus, and, at the request of the elector, authorized; the latter hoping, says the cardinal, that the university will truly prosper, having, besides the imperial foundation, the light of the apostolical splendor. Thus the Pope, in this case, assumes a place subordinate to the emperor, and the latter grants privileges before only proceeding from the former. A doubt, however, remained, although the cardinal had confirmed the establishment by Maximilian of the four faculties, whether valid degrees could be given in theology and canon law without special authority from the Pope; for which reason he expressly adds this authority supplementary.

Maximilian I., in the year 1500, granted a charter for the foundation of the University of Frankfurt, which corresponds in substance with that of Wittenberg, and which, like it, makes no mention of a papal bull. Pope Julius II. issued such a bull in the year 1506, and

---

* "*Studium generale sive universitatem aut gymnasium.*"

† "*In omnibus locis et terris R. Imperii et ubique terrarum.*" And in the imperial charter to the University of Frankfurt it is provided that those having degrees, "shall have license in whatever other universities, without further examination, to read, teach, and do all other things which the masters and doctors of any other universities may do."—*Becmann*, 10.

confirmed it by another the next year; and in both of these, he in his turn makes no reference whatever to the imperial charter, and provides for every thing as if no such thing existed.*

While the subsequnt founders of Protestant universities (of which Marburg was the earliest) naturally did not apply for papal bulls, still the Catholic emperors from time to time made grants to such universities. Thus, Charles V. did so in 1541, for Marburg; Ferdinand I., in 1557, for Jena; Maximilian II., in 1575, for Helmstadt; Ferdinand II., in 1620, for Rinteln; Leopold I., in 1693, for Halle; Charles VI., in 1737, for Göttingen; and Charles VII., in 1743, for Erlangen.

These grants were all similar in substance and in part word for word. But in the later ones, the rector or pro-rector, for the time being, of the university, at Erlangen the pro-chancellor, is granted the countship of the Holy Lateran Palace, and of the Court of Cæsar (count palatineship).† As such count palatine (pfalzgraf), he possessed singular privileges,—might appoint notaries; might appoint and displace guardians and curators; restore their honor to the infamous; legitimate illegitimate children of all kinds,‡ and create poets-laureate. These latter might freely read, write, and dispute upon the art (*scientia*) of poetry, in all countries of the Roman Empire, and everywhere; and in all places might enjoy the privileges, honors, &c., of poets-laureate.§

One circumstance relating to the University of Königsberg deserves special notice. Although Margrave Albert, in 1544, granted it a charter of foundation wholly Protestant in character, yet he, together with Sabinus, first rector of the university, applied to Cardinal Bembo,

---

* Whole portions are transferred word for word from the imperial charter to the papal bulls. An expression in the second bull seems to explain the matter. Julius II. mentions that his predecessor, Alexander VI., had already in the sixth year of his pontificate (1498), granted permission to the Elector John to found a university; which was two years before Maximilian's charter. The latter, it would seem, referred to the papal grant only in this, that he appointed as chancellor the Bishop of Leubus, whom Alexander VI. had probably designated for that office, and whom Julius definitely appoints, without any reference to the imperial charter. For a specimen of the imperial charters, see Appendix II.

† So the protector at Halle and Gottingen. Ferdinand II., in 1623, granted the count palatineship to the faculty of jurisprudence in Ingo!dstadt. This university, he says, "is the palæstra where we remember with kindly affection that our own youth was educated." For further information on this countship, see Dufresne, *sub voc., Comes palatinus* and *Comitiva.*

‡ The charter to Halle (Koch, i., 458), and that to Göttingen (Gesner, 6), enumerate "*naturales, bastardi, spurii, manseres, nothi, incestuosi.*"

§ Hedwig Zaunemannin, of Erfurt, composed a poem for the dedication of the University of Göttingen, ending with the lines:

> "Long may live this Muse's home;
> And prosperous it shall remain,
> Until the universe shall fall with crash and flame."

And upon this it is remarked—"This most noble virgin, for this and other most elaborate monuments of her talents, deserved to receive the poetic laurel from the university."

with the request that the Pope, for the certification of the university, would issue a bull granting it the right of conferring degrees in course. Bembo answered that the Pope would do so as soon as a copy of the imperial confirmation should be laid before him; as Königsberg was under the emperor's protection, if not actually under his authority. As the emperor, however, granted no confirmation, no bull was issued, and Albert found himself under the necessity of applying to King Sigismund, of Poland, for a confirmation. He accordingly issued one, in 1556, giving the university all and every the academical privileges,—jurisdiction, right of making its own statutes, right of conferring degrees in course, &c.; and all the privileges possessed by his own University of Cracow.*

D.—ORGANIZATION OF THE FIRST GERMAN UNIVERSITIES.

A. *Four Nations.—Four Faculties.—Rector.—Chancellor.—University Endowments.*

The charter of foundation and the imperial and papal grants of privilege having been issued, the university could now come into active life. The founder first invited teachers, who in turn gathered scholars about them. Teachers and students both, in Prague, Vienna, Heidelberg, and Leipzig, after the manner of the University of Paris, were divided into four nations, and each nation appointed a master of arts to stand at its head as procurator.

This division into four nations was laid down by Duke Rudolph in his charter of foundation to the University of Vienna in 1365;† but was more clearly defined by the university itself in 1366, and, as is expressly declared, upon the model of Paris.‡ The first nation, denominated the Southern (*Australis*), was chiefly composed of Southern Germany; the second, the Saxon, chiefly Western and Northern Germany; the third was the Bohemian, and the fourth the Hungarian. This division was modified by Duke Albrecht in his charter of 1384, so as to call the first nation, the Austrian; the second, the Rhenish, including Bavaria, Suabia, Alsace, Franconia, and Hesse; the third, the Hungarian, including also Bohemia, Moravia, and Poland; and the fourth included Saxony, Westphalia, Prussia, &c.

At Prague, great importance was found to attach to the division

* Arnoldt, 58, &c.; and Appendix XI.

† Schlikenrieder, 27. "We ordain that all the clerks (clerum) of the university shall be divided into four parts, of which each shall include masters and students from fixed and ascertained countries, constituting one nation according to the characters and circumstances of each."

‡ "We, considering that the venerable University of Paris is, by reason of its experience, under better regulations than others, have thought proper to divide our own university into four nations, as that is divided, after its model, although under different names."

into the four nations* of Bohemia, Bavaria, Poland, and Saxony. The Bohemian included also part of Silesia, and Moravia and Hungary. As the Polish nation included Prussia, Lusatia, Thuringia, and other German countries, the Bohemian nation differed from all the other three, which were almost exclusively German. Thus it naturally happened that the Germans often outvoted the Bohemians on university questions. The latter, irritated at this, petitioned the Emperor Wenceslaus in 1409, with Huss and Jerome of Prague at their head, to decree that thenceforward the Bohemian nation should have three voices and the three other nations only one. This was the reason why five thousand teachers and students left Prague, and why that university, instead of being a universal German one, was afterward exclusively Bohemian. The seceders went mostly to Leipzig, and caused the establishment of the university there, to which they also transferred the division into four nations. This division was only disused in 1830,† although it had long lost its place in the other old universities, and had very seldom been introduced into those founded later than Leipzig.‡

In Paris, besides the division into four nations, there was a second, altogether distinct from it, into four faculties, which also found its way into the German universities. The members of newly founded universities, thus divided into nations and faculties, needed first of all to choose a rector as their general head. At Vienna, Duke Rudolph's charter of foundation directed, still after the model of Paris, that the four procurators of nations should be the electors, and that the appointee must belong to the faculty of arts (the philosophical).§ But nineteen years afterward, in 1384, Duke Albrecht's charter allowed the rector to be chosen from either of the four faculties.‖ The election was made in like manner at Heidelberg. The first rector, Marsilius von Inghen, was here chosen, in 1386, after the Paris plan, from the faculty of arts. But as early as 1393, Konrad von Soltow, a doctor of theology, was chosen rector.¶

---

* Tomek, 9, 10. † Gretschel, 288.

‡ At Frankfort, there were four nations, called Marchcia, Franconia, Silesiaca, and Prutenica. But afterward, only the distinction into four faculties was preserved.

§ Schlikenrieder, 27.

‖ Schlikenrieder, 96. "The four procurators of the university must elect a rector, who shall seem to them fit for that office, a professor either in arts or in some other faculty." The Vienna statutes of 1384, prescribe that the electing procurators shall swear, before electing, "that they will not undervalue any faculty, nor prefer it to another, but will elect a fit person, to whatever faculty he may belong, so ordering that the rectorate shall not always remain in one faculty." Impartiality as to the faculties was promoted by the statutory regulation that the four procurators should not always belong to one faculty, but to several. Ib. 127.

¶ Schwab, 4, 12.

Down to the present time, the rector may be chosen from any faculty; and an alternation is usually had among them all.

The electors must be "actual teachers, or men recognized as fit for teachers."* In Erfurt alone, one student, selected from the philosophical faculty, took part in the election.†

The rector was the head of every university department, of management, instruction, and discipline; but was bound to govern himself by the statutes. About him was placed a senate, which varied extremely in composition and authority at different times and in different universities. Although, for example, at Prague, a "university congregation," of masters and students together, was erected, which met twice a year, and a special "university council" besides it, this general congregation soon fell into the background, and there remained only a congregation of masters, scholars being excluded.‡ The Vienna statutes admitted bachelors and those who actually read lectures (*actu legentes*) to the "general congregation," but adds, that this is to be the regulation only until there shall be doctors and masters enough, as in Paris, to fill the congregation.§ The chancellor, as we have seen, was usually appointed by the Pope, and in general was a high ecclesiastic,‖ whose especial duty it was to observe that the degree of master and licentiate were properly conferred, and he must himself confer the degree of licentiate (*licentia docendi*).¶

At the head of each faculty stood a dean, who was chosen from the masters who actually read lectures; and these masters formed the council of the faculty.

The endowments of the universities began, as we have already seen, with the gifts of the princes who founded them, and with the ecclesiastical properties and incomes granted them by the Popes. They were augmented by other gifts, especially by private legacies; Heidelberg, in 1391, received a grant of Jews' goods.** At the Reformation, the estates of dissolved convents, and afterward, in 1773, those of the dis-

---

* Meiners, *History*, ii. 172.

† Motschmann, i. 328.

‡ Tomek, 12.

§ Schlikenrieder, 131.

‖ At Vienna the Chancellor was Principal of the Church of All Saints, at Prague the Bishop of Prague, at Ingolstadt the Bishop of Eichstadt, at Leipzig the Bishop of Merseburg. The chacellor, in conferring the degree of licentiate, represented the Pope; using the words, "I, by authority . . . of the apostolical see, which I here represent, confer upon you the license to read," &c. (Zeisl, 37). In Tübingen, the appointment of chancellor passed over, after the Reformation, to the rector and senate; and he conferred degrees, not "by apostolical authority," but "by ordinary and public authority."—*Klüpfel*, 54.

¶ For more information as to the degrees of bachelor, licentiate, master, and doctor, see the description of the faculties. "In Prague, there was no distinction between a master and a doctor, except that the degree of master was commonly conferred in the faculties of theology and arts, and that of doctor in those of jurisprudence and medicine."—*Tomek*, 17.

** Häusser, i. 300.

solved Order of Jesuits, were given to the universities. In most of the charters of foundation, as in that quoted of Duke Rudolph of Austria, many immunities were granted to members of the university; freedom from imposts and tolls, right of hunting, right to retail wine and beer; most of which have subsequently been taken away, by reason of misuse of them, quarrels over them between the members of the university and the citizens of the university town, and great changes in Church and State.

Among the university endowments belong, as pecuniary aids to study, bursaries, free tables, stipends, &c., which will be afterward considered.*

B. *The Four Faculties.*

We shall proceed to consider the organization for instruction, and the discipline of the older universities.

We have seen that the division into four faculties was transferred from the University of Paris to those of Germany. These faculties are the same which our universities now include,—of theology, law, medicine and philosophy; which last was anciently termed the faculty of arts. We shall speak first of this latter.

1. *Faculty of Arts.*

This derived its name from the seven liberal arts; namely, the *Trivium*, including grammar, rhetoric, and dialectics; and the *Quadrivium*, including arithmetic, music, geometry, and astronomy. These seven were commemorated in the following memorial verse:

"Lingua, tropus, ratio, numerus, tenor, angulus, astra."

In the title "Master of the liberal arts," these seven are referred to. The relation of this faculty to the three others was very different at different universities and different times. At Paris, the rector was chosen from this faculty by the masters in it; and the rule was the same, at first, at Heidelberg and Vienna, as we have seen, after the Paris model. The situation of this faculty was very different at Tübingen, where it was subordinate to the three other faculties, only its dean and two other members belonged to the senate, and its professors received smaller salaries than those of the other faculties.†

These seven liberal arts were the subjects of instruction in the faculty of arts, and they included many subordinate subjects, as did, especially, dialectics. We have programmes of lectures from various universities, as Prague, Vienna, Ingolstadt, Erfurt, which all agree

* The same may be said of the various pecuniary helps furnished in later times, mainly by the growth of medicine and the natural sciences.

† Klüpfel, 7, 56.

substantially on this point. The dialectic, ethical, physical, and other works of Aristotle, in such translations as were then extant, are everywhere the principal theme.* Together with these are found a few other books, as for instance those of Petrus Hispanus and Bœthius, which, like Aristotle's, were included under the comprehensive term, dialectics.

In grammar were given lectures on Priscianus, Donatus, the *Doctrinale* of Alexander de Villa Dei, and the *Græcismus* of Eberhard von Bethune, which is a grammar in metrical Latin, in which Greek technical terms are explained; upon the same author's *Labyrinthus*, which treats of the difficulties of schoolmasters; and upon the *Poetria Nova* of the Englishman Gottfrid, which treats of the duties of masters.†

To the course of lectures on the four arts of the Quadrivium belonged those:

1. On the Algorism (Arithmetic).‡

2. On the work of Johannes de Muris, of Paris (1330), on Music.

3. On six books of Euclid and the *Perspective*§ of Johannes Pisanus (Geometry).

4. On the *Sphæra Materialis* of Johannes de Sacro Bosco,‖ the *Computus Cyrometricalis*,¶ the Almanac, and the Almagest of Ptolemy (Astronomy).

Masters, licentiates, and bachelors were permitted to read lectures. The *scolaris simplex*, the student, was at Vienna prohibited from reading; but at Prague, the statutes permitted a student to deliver lectures put into his hands on behalf of a master, who had previously revised them. Reading was termed pronouncing (*pronuntiare*).** The statutes of the University of Vienna say: "We direct each reader to pronounce faithfully and correctly, slowly and distinctly, distinguishing paragraphs, capital letters, commas, and periods, as the sense requires, in such a manner as to assist those who write after him; and that he do not pronounce any thing erroneous by deceit or fraud."

---

* See Appendix II. for the programmes of lectures of the faculties of arts at Prague, Erfurt, Ingolstadt, and Vienna.

† *Monumenta Universitatis Pragensis*, 1, 2, 560.

‡ Algorism or Algorithm (see *Monum. Univ. Prag.*, 1, 2, 550), is composed of the Arabic *al*, and the Greek *arithmos*. According to Renaud's *Mémoire Géographique sur l'Inde* (1849), the word signifies the Arabian author Al-Kharizmy, whose works, translated into Latin, spread the knowledge of the Indian system of numeration in the West: which system was then named after this author. My respected friend and colleague, Prof. Spiegel, drew my attention to Renaud.

§ This *Perspective* (a work on optics) is of the year 1280.

‖ For Euclid and Sacro Bosco or Busto, see this work, Part 1, 6, 7, 317, 326.

¶ For cyrometricalis, read chirometricalis, the art of finding the dates of the calendar by means of the fingers.

** *Monum. Univ. Prag.*, 1, 1, 13; and Zeisl, 146.

This extract is explained by another from the statutes of Prague of 1367. The masters, it is here said, have brought it into consideration, that the readers have permitted themselves to be guilty of many irregularities, disfigurements, and errors, from which much harm may come to the students, and much scandal to the whole faculty. Every *scolaris* has read what he chose and when he chose. Men have boldly committed to writing incorrect and unknown compositions, full of errors, and given them out as the works of eminent masters, to attract more hearers. Hereupon the faculty decreed that in future every master should read, either himself or by another, his own comments upon such work as should be selected from among the text-books by the faculty; and in like manner might read or cause to be read by another the writings of others, provided these were composed by eminent masters of the universities of Prague, Paris, or Oxford, and provided he have previously carefully revised them, and have secured a fit and skillful reader (*pronunciator*).

The bachelors, it was ordained further, should not read their own comments on Aristotle and other difficult works, but those of masters from Paris, Prague, and Oxford; but these must first be examined by a master, to see whether they are in reality the composition of such author, and correct.

No student shall presume to deliver lectures, unless he be authorized by a master.

According to these extracts, the teaching consisted in dictating the matter of the regular text-books, and in the speaker's or some other person's remarks upon them; and the notes taken down served instead of printed copies of the books.

Before the commencement of the lectures, the masters of Prague and Vienna met and agreed upon the books which each one should take to read;* and it was the duty of each, having chosen his book, to read it through if he had as many as two hearers.†

The permission to read at Prague the writings of Oxford masters had a great immediate influence upon that university, and also upon the Reformation in Bohemia and Germany; for in this manner Wicliff's teachings were imported into Prague, and widely disseminated by Huss.‡

* *Monum. Univ. Prag.*, i. 1, 13; Zeisl, B. 4.

† The masters who read were called *magistri actu regentes*, and *lectores*. The Erfurt statutes required them to read during three months of the year. And in those of Prague (Monum., i. 1, 81), it is prescribed that "none shall be called an actual reader (*actu regens*) who does not read his ordinary (book) as long as he has hearers." In Prague, one who has been five years master, and two years an actual reader, became a member of the Council of the Faculty, whose sittings were in the faculty-room (*stuba facultatis*).

‡ Palacky, *History of Bohemia*, ii. 2, 189.

The lectures were accompanied with frequent disputations, in which teachers and scholars took part. The regular disputation day was Saturday. *Sophismata* and *quæstiones*, after the fashion of theses, furnished the basis for the disputing. The purpose of them all seems to have been not so much to deal with the truth of the matter as with the form; they were dialectic fencing with all the tricks of sophistry; exhibitions of skill in arguing for and against the same proposition.*

In all the faculties the bachelors were lowest in grade, the licentiates next, and the masters next. To become a master it was necessary, at Vienna, to have studied two years, and to have heard lectures in the regular books. The candidate was examined, and was obliged to hold ten disputations. If he passed this examination, and received his bachelor's degree, he might receive the licentiateship at the end of the year from the Chancellor, after a sufficient examination. He might now become master at his option by a formal act of promotion, unless he preferred to remain a licentiate for the sake of avoiding the expense of the step.

According to the statutes of the Faculty of Arts at Ingolstadt, inasmuch as there was a distinction between those students who followed the way of the ancients (i. e., who adhered to the Realists), and those who followed the way of the moderns, or Nominalists, there was a separate dean and council for each "way."† At Heidelberg, Nominalism prevailed; its first rector, Marsilius von Inghen, having been a Nominalist. In Tübingen, the opposition between the Nominalists and Realists ceased only at the Reformation; Gabriel Biel being, here, "the last representative of the dying scholasticism."‡

Lectures, disputations, examinations, and even the daily conversation of the scholars (*scolares*), were in Latin. The Ingolstadt statutes say: "A master in a bursary shall induce to the continual use of Latin by verbal exhortations and by his own example; and shall also appoint those who shall mark such as speak the vulgar tongue, and who shall receive from them an irremissible penalty." In another place they say: "Also, that the students in their academical exercises may learn, by the habit of speaking Latin, to speak and express themselves better, the faculty ordains that no person placed by the faculty upon a common or other bursary shall dare to speak German. Any one heard by one of the overseers (*conventore*) to speak German, shall pay one kreutzer."

---

* In Melancthon's time there was at Wittenberg a disputation on one Saturday and a declamation on the next; which indicates that dialectics had at first predominated, but that at the revival of classical literature, rhetoric, under the influence of Cicero and Quintilian, came more into vogue.

† Mederer, iv. 70.

‡ Klüpfel, 30.

The very Latin of these quotations exemplifies the Latinity of that university, which was lampooned in the "*Epistles of Obscure Men.*" Nothing was said in them of classical studies.

2. *The Theological Faculty.*

The Theological Faculty of the University of Vienna declares, in the beginning of its statutes of 1389, that the Faculty of Paris is its model. In the first title of these statutes it is provided that every year, upon the day of St. John the Evangelist, a devout sermon shall be preached upon that "most profoundly speculative theologian," and the Holy Scriptures and purity of conscience shall be recommended to the students. The preacher shall choose a text which has a complete and intelligible meaning; not an expression unintelligible by itself, which he can interpret arbitrarily.*

The second title of the statutes treats seriously and ably of the morals of theological students. It says: "As knowledge and learning in the Holy Scriptures, which are to be attained by study and practice in theological faculty, are the rule of morals, and lead to true propriety of conduct, we consider it exceedingly wrong and most unseemly that theological students should not be distinguishable from all others by their virtues. The spiritual eye must be very clear from sin in order to discern the lofty themes of theology. That science itself teaches that only the pure in heart shall see God; and that wisdom cometh not into the sinful soul, nor abides in a body under subjection to sin. Therefore, students of theology must show by their whole life that they belong truly and really to the theological faculty; and a religious life must be the expression of their spiritual acquirements. Therefore, students of theology must be free from shameful vices, serious and modest in speech, decent, respectably clothed—no drinker, lecher, or brawler—an avoider of evil companions; must shun suspicious places, and must not run after idle amusements. The schools of theology must be not merely schools of science, but still more, schools of virtue and of good morals."

While in the faculty of arts more than thirty subjects of instruction were specified, the theological statutes name but two: the Bible, and the "*Four Books of Sentences*" of Petrus Lombardus, which were of the first rank as dogmatic authority. The bachelors who read upon the Bible were called Biblical, or *cursores*, from their reading their regular courses, or the Bible. They were to explain the text thoroughly, and to add good glosses, as was the custom in the cursory lectures at Paris.

---

* Zeisl, 8, 10.

He who wished to become *cursor* must have studied theology six years, and if not master in arts, must be well trained in opposing and answering. The *quæstiones* upon which the disputations were held in the theological faculty, were to be intelligible and seriously useful (*rationabiles et seriose utiles*) upon practical or speculative subjects, and clear, brief, and intelligible.

When the *cursor* had finished his Biblical course, he became *sententiarius*, and read for one or two years on Petrus Lombardus' "*Four Books of Sentences*." When he had come in his readings to the third book, he was called *Baccalaureus formatus*. When he had arrived at the end of the fourth book, he had yet to train himself at the university for three years in disputing and preaching, and in attending disputations, before he could receive the degree of licentiate or of master.

The *cursores* or *sententiarii* were not to deal with philosophical topics, which have no relation to theology; but were, at proper places, by logic or other arts, to endeavor to solve theological difficulties.

When the *sententiarius* had passed his examination for a licentiateship, the chancellor delivered it to him, saying:* "By authority of the Omnipotent God, and of the Apostles Peter and Paul, and of the Apostolical See, which I here represent, I give you license to read, dispute, and preach in the theological faculty, and to exercise all other acts of a master in the same faculty, here and throughout the world, in the name of the Father, the Son, and the Holy Ghost. Amen."

A few days after this, the new licentiate maintained a disputation; and on the day after the disputation the chancellor placed the master's cap on his head in the hall, as a token of the dignity of master, and said: "Begin now your teaching, in the name of the Father, the Son, and the Holy Ghost. Amen." Whereupon the new doctor (*novellus doctor*) began with an address in praise of the Holy Scriptures.

3. *Faculty of Canon and Civil Law.*

The statutes of this faculty, at Vienna, prescribe that before beginning the lectures, a solemn mass shall be held, and Sundays and feast days strictly observed.

The second title treats in earnest language of the morals of bachelors and students at law. They are to conduct themselves in an orderly manner, and to be quiet at lectures; not to shriek, howl, or hiss, or laugh indecently, and not to yell at strangers and new-comers. In other places, they are in words, gestures, and clothing, to show them-

* Zeisl, 37.

selves students of moral science; to shun vile companions, especially infamous persons, brawlers, and gamesters; neither to attend public dances, nor to direct others to them; not to carry weapons, nor to have them carried after them, and not to write any indecent compositions.

The doctors are to read honestly, to omit no part of the ordinary gloss, but to read clearly, wisely, and intelligibly, both to beginners and to those further advanced, and always to endeavor to be useful to their hearers. They shall make their lectures complete, and not too brief; and shall willingly answer, especially after lecture, such students as may ask questions on doubtful points. The doctors, especially such as read lectures in the morning, are forbidden to make it known to their hearers by handbills; the practice being objectionable, and allowed by no faculty of jurisprudence.

The teachers are also bound to give an honest statement of their hearers.

The doctors in civil law are to form one faculty with those in canon law, even at examinations. Neither bachelors nor students, but only doctors and licentiates admitted to the faculty, compose it (in the strictest sense), and no others can become deans.

The dean shall, during his official term, diligently visit the bursaries and the houses of the students at law.

A student who has heard lectures on civil law for two years, and on canon law for two years, may become bachelor. Before becoming a licentiate, he must have studied seven years, and must have received a *baccalaureate*.

But this term of years will not suffice without proof of learning; and learning will not suffice without good character and laudable morals.

"As our faculty," the statutes proceed, "is above all others bound to protect the sacrament of matrimony, and to reject every unlawful union, since both laws express themselves in various ways opposed to such, and as, moreover, the doctorate is an honor, we decree, like all the other faculties, that no illegitimate child, or child of a harlot, may become doctor or licentiate."

The bachelor must prove his attainments by examination and disputation; as must also the licentiate, at whose examination the chancellor or his substitute must preside.

At the conferring of the doctorate, the candidate receives the doctor's hat (*birretum*) and ring, the shut and the open book, the master's kiss and blessing; after which he reads and disputes. To the doctor presenting him (that is, to the *præses* of this disputation), the new doctor must give fourteen ells of cloth, at two florins an ell; to the beadle, six ells, at one florin an ell; and to every doctor actually lecturing, wine and confects.

4. *The Medical Faculty.**

Medicine, say the Vienna statutes, is a truly rational science, both as to its theory and its practice. We adhere to and obey civil dignitaries, the Pope, bishops, and prelates. A weakly, inefficient pastor injures the Church much. Dukes, counts, soldiers, and the common people, who should serve to protect the State, are, if they lose their health, entirely useless. It is a recognized truth, and on this we lay most stress, that medicine cares for men even while yet in their mother's womb, and from their birth, through all their life, to their death, both by preserving and curing.

The candidate for a baccalaureate must have heard lectures upon the work of Joannicius, the first or fourth of the canon of Avicenna, and some work on practice, as that of Rasis Almansor. If he is a master in arts, he must have heard lectures in the medical faculty for at least two years; if a mere student, for three. He must be twenty-two years old, born in wedlock, and not deformed in body. If princes or others, whoever they may be, shall apply for a degree for one unworthy of it, reference shall be made to the statutes in refusal, and to the oaths which have been sworn by the faculty.

A candidate for licentiateship, if he has a degree in arts, shall have heard lectures on medicine for five years; if not a graduate, for six years. If he is found fit in knowledge and character, without canonical impediments, and not too effeminate of countenance, he may receive his degree at the age of 26, but in strictness not until 28.

The *Aphorisms* of Hippocrates and Galen are to be the basis of the examination.

The promotion of licentiates to the doctor's degree must take place in the Church of St. Stephen; where the new doctor must deliver an address in praise of medicine, and afterward a lecture upon any portion of Avicenna, Hippocrates, or Galen.

The custom of conferring degrees in church was observed down to a much later period. Thus Rehfeld received his, in 1634, in the cathedral at Erfurt. Meifarth first preached from Sirach xxxviii. 1, 9; after which appeared a representative of Divine Providence, who directed the dean to take his seat. The latter, as *promotor*, then delivered a discourse on tobacco, after which Divine Providence directed the promotion to proceed, upon which the candidate was consecrated at the altar.†

* Zeisl, 73.

† Motschmann, ii. 316.

In Erfurt, the bachelor of medicine swore that he would observe all things to which the oath of Hippocrates, of Cos, binds every physician. This oath begins, "I swear by Apollo Medicus, and Æsculapius, &c., and by Hygeia and Panaceia, and all the gods and goddesses, calling them to witness that I will fully observe this oath."*

C.—MORALS AND DISCIPLINE.

Before treating these subjects I think it necessary to make a few general remarks.

Robert von Mohl, in 1840, published his "Historical Account of the Morals and Conduct of the Students at Tübingen during the Sixteenth Century." He drew such important facts as he found from the archives of the university, in which, as he says, are many records of the life and morals of the students. But he adds, that "many interesting pages of that life remain entirely unilluminated by them; as more especially, the praiseworthy qualities, the quiet virtues of industry, and of labor for learning, which have not given occasion for any record, while faults and excesses have called for official treatment and perpetuation."

What Mohl says here, with so much truth, of the matters recorded in the archives of the universities, is as true of most of the histories of universities. Everywhere in them are displayed vices, violations of discipline, outbreaks of abandoned students, brawls among themselves and with citizens, even murders, abominable immoralities, and these are often related at length. Among all these noisy, hateful, and lamentable wickednesses, the reader is in danger of overlooking the fact that at the same universities, and at the same time when the same wickednesses prevailed, were often studying, in quiet and unknown, youths who afterward, as men, were the pride and ornament of their country.

Vice should not be concealed. No one who knows men, especially the young, will put faith in any historian who finds every thing excusable and as pure as the angels.

And, on the other hand, the university historian would be to blame if he should give such prominence to every thing evil, as to make one believe, finding the history of the university only a "scandalous chronicle" of the vile tricks and vulgarities of vulgar students and professors, that only evil prevailed. The faults even of the instructors should not be concealed, but should be held up as warning examples, with religious seriousness; nor should the narrative ever remind the reader of the heartless tattle which is so often, unfortunately, to be heard relative to the occurrences of the present day.

* Motschmann, ii. 304.

The universities were not immaculate at any time, or in any country. No human corporation is faultless. They are all gone astray; the expression holds of all times and countries. Human sinfulness remains always substantially the same; and so, in consequence, do human sins. What Augustine related more than fourteen hundred years ago of the universities of Carthage and Rome, has remained true down to the present day. Even the *eversores** of whom he speaks, villainous students who took a devilish pride in leading astray newcomers, have been extant from that time to this. But at that same time there was at the University of Carthage with them that Augustine who, through God's grace, afterward became the greatest father of the Church, and the strictest in morals. How frightful was the moral condition of Paris afterward in the 13th century! A Papal bull of the year 1276 excommunicates such students of that period as celebrated festivals by feasts, drinking-bouts, and public dances, and even "did not fear to play dice in the churches and on the altars where they ought to worship God."

What horrible facts does Jacques de Vitry relate of the University of Paris! He says: "Everywhere in the streets and squares of the city, public harlots dragged students to their stews almost by violence; and if they refused to enter, they immediately followed them, shouting after them, 'Sodomite!'" In one and the same building there were schools above and a house of ill-fame below. In one part the harlots were quarreling with each other and with their pimps, and in the other the students were disputing and contending noisily. Jacques de Vitry, who relates these abominations, lived in the 13th century, and his account agrees only too well with the picture drawn of that century in the bull of excommunication just quoted. And in that same century the greatest of the scholastics, Albertus Magnus, Thomas Aquinas, Bonaventura, were students and teachers at the University of Paris. Thus it appears that from the earliest period to the present, good and evil have existed in the universities together.† At the same time it should not be denied that good may have prevailed more at some one time, and evil at another.

To learn what evils prevailed at some one university at one particular time, it is only necessary to read those parts of the statutes which refer to the conduct of students and professors. The evils which they

* *Confessions*, 3, 3.

† The worst period of the German universities falls, as we shall see, in the time of the prevalence of Pennalism, nearly from 1610 to 1661; and within the same period belongs the student-life of some most excellent men; as, Simon Dach, born 1605; Paul Fleming, born 1609; Johannn Franck, born 1618; Paul Gerhardt, born 1606; Otto von Guerike, born 1602; Martin Opitz, born 1597; and many others.

cite on particular occasions, had almost certainly already become general in the university.

To refer, for example, to the statutes of the four faculties at Vienna, already quoted. When the theological students are warned not to become drunkards and lechers, to avoid suspicious places, &c.; when the students of law are directed to be quiet at lectures, and not to shriek, howl, or hiss, to avoid vile company, infamous persons, and brawlers, gamesters, &c., and so on, as might be cited from these statutes, it may be taken for certain that those who drew the statutes were obliged to insert these warnings, by the most disagreeable previous experience. And the facts which vouch for such warnings are frequently to be found in the records of the universities.

The like is true of what the statutes say with reference to teachers. If, for example, some master at Prague had not lowered the established honorarium for lectures, to attract more hearers, the statutes would not have prohibited the doing so.

We may here insert some prohibitions from the Vienna statutes.* The students, these say, shall not spend more time in drinking, fighting, and guitar-playing, than at physics, logic, and the regular courses of lectures; and they shall not get up public dances in the streets. Quarrelers, wanton persons, drunkards—those that go about serenading at night, or who spend their leisure in following after lewd women, thieves, those who insult citizens, players at dice, having been properly warned and not reforming, besides the ordinary punishment provided by law for those misdemeanors, shall be deprived of their academical privileges and be ex-matriculated. These threats are directed especially against those who go about breaking into doors. Masters of different faculties shall keep the peace with each other; *beani* shall not be ill-treated; and at disputations no ribaldry or indecent gestures shall be permitted.

The pious earnestness of the expressions, not only of the faculty statutes, but of those of the University of Vienna, respecting the religion and morality of the students, is truly edifying. Sins, they say, darken the spiritual eye, so that it cannot discern refined truths. Though one in that condition should make great advances in learning, it would be in his hands a weapon for fearful wickedness, not a help upon the road to virtue. In schools of learning, a strict discipline must prevail. Holy Church can never gain by study, as long as men injure themselves by vice more than they are enlightened by instruction; for

* Schlikenrieder, 122 sqq. Compare the Ingolstadt bursary regulations, which provide that "those appointed to such by the faculty shall not spend more time at taverns, fighting-bouts, with guitar-players and lute-players, than in philosophy."—*Mederer*, iv. 97.

the destroying one single soul is so great an evil that it cannot be made good by the enlightenment with learning of innumerable others. Better that children remain at home in ignorance, but pure and innocent, than that they should go to school and be destroyed by sin.*

It was an object of solicitude to pious and conscientious men at all periods, that youth should lead moral lives at the universities, and should be saved from perversion. To this end the most various means were resorted to, but mostly without avail.

At the older German universities, as at Paris, bursaries were founded,† at which a number of students lived, under the strict supervision of a *Rector bursæ*, and receiving assistance from him in their studies. But many facts show that in these bursaries the students led lives any thing but moral, as did many of the rectors. These latter endeavored to attract new-comers to their bursaries; and in order to make themselves acceptable to them, overlooked their misdemeanors, cast aside all strictness of discipline, and even pursued abandoned courses in common with them; all for the sake of the profit to be made from the bursarii (*Burschen*). At Erfurt, each *Rector bursæ* took an oath, in the words, "I promise that I desire to be a faithful example to my *bursarii* in manners and learning."‡ And these same rectors drove a large trade in Naumburg beer, sold it like tavern-keepers to any one, neglected their duties as teachers, and by such courses grew rich, while their students ran down in circumstances, and became so poor that they had to give up their studies and go home.§

We shall hereafter see what means, either friendly or harsh, were afterward used to constrain the students to reputable lives and industrious labor.

IV. The University of Wittenberg, and its Relations to the Earlier Universities.

When the first German universities were founded, the period of the great profound scholastics was long past. Anselmus, Hugo de St. Victor, Roger Bacon, Thomas Aquinas, Bonaventura, belonged to the 11th, 12th, and 13th centuries. The later doctors in arts possessed, for the most part, only a technical skill in dialectic fencing, a fruitless power of playing with empty forms, without feeling any need of any real mental acquirements or progress. It is not to be wondered at that such a useless state of things should soon be attacked from more

* Schlikenrieder, 121.

† See App. XII., Bursaries.

‡ Also, to practice them in Latinity. Motschmann, i. 646. The oath is from the statutes in force before 1469.

§ Motschmann, 651. The Ingolstadt bursary statutes (Mederer, iv. 96,) provide that "The overseers (*conventores*) must expel from the bursary public gamblers and lechers, on pain of loss of office." Such orders had to be enforced by threats of punishment!

than one direction, and that in such an intellectual desert a longing should grow up for some living spring and the green of flourishing life.

In another part of this history I have sought to describe the contest between the ancient and dying scholastic system of instruction, and the young and vigorous classical system; the strife between the doctors in arts and the poets, as the two opposing camps were then called. We have seen that Cologne was the headquarters of the upholders of the ancient system; and that most of the champions of the new, either voluntarily or involuntarily, gathered into Germany, and in one place and another began to teach the new doctrines in universities and gymnasia.

About the end of the 15th and beginning of the 16th century, the new system found a home in the universities of Tübingen and Heidelberg: Agricola, Reuchlin, the youthful Melancthon, and others, arose at these places. The study of the classics did not suffice for them; a second and more profoundly comprehensive department of investigation was entered, namely, the exegetical study of the original text of the Old and New Testament,—a thing before unheard of.

There is a great resemblance between the great reformatory efforts of the latter years of the 15th century and those of its beginning, in which Huss was so influential. These efforts, so intimately connected with the study of the Scriptures and of the classics, found a point of concentration at the small but world-renowned University of Wittenberg, founded in 1502.*

To compare this with the earlier universities, we do not find it to differ in the mode of its foundation, nor in its first statutes, from those of Prague, Vienna, &c. It was founded by the Elector Frederic, and received grants of privileges from the emperor and the Pope. Its first statutes are dated in 1508. In them it is dedicated to God, and Mary the mother of God; St. Paul is made patron of the theological faculty, Ivo of the juridical,† Cosmas and Damian of the medical, and St. Catharine of the philosophical. St. Augustine was chosen as patron of the whole university.

In the year of the publication of these statutes, the Augustin Luther received the appointment of professor of ethics and dialectics in Wittenberg, became doctor of theology in 1512, published his theses in

* See Raumer's *History*, i. 127-213, 316-330; the descriptions of Luther, Melancthon, and the University of Wittenberg. The following account is intended in particular to elucidate the relations of this university to the early German ones.

† Grohmann, i. 108. Ivo was also patron of the faculty of law at Vienna and Erfurt. He was Bishop of Chartres in the 11th century, and served as a patron of the poor without pay. Motschmann, i. 147. St. Catharine was patroness of the philosophical faculty at Vienna and Ingolstadt.

1517, and in 1518 took Melancthon as his fellow-laborer in the great work of the Reformation, which was mainly based upon the teaching of the patron of the theological faculty, St. Paul,—upon the doctrine of Justification by Faith.

Wittenberg is strongly distinguished from the earlier universities, not only by its powerful Reformatory influence, but also by the new studies introduced there, and the new spirit and method in which they were pursued.

It is true that in the older universities lectures were read upon the Bible, but it was by beginners in the profession of teaching, the *Baccalaurei Biblici;* while at Wittenberg two doctors lectured in the Old Testament and two in the New, and that upon the original text. In the place of the mediæval dogmatics of the *Sentences* of Petrus Lombardus, appeared Melancthon's *Loci*, composed in the very spirit of the Reformation.

In comparing the courses of lectures in the older universities with those at Wittenberg, we find also in the latter the seven liberal arts, except music; but in none of them were the earlier text-books used, except in astronomy and geometry. At first sight it would appear that dialectics played a part in many respects the same as in the older universities; but further examination shows that instead of the mutilated translations of Aristotle formerly used, the Greek originals were introduced. Thus, the Wittenberg statutes say: "The professor of ethics shall read Aristotle's Ethics *in the Greek*, word for word;"* and in like manner is the professor of physics to read Aristotle's Physics. And where the original text is not made the basis of instruction, Melancthon's manuals of dialectics, physics, and ethics, composed with the most thorough study of Aristotle, are substituted for them. In like manner, Melancthon's Rhetoric was a text-book, in which he closely followed especially Cicero and Quintilian; and which, as he says, was intended as an elementary introduction to the understanding of the writings of both those authors, who were, in the middle ages, as good as forgotten. The entirely subordinate place previously occupied by rhetoric in comparison with dialectics, and its introduction to a higher one by means first of Cicero and Quintilian, and in general of the study of the classics, appears from the fact that in Wittenberg declamation alternated with disputation on the Saturdays, whereas previously there had been disputations every Saturday.

In grammar, great changes took place. We have elsewhere related how the scholars of Hegius in particular, as Busch, Murmellius, Cæsa-

* *Corpus Reformatorum*, x. 1010.

rius, &c., strenuously opposed the received grammatical text-books, particularly the *Doctrinale* of Alexander de Villa Dei, and how they were more than once persecuted for that reason by the adherents of the ancient scholasticism, especially the Cologners. The "*Epistles of Obscure Men*" was a prominent satire upon the vulgar lives, and the correspondingly barbarous style of these scholastics.

Melancthon's *Latin Grammar* was the result of the study of the classics, and both promoted that study and drove out the previous grammatical text-books.

Lectures upon the Latin and Greek classics were not given at all in the earlier universities, while they filled a very important place at Wittenberg. By the study of the Latin classics, the new Latin grammar, and a rhetoric based on that of antiquity, was gradually substituted for the barbarous mediæval Latin. Melancthon's historical lectures, also, took the place of Carion's *Chronicon*, as a new work.

The University of Wittenberg—mainly through Melancthon's influence during the 16th century—became a model for other Protestant universities. This will appear at once upon comparing, for instance, the lectures of the theological and philosophical faculties of Königsberg and Greifswald with those of Wittenberg; they will be found entirely similar in substance to the latter.*

While it thus appears that the University of Wittenberg was far in advance of the earlier ones in respect to learning and instruction, the question also arises, What was it as to morals and discipline as compared with them?

To judge from its statutes of 1546, it was in no better condition than Vienna, Tübingen, Ingolstadt, &c., had been before. These denounce the folly of such youths as imagine the university to be a place of unbridled license, and who by their bad example ruin many others; who destroy quiet and studious industry, disobey the rector, do not attend church, wander about by day and night, stir up disturbances, break into houses, rob gardens, commit thefts, and wantonly insult and injure others. They enact that none shall challenge another to fight; harlots are threatened with severe punishment; decent clothing is enjoined; immodest dancing† forbidden at festivals, and lampooners and liars are declared to be infamous.‡

* Koch, i. 604, 368, 372, sqq. Music is among the subjects of lectures at Greifswald. Ib., 379. Luther may be security that although there were no lectures on music at Wittenberg, music itself did not fail there. In part i. of this history, p. 178, an extract from his Table Talk is given, beginning thus: "On the 17th Dec., 1538, when Dr. M. Luther entertained some musicians, and they sang some beautiful motets and set pieces," &c.

† "We shall punish those who are immodest in dancing, and who carry young women round in a circle (waltzing?), in violation of the ordinary forms of decent dancing."—*Corpus Reform.*, x. 997.

‡ Ib. x. 995, &c.

Various discourses, drawn up by Melancthon, to be delivered by the rector before and after the annual reading of the statutes, prove the sad state of things which the statutes indicate clearly enough. Thus, one of these addresses, delivered in 1537,* says: "When I consider how at this time discipline is broken down and disorder prevails, deep grief seizes me. I see in spirit the severe punishment which shall overtake the obdurate. Never were youth so hostile to the laws; they are resolved to live according to their own desires only, and not to regard the wishes of others. They are deaf to the word of God and to the law. How few strive after profound and thorough learning! A few learn here and there something which will afterward be useful to them, and the rest learn nothing whatever."

"Let it not be imagined," says another of these addresses, "that universities are intended to assemble young men of leisure to amuse themselves and gamble. No; they are meant to foster divine knowledge and other good learning; they are meant to enlighten men around them by wisdom and virtue."†

It is scarcely necessary to observe that, despite the vices thus censured, to which part of the students at Wittenberg were addicted, yet at this same time there proceeded from the school of Luther and Melancthon most influential and excellent men; men like Trotzendorf, Camerarius, Neander, Matthesius, and many others.‡

It may perhaps be asked, How was it that such extraordinary teachers as Luther and Melancthon did not exert greater moral influence on these vicious students? The great number of them was one hindrance; and the more, as they gathered to Wittenberg from all the countries of Europe, and by reason of their differences in national character, were harder to manage than if all natives. It should also be remembered what requirements were made upon Luther, Melancthon, and the other teachers for the great work of the Reformation in church and school; how much they printed, what an extensive correspondence they kept up. Thus it happened that, notwithstanding their wonderful activity, very little time remained to them for personal intercourse with the students; and that only with such as sought them of their own accord;§ not with those who kept at a distance from them, living a low life, and desiring to be undisturbed in it. Lastly, the history of the Reformation shows that the students in various ways misinterpreted for evil the newly rising intellectual freedom, and, not

---

* *Corp. Reform.*, x. 934. † Ib. x. 939.

‡ Compare the previous remarks as to the existence at the same time of good and evil at the universities.

§ For Melancthon's kindness to such, see this work, part i. 189.

having any religious adaptation to it, foolishly and wildly broke over all bounds. To understand this state of things, it is only necessary to recall the excesses which forced Luther to leave the Wartburg and return to Wittenberg to restore order there.

V.—History of the Manners of the Universities in the Seventeenth Century.

We have described the dark side of the discipline at Wittenberg in the 16th century. At the other universities, Protestant and Catholic, the students were in a similar condition of disorder. Thus at Tübinger, Königsberg, Greifswald, Ingolstadt, the statutes prohibited drinking, gaming, lechery, fighting, street tumults, &c.; the same excesses which are threatened with punishment by the statutes at Wittenberg.*

It would seem that such insubordination could not be exceeded. It was, however, during the 17th century; a period when wickedness was more wanton, influential, and universal than before.

But in order the better to describe the peculiarities of this terrible demoralization, something must first be said of the deposition.

A.—Deposition,

Called, also, *Beania.* "Beani" were those who are now called by the universally received term, which needs no definition, of "Foxes." The word is derived from the French *bec jaune*, yellow-bill.† The Beania or Deposition was a strange ceremony by which the Beani were received to be students.

In a dissertation of the Swede Fryksell, there is a description of a Deposition which the author attended in 1716, at Upsala; and which, from the illustrations accompanying it, seems to have been precisely like the German ones.‡

"The principal of the ceremony, called Herr Depositor," says this author, "caused the youths who desired to be received into the class of students to dress in clothes of various patterns and colors. Their faces were blacked, and long ears and horns were fastened to their hats, whose brims were fastened down smooth; in each corner of their mouths was inserted a long boar's tusk, which they must hold fast, like two little tobacco-pipes, during the subsequent beating; and on their shoulders were placed long black mantles. Thus hideously and ridiculously clothed, like those whom the Inquisition has condemned to the flames, the Depositor dismisses them from the Deposition-chamber and drives them before him with a stick like a herd of oxen or asses, to a hall where the spectators are awaiting them. Here he arranges them in a circle, in the middle of which he stands, makes faces at them and silent reverences, ridicules them for their absurd appearance, and then delivers a discourse to them, proceeding from burlesque to earnest. He speaks of the vices and follies of youth, and shows how necessary it is for them to be improved, disciplined, and

---

* See Klüpfel, 21; Koch, i. 387-393, 592-595.

† *Beanus* was defined, acrostically, *Beanus est Animal Nesciens Vitam Studiosorum.* Instead of *Beani*, *Bacchanten* is often found; and instead of *Fuchs* (Fox), Meyfart says *Feux.*

‡ *Dissertation on the Origin of the Initiation of New-Comers into Universities*, 1755.

polished by study. Then he asks them various questions, which they must answer. But as the swine's tusks which they hold in their mouths hinder them from speaking distinctly, they make a noise more like swine's grunting; whereupon the Depositor calls them swine, gives them a light beating with a stick over the shoulders, and a reproof. These teeth, he says, signify excesses; for young people's understandings are obscured by excess in eating and drinking. Then he produces out of a bag a sort of wooden tongs,* with which he takes them about the neck, and shakes them about until the tusks fall down on the ground. If they are docile and industrious, he says, they will get rid of their tendencies to intemperance and gluttony, as of these swine's tusks. Then he pulls off their long ears, by which he gives them to understand that they must study diligently, unless they wish to remain like asses. Then he removes their horns, which signify brutal rudeness, and draws out of his bag a plane. Each *Bean* must now lie down, first on his stomach, then on his back, and then on each side, while the Depositor planes him his whole length in each position, saying, 'Literature and liberal arts will in like manner polish your mind.' After some other laughable ceremonies, the Depositor fills a great vessel with water, which he pours upon the head of the novice, and afterward wipes him with a coarse towel. The buffoonery being ended by this washing, he admonishes the planed, scrubbed, and washed assemblage that they must commence a new life, strive against wicked impulses, and lay aside evil habits, which will envelope their minds just as their different garments envelope their bodies."

This account was illustrated with cuts, and it and they appeared in a little book published in 1680.† The frontispiece represents all the instruments of deposition,‡ and the remaining cuts the use of them, and under each is a brief explanatory rhyme. In the first the *Beanus* is having his hair cut off, in the second his ear cleaned with an enormous ear-pick, and underneath two lines, importing—

> "Let your ears be closed to protect you against fools;
> I cleanse you for learning, not for vile buffoonery."

Further on, his Bacchant's teeth are shaken out, his hand filed, a beard painted on him; he is hewed with an axe, planed, bored; the horns are taken off him,§ and he is measured with a measure.

Besides the explanations already given of the meaning of these ceremonies, there are many others substantially similar. Thus, one writer‖ says:

---

* "With legs which stretch out and draw back in zig-zag"—an instrument very vividly represented in the accompanying cuts.

† "*Ritus Depositionis. Argentorati, apud Albertum Dolhopff.* 1680."

‡ These are named in the following hexameters:

> "*Serra, dolabra, bidens, dens, clava, novacula, pecten*
> *Cum terebra tornus, cum lima malleus, incus,*
> *Rastraque cum rostris, cum furca et forcipe forpex.*"

§ H. Conring (*De Antiquitatibus Academicis*, Dissert. iv. p. 122) says, "The initiation of new students, which we call *the Deposition of the horns.*" Does this give rise to the phrase, "He must get rid of his horns first?" Another derivation of "*Deposition*" is, from the putting off their Beanus-ship upon a goat; or their rustic manners, with it. See *Monum. Univ. Prag.*, i. 2, 553. The phrase reminds us of Leviticus, xvi. 20–22.

‖ "*Short Account of the Academical Deposition, for New Gentlemen Students and Others*, by F. B. Pfenning, Imperial Notary Public and Depositor in the University of Jena." Unfortunately without date.

"The hat and horns represent a wanton, wild, and insubordinate nature, like that of an obstinate ox; the Bacchant's teeth represent a man who is like a wild boar, and when the Depositor takes them away from the new student, there should also be taken away all such wild, snappish, and devouring qualities. The great axe and plane allude to coarse, unpolished, and boorish manners. And as *eruditus* means nothing else than an image hewn and shaped out of a rough block, thus should a student be *erudite* from such coarse, unpolished manners; that is, hewn and planed, so that after the Deposition he may be a polite and well-mannered student. The comb, shears, knife, and soap, refer to purity of body and soul; and the auger means, 'that by pains and industry, men in like manner pierce into, investigate, and discover the secrets of nature.'"

The above account of the Deposition at Upsala omits a concluding act of the ceremony which was practiced both there and in Germany.* After the Beani had gone through all their symbolical annoyances, they were brought to the dean of the philosophical faculty, who examines them about their school-knowledge, and admonishes them how to use it in studying and in life. Then he consecrates them, putting salt in their mouths, and pouring wine on their heads. The salt was a symbol of wisdom, and reminded them of the words, "Let your conversation always be salted with salt;" the wine signified purification from the dirt of the *Beania*, and admonishes the student thenceforward to lay aside all uncleanliness, and to live a pure life.

Most writers on Deposition state that in ancient times, at Athens, Constantinople, and Berytus, the novices were subjected to the same annoyance.†

That the ceremony of Deposition, at the German universities, was not merely a piece of buffoonery invented by the students, but was reckoned an officially authorized ceremony, appears, for example, from the following statute of the University of Erfurt: "No one shall be enrolled as a student who shall not previously have undergone, here or elsewhere, the rite of *Deposition*, anciently established.‡ In like manner, by the ancient statutes at Prague, no one could be admitted to the baccalaureate examination who had not undergone Deposition. The ceremony was permitted to be performed, however, immediately before the examination or during it, in the presence of the master.§

The Greifswalde statutes of 1545 say,‖ "The Deposition is to be

---

* Fryksell (p. 17) says, "We learn from Freinsheimius that salt and wine were commonly brought in here (at Upsala) as at other universities;" and he cites an address of Freinsheim at a Deposition at Upsala in 1645.

† So Conring, who gives an extract from Gregory Nazianzen, in which the latter mentions the usual annoyances of novices at Athens; which carries the custom back into the fourth century. In the sixth, the Emperor Justinian forbade the tormenting of novices coming to Constantinople and Berytus. The statutes of the University of Vienna of 1384 say: "Also, let none presume to vex the new-comers, who are called *Beani*, with exactions not due, or to molest them with other injuries or contumely."

‡ Motschmann, i. 797; and he says (1st continuation, p. 465), "The chief beadle conducted the Deposition in the faculty-room."

§ *Monum. Univ. Prag.*, i. 1, 125.

‖ Koch, i. 367.

kept up. Such *Beani* as feel themselves free from school discipline, are inclined to idleness, and think themselves exceedingly learned, are to be somewhat sharply admonished during the Deposition how trifling their learning is, and how much they have yet to learn."

Opinions of the Deposition were very different. Melancthon said, "This vexation may remind you that you must meet in life many troubles and difficulties, which are to be borne with patience, lest impatience bring you into worse condition."

Luther's views were similar. Matthesius relates that at one Deposition, Luther himself "absolved" the novices. Among many other beautiful remarks, he said, "This was only a child's Deposition; when they grew up and served the people in church, school, or state, they would then really 'depose' their parishioners, pupils, and citizens. And this annoyance accustoms the children from their youth to endurance; and he who cannot endure and listen to any thing, will not do for a preacher or governor."*

"When Martin," it is related elsewhere (Luther's *Table Talk*, Walch, xxii. 2232 and 2233), "was at a Deposition, he 'absolved' three boys, saying, 'These ceremonies will also be of this service, that they will make you humble, not pompous and presumptuous, nor accustomed to wickedness. For such vices are frightful monstrous beasts, which have horns, and are not good for students, but do them harm. Therefore be humble, and learn to suffer and have patience, for you will be passing through a Deposition all your lives. . . . . When any thing befalls you, do not be mean-spirited, cowardly, and impatient . . . . but be bold, and endure such a cross with patience, without murmuring: remember that at Wittenberg you were consecrated to endurance; and you can say, when such a thing happens, Well, I began to be "deposed" at Wittenberg, and it will last me all my life. Also, this Deposition of ours is only a figure and picture of human life, in all manner of ill-fortune, trouble, and discipline. Pour wine on their heads, and absolve them from being *Beani* and *Bachants*.'"

Later writers, again, spoke with contempt of the Deposition, and called it a stupid buffoonery† and a barbarous custom.‡

These opponents lived during the 17th century, in the time of the terrible custom of Pennalism; and in the shameful abuse of the Pennals they saw only an extension of the Deposition. The Deposition, says Weisius, is finished in an hour, while the vexations of the Pennals

* Matthesius' *12th Sermon on Luther.*

† Conring—"The folly of petulant students." Conring died in 1681.

‡ "Put away this barbarism from Germany," says Limnäus, who was inspector of studies at Ansbach. He died in 1665.

last a year.* In Jena, Valentin Hoffmann came out in defense of the Deposition,† saying that "the barbarous and barbarously named custom of Pennalization, though it looked much like the Deposition, was nevertheless as wide as the heavens apart from it, since the Deposition was not private but public, and conducted by some one appointed by the authorities."

Although we may well believe the respectable and officially appointed depositor Hoffmann, still there are many reasons for believing that the Deposition was what gave its origin to Pennalism, as it certainly was what the latter falsely claimed to resemble. Luchten, in his "*Oration against Pennalism*," says that "the *Schorists* do not pass over those who have been 'absolved' by Deposition. From Beanism, they tell them, you are free; but you are now Pennals; you must remain in that equally shameful condition, and cannot escape from it in less than a year."‡ The same appears from the above cited description of the Deposition in Upsala. After the ceremony of Deposition, it is said, the Depositor declares that the Beani are thenceforth free students, but that they must still for six months wear the same black mantle used at the Deposition, and must every day offer themselves to do service to their older fellow-students of the same nation, both in their rooms and at taverns, and must do all things which they are commanded, and endure all reproaches and abuse. "And this," adds the French relater, "is what they call *les Pénales*."§

This unfortunate similarity between the Deposition and Pennalism, would, of course, at a time when all means were resorted to to put down the latter, destroy the former also. Thus, the Deposition was discontinued at Tübingen in 1717, although new students continued to be examined on their school studies by the dean of the philosophical faculty.‖

The statutes of the University of Halle, of 1694, also put an end to the Deposition. "At the same time," they say, "we retain the purpose for which a judicious antiquity established that ceremony; namely, that the students may be examined by the dean of the philosophical faculty, may be admonished of the piety, modesty, and manners which

---

* "*Q. D. B. V. ritum depositionis academicæ.*" Præses Sonftius, respondens Weisius: 1697, Wittenberg.

† *Praise of the Deposition of Beani;* pronounced in 1657 by Valentine Hoffman, Depositor at this University. 2d ed. Jena, 1688.

‡ Luchtenius. In *Chrysander*, p. 42.

§ Fryksell, p. 17. "*Ce qui s'appeloit les Pénales.*" The relater seems to derive it from the French pénal (*pœnalis*).

‖ Arnoldt, i. 234: and he gives, at p. 414, an extract from M. Sahmen's "*Dissertation on the Ceremony of Deposition.*"

befit an ingenuous youth; that advice for the prosperous beginning of their studies may be supplied them; and that, evidence of this being given, they may be admitted to the study of letters, if their age permits, by the use of wine and salt, and dismissed."*

In Jena, the Deposition was restricted to this: that the instruments of martyrdom were only exhibited to the new-comers, their use explained, an appropriate admonition given, and then, as before, they were taken to the dean of the philosophical faculty, who examined them, and instructed them how they ought to live and to study.† In Wittenberg, the practice was discontinued in 1733; and sixteen groschen, which the Depositor had received from a *Beanus*, were handed over to the philosophical faculty.‡

B.—PENNALISM.

The Deposition, in spite of all the tragi-comic annoyances to which the new-comers had to subject themselves, was still, as we have seen, intended in earnest; was even recognized, and indeed commanded, in the academical statutes, and performed in the presence and with the help of the dean of the philosophical faculty.

Unprincipled older students perverted the practice, however, in a dishonest manner, into the devilish caricature of Pennalism. This has been described to us by many cotemporaries, even in many official papers, in royal rescripts, and in a decree of the Diet of Ratisbon; all of which agree so perfectly that we cannot, unfortunately, doubt at all of the actual existence of this imp of the devil.

We have already seen that the university statutes and annals show that at all times dangerous vices and disorders were arising in all the universities.

In a discourse by Prof. Wolfgang Heyder, of Jena,§ in 1607, the whole repulsive life of a rude, disorderly student is described in the strongest language; but Pennalism is not alluded to in it. But only a few years later, about 1610 and 1611, it first appeared,‖ and for fifty years, until 1661, it had possession of the universities. The flourishing season of its tyranny fell in a most terrible period for our country, in that of the Thirty Years' War; in those years when it seemed as if evil had completely gained dominion over good.

---

* Koch, i. 478.

† Pfenning; at the end.

‡ Grohmann, iii. 47.

§ See Appendix VIII.

‖ In the ordinance of the University of Jena, relating to the entire disuse of Pennalism, dated in 1661, it is said that fifty years and more ago it had come thither, and that a prohibition of it had appeared as early as 1610. (Schöttgen, 81.) Luchtenins, at Helmstadt, delivered an address in 1611, at the conclusion of his vice-rectorate, in which he says, "A contagious plague has even now (*pridem*) attacked our university, coming I know not whence"—namely, Pennalism.

What now was the distinction between Pennalism and the other previous vices of student-life; and how did it come to pass that even governments allied themselves together and sought all possible means of exterminating it?

The reason was, that this case was not one of excess by a single person, as had previously happened, but was a real conspiracy, an organization of bad men, by means of which older and abandoned students exercised the harshest tyranny over the younger, and made all discipline impossible. Nor was this organization confined to one isolated German university. The ringleaders in all of them had entered into a league for the maintenance of their villainous scheme, for the prevention of all discipline, and the frustration of all the regulations of academical authorities.

If it is asked how this hellish league could establish itself in so few years, it may be said that the existing ceremony of Deposition was an assistance to it. And when one generation of elder students had, under the cloak of inflicting only the usual annoyances, established complete authority over the new-comers, and kept them for a year in the harshest manner, under the indecent and abominable Pennal service, it was endured in the hope, after the Pennal year was ended, of taking a place among those who should in turn tyrannize over new-comers. Thus the government of these tyrants propagated itself from one generation to the next.

The older, or tyrannizing students, were called *Schorists*, "because they cut off (*abgeschoren*) the hair of the younger students, and also gave them a good dressing down, or, as their vulgar dialect had it, sheared (*geschoren*) them." They were also called *Absoluti*, as being freed from the Pennal obligations.*

The name (Pennals) of the subject-students has been variously derived. It might, very evidently, have been derived from the wearing of such a bunch of feathers as is even now used in schools under the name of Pennal;† those students were intended to be ridiculed by it who industriously made notes of the lectures.‡

The mode in which the Schorists apprehended the new-comers is given by Schröder. "When young people," he says, "come to the university, they have scarcely set one foot inside a door, or house, or city, before one of these national brothers waits upon them to inquire, 'Will you come to the magnificus, and promise to obey him in all proper things?' 'What magnificus?' they ask. 'You have no friend near him,' it is answered, 'and his opinion of you will be small. We

---

* Schöttgen, 16. † Ib. 13. ‡ For other nicknames of the Pennals, see Appendix IX.

will advise you how to arrange matters so that you shall thank us all your lives. Follow our advice with cheerfulness, or you will have to follow it in sorrow; join yourself to the nation; a year soon goes by; lest they treat you so that you will have cause to curse them all your life.'

"To accomplish their designs they used both deceit and force. As for the former, they pretended that their organization and meetings established love and friendship,—as the Epicureans were accustomed to do, probably; that is, by great glasses, beakers, and cans. There they bound themselves to each other, with cursing and swearing, to live and die like brothers for the welfare of each other. But scarcely would an hour or half an hour go by, when from one word, or one cup which one had got more or less than another, arose a great quarrel; and those who a little before had been willing to praise each other to the heavens, both by word and writing, were abusing each other and pulling each other by the hair."*

We have many descriptions of the vile and abandoned student-life of the period of Pennalism; the following very lively one is from the pseudonymous Philander von Sittewald: †

"Meanwhile I saw a great chamber; a common lodging-room, or museum, or study, or beer-shop, or wine-shop, or ball-room, or harlot's establishment, &c., &c. In truth I cannot really say what it was, for I saw in it all these things. It was swarming full of students. The most eminent of them sat at a table, and drank to each other until their eyes turned in their heads like those of a stuck calf. One drank to another from a dish—out of a shoe; one ate glass, another dirt; a third drank from a dish in which were all sorts of food, enough to make one sick to see it. One gave another his hand: they asked each other's names, and promised to be friends and brothers forever; with the addition of this clause, 'I will do what is pleasant to you, and avoid what is unpleasant to you;' and so each would tie a string off his leather breeches to the many-colored doublet of the other. But those with whom another refused to drink acted like a madman or a devil; sprang up as high as they could for anger, tore out their hair in their eagerness to avenge such an insult, threw glasses in each others' faces, out with their swords and at each other's heads, until here and there one fell down and lay there; and such quarrels I saw happen, even between the best friends and blood relatives, with devilish rage and anger. There were also others who were obliged to serve as waiters and pour out drink, and to receive knocks on the head and pulls of the hair, and other similar attentions, which the others bestowed on them as if on so many horses or asses; sometimes drinking to them a dishful of wine, and singing the Bacchus song, or repeating the Bacchus Mass—'*O vitrum gloriosum!*' Resp. '*Mihi gratissimum!*'—which waiters were termed by the rest, Bacchants, Pennals, house-cocks, mother-calves, sucklings, quasimodogeniti; and they sang a long song about them, beginning—

'Proudly all the Pennals hither are gathered,
Who are lately newly feathered,
And who at home have long been tethered,
Nursing their mothers.'

And which ends—

'Thus are all of the Pennals treated,
Although they all are very conceited.'

---

* Schröder's *Trumpet of Peace*, 33; in Schöttgen, p. 40; and compare Meyfart's description, Appendix X.

† *Sixth Tale*, Part i. Given by Schöttgen, p. 35.

"At the conclusion of these ceremonies and songs they cut off their hair, as they do that of a professing nun. From this, these students are called *Schoristen*, also *Agirer*, *Pennalisirer*; but among themselves they call each other gay, free, honest, brave, or stout-hearted students.

"Others I saw wandering about with their eyes nearly shut, as if they were in the dark, each with a drawn sword in his hand, which they would strike on the stones till the sparks flew; then would cry out into the air so that it would give one a pain in the ears; would assault the windows with stones, clubs, and sticks, and cry out, Here, Pennal! here, Feix! here, Bech! here, caterpillar! here, Mount-of-Olives-man! with such a tearing and striking, driving and running about, cutting and thrusting, as made my hair stand on end. Others drank to each other off seats and benches, or off the table or the floor, under their arms, under their legs, on their knees, with the cup under them, over them, behind them, or before them. Others lay on the floor and let it be poured into them as if into a funnel.

"Soon the drinking-cups and pitchers began to fly at the doors and the stove, and through the windows so outrageously, that it provoked me; and others lay there, spewing and vomiting like dogs."

A second description of this abominable student-life is given by Schöttgen, from a work published at Giessen,* which states that "the Schorists, at the Pennal feasts, when they have eaten and drank to their satisfaction, are accustomed to carry off movables, books, manuscripts, clothes, and whatever else they happen to find; and, moreover, to be guilty of all manner of insolences, such as breaking down and destroying stoves, doors, windows, tables, and chests.

"And, further, the younger students have been made to copy all sorts of writings, to wait, to go of errands, even ten and twenty miles and more. If one of these *maleferiata* and Pennal-flayers happens to choose to have something copied, the junior must be at hand to serve as his scribe; has he guests and friends with him, the young man must be there to wait; is there any thing else to be done or to be obtained, or to bé brought from any of the neighboring villages, the young fellow must go at his order, and be his servant, messenger, and porter. Does he choose to walk, the junior must attend as his body-guard; is he stupidly drunk, the novice must not flinch nor budge from him, but must remain close at hand as if he were his master, must serve him and help him along the street. Is he sick, the juniors must wait on him by turns, so that he need never be alone; does he wish for music, if the junior is skilled in it he must be his musician, all night long if he desires it. Is any thing else whatever required, the new-comer is set about it, and he must be forthcoming, even if he were sick in bed from his discipline, and at midnight. Does the older student get into a quarrel or a fight, the junior must carry his sword to him, and be ready for assiduous service in the matter. Would he gratify his vile desires with blows, the junior must suffer the blows and boxes on the

* Schöttgen, p. 46; from "*Pennalismi Abrogatio et Profligatio ex Academia Hasso Lisena.*" Giessen, 1660, folio.

ear which come from his cursed and devilish passion; must patiently endure the most shameful personal abuse, and must let the other work his entire will upon him as if he were nothing but a dog. In short, he treats him like a slave, after his own hateful will, almost more harshly than the harshest tyrants or most shameless men could do; and what is still more, although these tormentors inflict the most unendurable tortures upon these young people, they must preserve perpetual silence about it, and must not dare to open their lips or complain to any one, even to the academical authorities; or otherwise they will never be 'absolved' and admitted to become students; which threat terrifies them so much, that they would suffer the most severe and vilest shame and torment ten times over rather than to inform any one about it."

We find a third description in a rescript of Duke Albrecht of Saxony to the University of Jena, in 1624.* He says: "Customs before unheard of—inexcusable, unreasonable, and wholly barbarian—have come into existence. When any person, either of high or low rank, goes to any of our universities for the sake of pursuing his studies, he is called by the insulting names of Pennal, fox, tape-worm, and the like, and treated as such; and insulted, abused, derided, and hooted at, until, against his will, and to the great injury and damage of himself and his parents, he has prepared, given, and paid for a stately and expensive entertainment. And at this there happen, without any fear of God or man, innumerable disorders and excesses, blasphemies, breaking up of stoves, doors, and windows, throwing about of books and drinking-vessels, looseness of words and actions, and in eating and drinking, dangerous wounds, and other ill deeds; shames, scandals, and all manner of vicious and godless actions, even sometimes extending to murder or fatal injuries. And these doings are frequently not confined to one such feast, but are continued for days together at meals, at lectures, publicly and privately, even in the public streets, by all manner of misdemeanors in sitting, standing, or going, such as outrageous howls, breaking into houses and windows, and the like; so that by such immoral, wild, and vicious courses not only do our universities perceptibly lose in good reputation, but many parents in distant places either determine not to send their children at all to this university—founded with such great expense by our honored ancestors, now resting in peace with God, and thus far maintained by ourselves—or to take them away again; so that if this most harmful state of affairs is not ended and removed out of the way at the begin-

* Dated Dec. 9; given by Meyfart, p. 205.

ning, it may well happen that very soon no students whatever will be left in the place, and that this institution, which even in these careful and perilous times is so useful in advancing the glory of God, spreading abroad his name, which alone makes blessed, the promotion of all good and liberal arts, and the maintenance of spiritual and temporal government, which depends on them, may go entirely to ruin."*

Much influence was exerted by a work upon Pennalism, entitled, "Christian Recollections of the Orders and Honorable Customs introduced in many of the Evangelical Universities in Germany, and of the barbarous ones now for some years crept in during these miserable times, by Johannes Matthæus Meyfart, Doctor in the Holy Scriptures and Professor in the Ancient University of Erfurt: Schleissingen, 1636." The author will be remembered by many readers by his hymn, "Jerusalem, thou lofty builded city," and by his two works "On the Heavenly Jerusalem," and "On the Four Last Concerns of Men." It may be imagined what the feelings of one who found such pleasure in the great themes of eternity would be in respect to the immoral and vicious courses of the students of his university.† In severe anger against it, he describes it in the coarsest terms, only caring to make his account true and comprehensive. His anger sometimes carries him beyond moderation, and even to injustice to the Lutheran Church; but the substantial truth of his description of Pennalism is shown by its agreement with those of his contemporaries.‡

Although in earlier times part of the students lived immorally, still new-comers could easily avoid them, and follow their own course. But during the ascendency of Pennalism this was substantially impossible, as appears by a letter of the well known Schuppius to his son, who was about entering the university. He says to him: "You may imagine that at the universities they sup clear wisdom up by spoonfuls, and that no folly is to be seen in any corner, but when you come there, you must be a fool for the first year. You know that I have spared no pains or money upon you, and that you have not grown up behind your father's stove, but that I have carried you about from one place to another, and that already a great lord has looked upon you with pleasure and given you a place at his table. But you must forget this. For it is a part of wisdom to be foolish with the age, and to give in to its manners so far as conscience will allow. Let yourself be plagued and abused for this year, not only in good German but in slang. When an old Wetterauer or Vogelsberg Milk Cudgel steps up

* Luchtenius says of Pennalism, even in 1611: "It cannot be said how it produces all manner of corrupt ways, destroys all discipline, and evidently cools down a love of learning."

† Meyfart was born at Jena in 1590, and died at Erfurt in 1642.

‡ Appendix X.

and pulls your nose, let it not appear singular to you; endure it, and harden yourself to it. '*Olim meminisse juvabit.*' I warn you faithfully against becoming yourself one of the gang of Schorists after the Pennal year is over."* Whether the son followed this advice after enduring the frightful Pennal life for a whole year, is very doubtful.

"The end of the Pennal year," says Schöttgen, "was the absolution; in which a member of the whole Landsmannschaft 'absolved' them, after the conclusion of the year, and declared them real students. For this purpose the poor Pennal was obliged first to go round to all the members of the Landsmannschaft, and request them to permit him to be released from his slavery. If he found grace in their eyes, he had now to furnish an absolution feast. After this he was a student, and there forthwith entered into him seven evil spirits, who made him torment the Pennals just as he had himself been tormented."

The various governments now undertook to put an end to these evils, but after a time they found that successful efforts were impossible singly. For if an ill-conducted Schorist were sent away from Leipzig, he would go to Jena, and be received with open arms by his companions there. For this reason several universities, as Wittenberg, Königsberg, Marburg and others, associated together and made statutes in common against the practice.† Still they accomplished no more than other single universities with their innumerable prohibitions and severe punishments.

In 1654, the German princes took occasion, at the Diet of Ratisbon, to procure the following ordinance:‡ "Whereas we have taken into careful consideration the severe and bitter afflictions, especially the bloody and wearisome war, with which Almighty God, in his justice, is disciplining our beloved fatherland and the German nation, together with other neighboring kingdoms and countries, and have still more ripely considered the causes whereby these evils have come upon a country and people so remarkably prosperous, we have found not to be the least, among other fearful vices which have come into vogue notwithstanding both the first and second tables of the Ten Commandments of God, that most harmful and disorderly custom which has crept into the universities of Germany, called Pennalism; by which certain young persons, reckless, wicked, evil-trained, and neglecting all Christian discipline, waylay in the most scandalous manner those who come from other places to the universities from trivial-schools, pæda-

* Schuppius' "*Friend in Need*," i. 252.

† These statutes are given in Arnoldt (i. 438), and were confirmed by Elector George William. (Ibid. 444.) Schöttgen (p. 140) gives the same information from the orations of Schuppius.

‡ Schöttgen, 149.

gogiums, or gymnasiums, to acquire various learning in the classical tongues, liberal arts, philosophy, or in the higher faculties, as well as those who are born and brought up in the places where such universities are,—who treat them barbarously, not only with insulting scoffing gestures and words, but with dishonorable and abominable abuses and blows, and often demand of them such service and waiting on as a reasonable master would hesitate to require from the least of his servants, —but also oblige these new students, at coming and going, and whenever else they choose, to furnish them with feasts and entertainments; so that the money which their parents, often with the utmost difficulty, in these times, when money is so scarce, have given them to maintain them through the year, must be squandered in one and another drinking-bout and feast; so that many good minds are driven desperate by such 'exagitations' and 'concussions;' and the result is, that many well-begun courses of study are obstructed, and parents disappointed in the hopes they have conceived, as well as the church, the government, schools and the commonwealth, deprived in the most unjustifiable manner of useful instruments."*

But this ordinance in like manner failed of its effect; and successful steps in the business were only first taken from 1660 to 1662. Saxony was first; Pennalism being driven out from her universities of Wittenberg, Jena, and Leipzig, by the regulation that a student expelled from one of them for that reason, should not be admitted into either of the others. This example was followed by the universities of Helmstadt, Giessen, Altorf, Rostock, Frankfurt, and Königsberg. In 1664, Elector Friedrich Wilhelm powerfully confirmed the Königsberg anathema against Pennalism, by an edict, in which he expresses great indignation against the mode in which students newly come to the university are "held in servitude for a year," and demoralized through and through. And he adds: "This vicious and disorderly life so well pleases the Pennals, that they forget their freedom, and take so much pleasure in their servitude, hard as it is, that they not only do not shame to recognize this slavery by assuming disreputable costumes and other outward distinctions and disgraces, but even hold them a credit; and thus come to respect the usurped authority of their disorderly seniors more than the regular power of the established academical magistracy."†

It was only after the extinction of Pennalism, which was finally destroyed about 1660, that well-meaning students could employ their time well at the universities. This appears by the following letter

* This ordinance is followed by the prohibition of Pennalism issued by Duke Eberhard of Würtemberg, in 1655. (Klüpfel, 184.)

† Arnoldt, i. 446.

from Dr. Haberkorn, at Giessen, to Dr. Weller, April 6, 1661.* He writes: "The condition of our university since we have utterly destroyed the Pennal system, is quiet and prosperous. The number of students does not decrease, but increases. The ridiculing and other features of the accursed Pennalism have entirely ceased, so that I hardly seem to be rector, although I yet hold that office. Many parents thank God with uplifted hands, and wish our university much of the divine blessing. I remember to have earnestly urged your high-worthiness, at Frankfurt, to push your efforts to banish this hell-hound out of all the universities in the Roman Empire; but that in spite of all the pains that could be taken, it could not be done. Now, however, I doubt not your high-worthiness will make use of your great influence and good fortune, to banish this deviltry at least out of the Saxon universities. For our example shows clearly that the object is proved practicable, and that the devil will fail of his purpose, however much pains he takes to maintain his kingdom of Pennalism."

To return once more to the history of that vile custom. It has been observed that the old practice of the Deposition may have given rise to Pennalism, and that it was made a cloak for it; and also, that thoroughly organized societies of students made opposition to all discipline, and this not only in single universities, but that there existed a league embracing several of them, which prevented the operation even of the severest regulations.

These societies we have referred to as "nations;" but they had nothing in common with the "nations" of an earlier period. The latter, as we have seen, were openly established and recognized corporations, who elected procurators, took part in the government of the university, &c.; whereas the "nations" of the 17th century corresponded to the "*Landsmannschaften*."† This is clearly shown by a "programme" issued by the University of Leipzig in 1654, at expelling a Schorist. "From this," says Schöttgen,‡ "we see that the Schorists had their 'nations,' and in them *seniores*, *fisci*, and a fiscal officer; that they had a correspondence with other universities, and that when one university would endure one of their number no longer, they pro-

---

* Schöttgen, 111.

† It has been stated that Duke Rudolph organized four "nations" at the University of Vienna, as having taken that of Paris for a model. Each of these included students from the most different and distant countries:—e. g., the Saxon nation included Treves, Bremen, and Prussia. The *Landsmannschaften*, on the other hand, belonged to the countries after which they were named. Thus, in the 17th century, at Tübingen, the students from Hohenlohe organized the New Würtemberg *Landsmannschaft;* those of Ulm the Danubia; those of Old Würtemberg the Würtembergia, and the Swiss the Helvetia. (Klüpfel, 293.)

‡ Schöttgen, 103. The "nations" thus broken up at Leipzig, had no relation whatever to the four old "nations" which existed from the foundation of the university until 1830.

vided for him elsewhere; that they held those dishonorable who revealed any matter to the authorities, and persecuted them everywhere." From a similar document of November 13, 1659, we see in still greater detail, "that each 'nation' had its seniors, directors, fiscal department, and even its beadles, who held their offices by turns, some for a longer and some for a shorter time. New-comers had to submit to be 'inscribed' in one of these. They were cited before the Schorists, and their cases adjudicated; and every one who according to this tribunal was guilty of any thing, was fined in money or in an entertainment. Any one who told tales out of school, or went to the authorities to complain, was held dishonorable."

What a devilish sort of authority the "seniors" of these nations practiced, appears from an example given by Schöttgen.* In 1639 a student named Holdorff complained to the prorector at Rostock, that "as his Pennal year was out some days since, and he was required to proceed to Copenhagen to enter into an employment there, he had gone to Höpner, as senior of his nation, and had asked to be absolved. He answered, however, that it had been decided in the nation that he must stay six weeks over his year; and therefore he required him to stay. He went to him again and asked amicably that he might be absolved; to which Höpner answered that he must remain, and should; and that if he did not complete his year, and six weeks, six days, six hours, and six minutes besides, he would be *sent for.* He asked him a third time to absolve him; but Höpner answered no less positively that if he did not stay, and went, he would surely be sent for." Höpner afterward cited Holdorff before him, and because for fright he did not appear, that senior and four others broke into his lodgings at night with drawn swords.

As the tyranny of Pennalism was based on these nations, and operated by means of them, Elector Friedrich Wilhelm, in the rescript already quoted, ordains with great justice, "that the most injurious system of Pennalism, as well as the national organizations, shall be wholly broken up and destroyed."† The truth of the further allegation in the same rescript, viz., that Pennals have become so corrupted by their disorderly life that they have forgotten their freedom, and take pride in their severe servitude, appears from the following fact. When the Elector of Saxony's ordinance against Pennalism in Leipzig was published in 1661, "more than two hundred Pennals got together,

* P. 94. Schöttgen took the account from a university protocol.

† Arnoldt, i. 448. The attempt made by the University of Königsberg, in 1670, to legalize four nations—Pomeranian, Silesian, Prussian, and Westphalian—and to exercise authority over them, failed. Arnoldt, i. 261.

and foolishly swore to adhere to the practice of Pennalism, and not permit it to perish. They, however, soon thought better of it."*

But were these associations destroyed, together with Pennalism, in the year 1662? By no means. We shall see that the *Burschenschaft* substantially put an end to Pennalism, although it may be said to have continued to exist in the *Landsmannschaften*, but not in its earlier coarse and abominable phase.

VI. History of the Universities in the Eighteenth Century.

A. Nationalism.—The Landsmannschaften.

Pennalism, as we have seen, was based upon the national organizations. When it was suppressed, in the year 1662, it was asked whether it was extirpated from the roots, or, in other words, whether these organizations also were suppressed? The answer given was, by no means. It is, however, not easy to substantiate this answer by facts. The national organizations being strictly forbidden, it was necessary to conceal their existence by all possible means. The statutes of one of the *Landsmannschaften*, for example, provide that a new member, at his entrance, shall give his word of honor "that he will never reveal what happens at any time within the society, that he will always be diligently watchful against renouncers (students belonging to no society), and will never reveal that such a society exists, and will even endeavor to cause the contrary to be believed. But in case he shall be seriously questioned on the subject by the police or the rector, he must lie stoutly, and be willing to give up his existence at the university for the sake of the society."*

In such secrecy, it is natural that the *Landsmannschaften*, as long as they were prohibited, should come to light only occasionally. We will give a few examples.

In 1682, twenty years after the suppression of Pennalism, there arose a great tumult of the students in Leipzig, upon the prohibition of the national organizations by an electoral rescript, and it required the severest penalties to carry out the rule.†

In 1717 there arose, all at once, at Halle, a multitude of *Landsmannschaften;* Meiners names twelve. They chose seniors and subseniors, and openly wore colors as marks of distinction, as those of the Marches of Pomerania, &c. These associations were immediately prohibited by a royal rescript.‡

The *Landsmannschaften* were forbidden at Rostock § in 1750, at

* Haupt, 204. † Gretschel, 274.

‡ Meiners (*History*, iv. 163) says that these associations were in fact suppressed. But *quære.*

§ Ib. pp. 163–174.

Jena in 1765 and 1778, at Kiel in 1774, at Göttingen in 1762, at Erfurt in 1794, in Prussia and at Altorf in consequence of the decree of the diet of 1795. In 1816, when the *Burschenschaft* was organized, *Landsmannschaften* existed in most of the universities, and a contest took place between them and the *Burschenschaft.*

From two of these academical prohibitions, it appears that Pennalism still survived in the *Landsmannschaften.* Thus the Rostock law of 1850 says: "Pennalism, that barbarous custom, barbarously named, having been driven into exile from our universities, for their good, let Nationalism also, with the evils which come with it, be put away from our course of education. Therefore, if any one shall attempt to set on foot any thing either of the name, or the thing itself, who shall assume the title of senior, . . who shall subject to himself new-comers or others, or annoy them, or shall exact money from them, even a penny, him we shall estimate altogether unfit to be a member of this academy."

The law of the University of Kiel, of 1774, is still more severe: "Any one daring to introduce or establish the infamous custom of Pennalism, condemned and proscribed by all good and wise persons, or to call together seditious assemblies, or to set up the national societies, or to annoy students lately come to the university, by the exaction of money, or entertainments, or other unjust treatment, shall be subjected to penalties, to be determined in each case, and shall be put away, as an enemy and traitor to the university."

That Pennalism still prevailed in Göttingen, appears from a rescript of Münchhausen to the university, of 1757; which directs care to be taken, "that neither shall newly arrived students, by the post or other conveyance, be made sport of; nor shall such students as use, for their own pleasure, to form the acquaintance of new-comers, and to that end to put themselves in their way, obtain them lodgings and strike up friendships with them, be permitted to practice such presumptuous means of corrupting young persons."*

Klüpfel† gives a striking sketch of the *Landsmannschaften* or Corps.

"Each Corps," he says, "is divided into regular and irregular members, *Corps-burschen*, and *Renoncen.* Only the former are full members of the association, and form its nucleus; the others, as their name indicates, are such as do not claim full members' rights, but attach themselves to the Corps for the sake of its protection and influence. In like manner the *Renoncen* are in a sort of novitiate, where every one wishing to join the Corps has to remain for a time,

---

* Meiners, ii. 210.

† Pp. 293–398. It must be understood that Klüpfel's description does not apply equally to all the Corps (*Landsmannschaften* National Societies), and much less to all their individual members. I know very estimable persons, and myself had excellent pupils, belonging to Corps of the better sort. But this does not impair the general correctness of his picture.

until he can claim full membership. Admission is attended with certain ceremonies, frequently with a sort of catechisation on the *Comment* and principles of the association, the attaching a ribbon, the communication of the cipher of the association, and the kiss of brotherhood. At the head of the organization, and chosen from among members, for one year, stands a senior, a consenior, a secretary, and a number of special committeemen (*weitere Chargirte*), proportioned to that of the members. All these together constitute the council, which resolves absolutely upon all matters connected with the Corps, attends to its connections abroad, presides at its regular festivals, and to which the unconditional obedience of every member is due. Each Corps has, besides, minor distinctive peculiarities, to which it is a point of importance to adhere without variation. The various Corps are connected together by their common object of maintaining the *Comment*,* and of keeping up their fantastic and brilliant phase of student-life. The co-operation necessary for these purposes is kept up by the convention of seniors, and the convention of committeemen. These hold the place of supreme authority among the students, and seek to maintain their position by means of the rule, that every student who would have a voice in public matters must belong to an association and act through his Senior; that the Convention of Seniors alone shall give laws, direct festivals, and put forth decisions; and that any one opposing its determinations or disobeying its decisions on points of honor, &c., shall, by so doing, incur the condemnation of infamy.

"From these societies, and among them, there grew into existence a kind of student-life, social among its members, and jovial to others. Their members had frequently been friends at the inferior schools; each upheld all, and all each: the consciousness of belonging to an organization gave a certain confidence and freedom to their manners; prominent and favorite persons, such as every Corps contained, planted and cherished a cheerful and bold spirit. At the same time, each society strove to outdo the rest in the splendor and solemnity of their society and anniversary feasts; and there was always a magnificent display when whole Corps, with all their dependents, met at some festival, and the society colors vied with each other in display.

"But dangerous and grievous harms began to show themselves, derived from the Corps organization.

"The *Circuli Fratrum*, or circles of brothers, were intended to be societies of intellectually educated young men, of an age most susceptible to lofty ideas, and who were summoned to mental growth in an atmosphere such as, when kept in motion by the flights of genius, will stimulate the noblest powers. But these circles became too exclusively mere open convivial societies of good-fellows, aiming chiefly at pleasure, and very often at exceedingly material pleasures, without any higher purpose, or broad and inspiriting beliefs. This emptiness and insipidity must, of course, very soon become irksome to intellects and spirits of the higher class. These would not suffer themselves to be hidden under showy externals and pompous public appearances. The brotherhood among the brethren of the societies, which was held up as one of the chief aims of the organization, was not always that true friendship so delightful to the hearts of the young, which forms a basis for lifelong associations, although the Corps-statutes expressly prescribe such; for the real basis of friendship was frequently wanting, namely, true respect, arising from noble aims and goodness of character. The Corps was altogether unfit to be a school for such virtues; the system of subordination to the seniors was opposed to noble impulses. The ambition of becoming one of that number perverted and destroyed friendship. The less the interest felt in intellectual things, so much the greater was the power of sensual influences; and the principle adopted by the Corps, that the private life of a member was no concern of the whole body, as long as he did not endanger what the *Comment* held as their honor, inclined towards a tolerance in respect to morals. which was only too well adapted shamefully to pervert the moral perceptions of a young man, and to lead him off into a vicious course of sensual and dissolute indulgence in which many have been ruined, but from which the Corps, as such, never saved one.

"The state of feeling within these societies may be judged of from the pro-

* A sort of constitution.

visions in the statutes and the Comment, which require that any member having a venereal disease shall notify the fact at the beer-house (*Kneipe*), and shall suffer a penalty if he fight a duel while ill. It is demonstrable, also, that the Corps-festival often ended in mere orgies; and many unfortunate and perverted youth were first induced to procure membership and standing in societies for the sake of their vicious indulgences. At Tübingen, it has happened that a whole Corps has become corrupted. This same low condition of morals is indicated more and more by the meetings at the *Kneipe*, where the beer-laws (*Bier-Comment*) were so easily made an instrument of vulgar drunkenness, and where the abilities of honor, as well of individual members of the same Corps, as of the different Corps themselves, was determined by the standard of their capacity for drinking, whose highest grade, that of Beer-king, was given for the ability to dispose of eighty pints (*schoppen*).

"With this coarseness and even vulgarity of tone, which soon prevailed in the Corps, was connected the misuse of the Comment as a stimulus to dueling, and the bullying (*pauksucht*) and 'renowning' which were its consequences. No one was thought honorable except such as were ready to give satisfaction on the dueling-ground; and he was a jolly respectable Bursch, and the pride of his society was such a one as had already fought many duels, and was known as a keen and powerful swordsman. To become such was the aim of their ambition. Quarreling, insults, provoking conduct, a touchiness carried so far as to be ridiculous, and innumerable duels were the consequence. To make up the full number of a hundred duels was the only ambition of many students; and while learned studies suffered in this state of things, social life was an unpleasant existence upon a continual war-footing, in which those unacquainted with weapons were entirely defenseless. Indeed, to behave toward these last in a manner usually reckoned utterly dishonorable, was no prejudice to the honor of a *Bursch*, and to break one's word of honor to a *Philister* was only a matter of sport. The societies were also in a state of constant excitement and irritation against each other. The privilege of changing freely from one Corps to another availed nothing; for any one who had insulted one, was obliged, before he could enter another, to fight duels all round with the former; nor could a new Corps establish itself on a received footing except by fighting itself into recognition. A continual rivalry, also, gave abundance of occasion for constant quarrels, which ended in duels for the honor of each man's country; in which every member of the Corps, as the lot or the decision of the senior should determine, was obliged to fight for the honor of the society. In this manner it came to pass, lastly, that the whole body of students were, by means of the Corps, only divided into larger parties; and that much the largest number had to submit to be tyrannized over by a minority of the members of the Corps, and even by a still smaller number, namely, the Convention of Seniors, which, as we have seen, was constituted by no means of the most respectable, but only of the most bullying of the students."

With this description of Klüpfel's may be compared the Comments of two of the Corps, given in the Appendix, and agreeing entirely with him.* The Comment treats chiefly of honor, how it may be preserved, attacked, and regained when lost. The sword is the talisman of honor. Accordingly, much of the Comment discusses the duel, and how it may be occasioned and fought. Nothing is said of good morals; and, on the contrary, more than one paragraph betrays how low was the condition of the Corps in this respect, and proves only too clearly the truth of Klüpfel's description.

This author cites, in another place, the technical terms of the societies. The Comment defines the names Fox, Brandfox, Young Bursch, Old

---

* See Appendix III.

Bursch, Mossy Head.* "Every student not a member of a society is a renouncer." One not holding himself subject to the Comment was a "savage" or a "finch," and on such, when opportunity offered, punishment was inflicted with a whip or a stick.

"The Comment," observes Klüpfel, "was probably modeled upon the ceremonial of the later chivalry and court life, as developed at the court of Louis XIV. Most of the French technical terms used in it are from this source."† Such words, in part in distorted forms, are numerous; including *Comment, Comment suspendu, Satisfaction, Avantage, Touche, Secundieren, Renommieren, Renonce, Maltraitionen, Chargierte*, &c.‡ According to Klüpfel, the rapier with the plate-shaped guard came also from France.§

After the period of the dominion, and indeed tyranny, of the *Landsmannschaften*, in the German universities, dating from the sixteenth century, there arose against them, in succession, two violent adversaries; first the Students' Orders, and afterwards the Burschenschaft. The latter, as we have seen, definitely put an end to Pennalism.

B. Students' Orders.

These arose about the middle of the eighteenth century. The first prohibition of them appeared at Göttingen, in 1748, and was repeated in 1760 and 1762.‖ In the latter year appears the first trace of the same at Erlangen,¶ in 1765** at Tübingen; in the same year, 1765, appeared the first prohibition of them at Jena, and another in 1767.†† A third came out in 1795, in connection with an imperial edict against secret societies; and a similar one was then issued in the Prussian universities and at Altdorf.‡‡ In 1802, Meiners announces, with satisfaction, of Göttingen,§§ that "it is now some years since the strictest inquiry could detect any of the orders at our university;" although he naïvely adds, in a note, that "within a very short period traces of an order have been discovered." An accident, as I myself remember, led to this discovery. A student was drowned, and in sealing up his

---

* Comment (App. III.), § 16–22. For Fox, was used, in the seventeenth century, Feux. Schöttgen's very full list of nicknames of Pennals contains no other now used. The name Schorists, for students who have passed through their Pennal year, has also gone out of use.

† Klüpfel, 182.

‡ Butmann would even derive *Verschiss* (dishonor), from *verjus*.

§ Klüpfel, 184. The opinion of those who find, in the present students' duels, a trace of the mediæval German chivalry, is contradicted by Klüpfel's view, which is certainly correct, of their French origin. There is a difference as wide as the heavens between a *chevalier* of the time of Louis XIV. and a German *Ritter* of the time of Hohenstaufen; and as much between a duel upon a point of honor and a decision of God by means of a joust.

‖ Meiners, "*Constitution and Administration of the German Universities*," ii. 296.

¶ Englehardt, 177.

** Klüpfel, 279.

†† Meiners, "*History*," &c., iv. 169.

‡‡ Ibid., 174.

§§ Meiners, "*Constitution*," &c., ii. 302.

effects, a list was found of names of members (*Konstantisten*). Thus the orders lasted until the first years of the nineteenth century. At the time of the rise of the *Burschenschaft* (1816), they seem to have disappeared. I find no record of any contest of the *Burschenschaft* with the orders, but only against the *Landsmannschaften.*

What distinction existed between these Orders and the *Landsmannschaften* or *Nations?* There must have been one, because they were always at enmity. Meiners says that they had much in common in their organization, and that the orders differed from the *Landsmannschaften* "only in that they admitted members without regard to their nationality." This was, it is true, one distinction, but not the only one; a second was, the adoption by the orders of symbols analogous to those of the Free Masons. Thus, there were found, in 1765, "traces of a lodge of Free Masons among the students at Tübingen." Klüpfel says, "most of the orders in the universities were off-shoots of Free Masonry."* In like manner, Englehardt says† that the Order of the Cross, founded in 1762, was organized throughout in the forms of Free Masonry. "In the place of assembly of the order, there was a basin with water, whose symbolic meaning was explained to those initiated; a statue of friendship, and one of virtue, skulls, a cross of the order, with sun, moon, and stars, and a crucifix." The university senate reported, in 1767, that it had taken away some insignia of an order from some students, and that the orders, in spite of prohibitions, were universal, both in Erlangen and the other German universities, and that scarcely a student could be found who did not belong to an order.

In 1770 the Order of Coopers was discovered, which held lodges, had degrees, and had a destructive influence.‡ The Black Order, or Order of Harmony, arose in 1771, at Erlangen, and had members in Nuremberg and Coburg. Its grand lodge was in Brunswick. In 1797 were found in the papers of this order catechisms of the first, second, and third grades, with symbols having an ethical signification. "The ceremonies of admission were adopted from the Free Masons, with whom the Black Order seems to have maintained very friendly relations. The statutes of this order named Pythagoras as their first known master." So much will serve to describe this order as such; and it also appears that they were not confined to the universities, nor to students. The same was the case with the Constantists, who existed at Halle in 1786, and had afterward (about 1798), members in civil and military stations at Berlin. Their laws seem to have included

* Klüpfel, 280. † Englehardt, 178. ‡ Ib., 180, 183, 184.

the reckless jacobinical religious and political opinions; and the Prussian ministry believed "that the revolutionists sought to make use of the students in their designs."*

From the foregoing, it seems that the orders were especially active in the second half of the eighteenth century, and only lasted into the first years of the nineteenth century; that they were entirely distinct from the *Landsmannschaften*, having no regard for nationality, as the latter did; having also symbols and degrees, and being in connection with orders outside the universities; neither of which was the case with the *Landsmannschaften*. Considering the existence of so essential differences, it is not to be wondered at that the two organizations were in a state of bitter enmity.

VII. History of the Universities in the Nineteenth Century.

Introduction.—My own Academical Experience.

From the description of the *Landsmannschaft* and orders, I might pass at once to the Burschenschaft. But the question might justly be asked, Were there not, in these earlier times, some students who did not belong to these orders; or would it not be worth while to consider them? There certainly were many such; but it is difficult to find much information about them, for the very reason that they did not swear to any standards or emblems, nor were organized as an associated body, under common statutes. They did not, however, live in entire isolation, but in friendly circles; and they were united by a friendship which needed no statutes. These circles, moreover, had a very definite character: a common ideal, common labor, endeavors after a common purpose.

I have known several such circles, and have belonged to them. It appeared to me that a simple description of my own student-life will afford a more lively picture of such a circle, than to give an abstract characterization of them.

But the idea carried me further. Why should I, I asked, confine myself to my experience as a student? Why not add that of my life as a professor?

I entered the university in the first year of this century, 1801, and from that time to 1854, with comparatively small intervals, I have lived in the German universities. Having been a professor since 1811, I have, as such, stood in close personal relations with the students, and have taken sincere and active interest in their weal and woe.

I give, therefore, after ripe consideration, an account of all that was

* The Jena ordinance against the Orders, in 1767, names the Orders of Hope (Esperance), that of Concord or of the Cross, the Coopers', and that of the Lilies.

important in my academical life and experience, in chronological order; having had excellent opportunities of consulting the best oral and written sources, and testimony on the spot, as to matters at a distance, and having observed the influence of whatever happened, upon the university where I might happen to be at the time.

A. Going to Halle, in 1799.

Preliminary View.

Fifty-five years have passed since my first glance into university-life. I had left the Joachimsthal Gymnasium, at Berlin, and was going to visit my elder brother, Friederick, then a student at Halle. He, and other previous school-fellows, took me with them to the lectures. There I heard, for the first time, F. A. Wolf, whose lecture-room was crowded full, and who made a profound impression upon me. I thought it very singular, during the lectures of Master Güte on Isaiah, to hear the poor old man every moment interrupted by "Pst!" on which, according to the custom, he was obliged to repeat what he had been saying. I also visited the fighting-rooms, where I was introduced to the greatest fighter and bully for the time being. He was a great stout *Bursch*, in very simple costume—shirt, drawers, monstrous pantaloons, and on his head a lofty *stürmer*, i. e., a three-cornered hat, with one corner brought forward to protect his eyes. This ogre made such an impression upon me, that I was at the trouble, some years afterward, of inquiring what had become of him. I found that he had become tutor in the family of a miller, where he had every thing free, and a fixed daily allowance of nine pots of beer. There could scarcely be a greater contrast than after this visit to the fighting-room, an excursion which I took on the Saale by moonlight, in listening to the melancholy notes of the French-horn at a distance. This short visit to Halle was a foretaste, indeed, of all the pleasures and sorrows which I experienced there some years later.

B. Göttingen.

Easter, 1801, *to Easter*, 1803.

I left the Gymnasium at Easter, 1801, and went, in company with my friend, now Privy Councillor of Finance, Sotzmann, to Göttingen, by way of Thuringia.

We passed through Weimar. How glorified, to my youthful imagination, did every thing appear in this home of the greatest genius of Germany! I watched everywhere for Goethe, Schiller, and Herder. I had, however, only the pleasure of becoming acquainted with the latter, my father having given me a letter of introduction to him. He received me in a very friendly manner, and invited me to supper, where I found Consistory-Councillor Günther. It may be imagined how I hung upon every word from Herder. Fifty-three years have passed since that evening, but I can yet hear his observations on the idea of character. As he was in the habit of doing in his writings, he did orally; beginning with the word itself, as derived from χαρασσειν, &c. From various remarks of Herder and Günther, I saw, with sorrow, that there was a division among the heroes of Weimar; a division with which I afterward became acquainted from Goethe's "Truth and Poetry from my Life." As I write this title, I lose all courage to give a more detailed account of Herder, in thinking of Goethe's incredibly correct and most masterly description of him.

On arriving at Göttingen, I took lodgings in the house of an instrument-maker named Krämer, which I mention for a reason that will soon appear.

My father intended me for a jurist. I commenced my studies by attending lectures on the Institutions, from Councillor Waldeck, taking notes industriously. At the same time I procured a book then universally used, Höpfner's Institutions, and made use of it in studying, along with my notes on Waldeck's lectures. To my astonishment, I found such an entire agreement between the book and my notes, that I gave up taking notes at all, but took Höpfner to lectures, to follow along in it. Unfortunately, I sat pretty near the lecturer's chair, and Waldeck espying my book, his keen eyes recognized it. To do this, and to break out into the most violent and pitiless attacks upon Höpfner, were the work of the same moment. My situation was not the most comfortable, as I had not the remotest intention of provoking old Waldeck. He did not, however, lay it up against me, but was very friendly, when I attended his lectures on the Pandects, in the winter term, and afterward gave me an excellent testimonial, earned, however, with infinite discomfort. He lectured on the Pandects three hours daily!

He belonged entirely to the old school of jurists; his edition of Heineccius' Compendium of the Institutes is now used only at Coimbra.

In the summer term of 1802, I attended the lectures on civil law of one who prepared the way for the subsequent school of Savigny—namely, Hugo. His lectures, in connection with which we had questions in jurisprudence to solve, were marked by critical acumen; and his relentless controversial powers, not seldom directed against Waldeck as a representative of the old school, did not at all displease us. Hugo also wrote the sharpest reviews in the Göttingen papers, otherwise chiefly of a neutral character. I remember one such, an attack on Malblanc's Pandects, under which a reader had written "*Hunc tu Romane caveto.*"*

In my fourth term I turned my attention, with my father's consent, to political economy, attended Sartorius' lectures on politics, and studied for myself, Smith's celebrated work on the Wealth of Nations. These, my professional studies at Göttingen, I pursued, in truth, not with much love of them, but still constrained myself to a considerable degree of industry.

In each term I attended one or two courses not juridical. Thus, for two terms I attended the valuable mathematical lectures of Thibaut, brother of the celebrated jurist; and applied myself with the greatest assiduity to algebra, in which my friend Sotzmann gave me the most faithful and patient assistance.

At another time I attended Blumenbach's lectures on natural history. Most of his hearers cared little for any knowledge of the subject, but attended for the amusement of the entertaining accounts—of shaved bears, earth-eating Otomaks, &c.—which he used to narrate with superabundant humor. After the lecture we often went to Pütter's house, where we were entertained with a quartette, in which he himself played first violin. The excellent old man used to be pleased to have us for an audience.

I also attended Blumenbach's lectures on mineralogy, without having the remotest idea that I should ever myself become a professor of natural history and mineralogy.

A course by Fiorillo, on the history of art, was very instructive, although he did not speak German very correctly. Thus he would say, that "in this century there arose a fury for spires;"† meaning a passion for building them. His principal subject was the history of painting. He described the various schools of painting, and the most celebrated artists of each; mentioned the localities of the chief works of each master, and exhibited copper-plates of the most remarkable. In connection with Fiorillo's course, I made excursions to Cassel, only five miles distant. Tischbein, director of the valuable collection of paintings there, was very kind in giving access to them. I became quite intimate with Hummel, from Naples, a shrewd and agreeable man.‡ In Göttingen I made the acquaintance of Riepenhausen, the engraver on copper. His two sons, both known as artists, and of whom one is

---

* Savigny has given an excellent account of Hugo.

† The mispronunciation cannot be transferred to English.—[*Trans.*]

‡ Napoleon had the Cassel gallery carried to France, and its finest pictures, such as Claude Lorraine's Four Hours of the Day, were made over to the Empress Josephine, at Malmaison, and afterward were taken to St. Petersburg by Alexander.

yet living at Rome, were my friends. Among the works of the father are his widely known copies of Hogarth's pictures, to which Lichtenberg wrote an explanation. Riepenhausen possessed a treasure of Dürer's engravings, from copper and wood, then valued only by a very few amateurs, and consequently not so costly a luxury as at present. The oftener I examined these, the more I liked them; and now I cannot look enough at the St. Jerome, the Hubert, the Melancholy, and many others.

My elder brother, a student before me in Göttingen, was well known to Music-director Forkel. I inherited the acquaintance, and the more easily, as he and I lived in the same house. At this time he stood quite alone in the musical world. A scholar of Emanuel Bach, of Hamburg, he had an unbounded reverence for Emanuel's father, the great Sebastian Bach, and played his compositions for piano-forte and organ in a masterly style, after the manner which had descended from him.* Almost all other music was strange and unpleasant to him, and his over-severe criticism upon the celebrated and splendid overture to Gluck's Iphigenia in Aulis, gave dissatisfaction to many, and with good reason. This criticism would, of course, be unfair, because Forkel judged of all music, even Gluck's, by the pattern of that of Sebastian Bach. One who should take Palladio for the normal architect, or Michael Angelo for the normal painter, would judge wrongly of the Strasburg Minster, and of Correggio. Thus, as Forkel disliked all the universally liked modern music, the friends of it disliked him; and many left him, also, because they were entirely unable to comprehend Sebastian Bach's compositions. By means of my brother, I took piano-forte lessons of Forkel. He made me begin, not on his grand piano, but on a common Silbermann's instrument, with learning the touch, and the production of a pure tone, and then proceeded to exercises, and thence to the "Inventions" which Bach wrote for the piano.

I studied, also, modern languages. I took French lessons of a French abbé, who, with undoubting self-sufficiency, considered French literature elevated high above that of all other nations. He hardly knew what to say when I praised Shakspeare—that "*monstre.*" I remember how, once, he was almost beside himself at my translating to him a passage from Lessing's "Dramaturgy," beginning with the words, "Let any one name to me a composition of the great Corneille which I cannot improve. What will you bet?" "Who is this Monsieur

---

* Forkel published several collections of Sebastian Bach's compositions for the piano. But the works of this profound master were not valued by the public at large, until Mendelssohn, in 1828, summoned to life some of them, which had slept as silent as death, in manuscript, for a hundred years.

Lessing," he asked, "who dares to come out in this way against the great Corneille?" And the explanations which Lessing added could not satisfy him at all.

I learned Spanish with the theologian Tychsen, who was long employed in the Escurial; and with the friendly and thorough Beneke, I read Shakspeare.

With my love of art was connected also love of nature. In every vacation I used to take journeys. At Whitsuntide, 1801, with Meckel, the anatomist; Luden, the historian; and some other friends, I visited the Hartz. There was collected on the Brocken a cheerful company of some forty students from different universities.

In the Michaelmas vacation of 1801 I went to Hamburg; at Easter, 1802, to Berlin; at Michaelmas, 1802, to Switzerland, and down the Rhine, from Basle to Coblentz. As appears—or ought to—my journeys were mostly on foot; as, fortunately, the seductive railway was not in existence;—fortunately, I mean, in reference to the journeys of students. Not that I would have them, as I did in my youth, plod through the sandy deserts of the Mark, Pomerania, and Luneburg, on foot; although even those routes have their enjoyment when traveled with congenial and cheerful friends, who, in spite of wind and weather, bad roads, and worse inns, remain courageous and cheerful, and never despair as long as the money lasts. But I heartily pity those students who go from Frankfort to Basle by railway, and see all the magnificence of the Rhine and its beautiful mountains, with their castles, and strong old towns, flit swiftly past their eyes without leaving one single fixed and clear picture.

The custom of students' journeys began first to obtain, as far as I know, in the beginning of this century; especially long ones. When, in the Michaelmas vacation of 1802, I went from Göttingen to Stuttgart, with four acquaintances, and challenged them there to proceed with me to Switzerland, the thing seemed to them impossible. They were so far from accepting my proposal, that one of them made a wager with me that I would not enter Switzerland. I won the wager.

Traveling is of the greatest value to students. How otherwise could they use their vacations? Most of them go home. The more indolent of them are often an annoyance at home, and even to the whole neighborhood, by their foolish tricks, and return, tired out, to the university, having learned nothing in the vacation, but forgotten much. And even to the industrious, the season is not one of active exertion. They probably do not desire to be entirely at leisure, and often fall into an unfortunate way of half working and half not, in which their heart is only half in what they do. So they return to the university without being either satisfied or refreshed with their vacation.

The case is far otherwise with students who spend their vacation in traveling. To begin with a very obvious remark, it is a good thing that the money which others often waste so uselessly, should be spent in a pleasure so elevating as that of traveling.

Traveling—that is, of industrious students—makes a pause in their studies, so that they do not work, year in and year out, like soulless machines wound up and set going. This pause, moreover, is not a useless, wearisome, and enervating idleness; on the contrary, traveling necessarily excites a most vivid activity of mind; for the traveler cannot be satiated with examining all the beauty which appears everywhere, in nature and art. I shall never forget how overpowering was my first impression upon seeing the Alps, the Rhine country, the ocean; and the Strasburg Minster, the cathedral of Cologne, and many other such things. All such things are deeply impressed on the mind of the youth, and he collects in his memory a treasure of splendid pictures which he can recall with pleasure in after years, perhaps when unable to leave home. How he will learn, also, in such journeys, to know his beautiful German fatherland, and to love it with youthful affection! But enough of traveling, the pleasure of my youth, and by the memory of it, of my old age.

Having sketched the bright side of life at the University of Göttingen, I must not hide the dark side.

Whoever has read, with attention, Meiners' "Organization and Management of the German Universities," has found an account of this dark side in the former days of Göttingen. The book appeared in 1802, when the author was prorector there. His description throws the strongest light upon the traits of the University of Göttingen; and how does he begin? What does he say, for instance, of the students? He speaks especially of those from leading families; who, he thinks, give tone and character to the university. As at that time such young men "of condition" studied almost nothing but jurisprudence, this fact seems to have been the cause of Meiners' statement, that in Germany jurisprudence "undeniably held the highest place, medicine the second, theology the third."

Meiners discusses the duel like a pedant trying to appear a man of the world, and therefore quite unable to "touch the honor" of those of high condition; and, indeed, having more consideration for that than for his own duty as *magnificus*. He repeatedly uses the term "a young man of condition," in speaking of challenges and duels by such persons.

His tone is very different in speaking of the poor students of his third faculty, the theological. "At our university," he says, "the period seems to me not far distant, when it will be universally considered not only punishable, but ridiculous, for future teachers of Christ's religion to be demanding satisfaction with the sword for insults received." These future teachers of Christ's religion, then, were at that time never persons "of condition."*

Among other objections to the examinations at Göttingen, Meiners cites this: that the wealthy would go to other universities to escape them; and that they would occasion "still fewer well-born and wealthy young men to devote themselves to the sciences than heretofore." But he says nothing against the half-yearly examinations of the poor beneficiaries (mostly theological students). While he is very tender of all considerations which might restrain the wealthy and well-born from studying at Göttingen,† he gives advice, on the other hand, for preventing the poor from attending the university. "Even a moderate number of industrious young persons," he says, "with whom no fault can be found, who cannot support themselves through the course, are a great evil."

Meiners' remarks on gaming, as follows, are also characteristic:

"Playing hazard will never be stopped at universities where many wealthy young men of family are gathered together. . . . Sons hear and see it going on from their earliest childhood, and imitate their fathers in it as early as possible. . . . A few years since, certain persons convicted of playing hazard, declared before the court that they had played the game from their childhood in their parents' houses, that they thought it justifiable, that they knew no other game, and that they should continue, when they had leisure, to play it; and they were content to suffer the legal penalty for it when discovered. Even tutors believe it to be a good plan to play hazard under proper oversight—on the principle of acquainting young people with such games, and of teaching them early to play with moderation."‡

Every count sat, at lecture, at his own table—the "count's table;" they were addressed separately, at the beginning of the lecture, by the title of "High and well-born lord count," and paid a double fee.§

These quotations sufficiently show that, when I came to Göttingen, students from high families did actually give tone and character to the university. This shows why Meiners laid so extraordinarily much stress on the behavior of the students; caring more for the varnish on their education than for the education itself. He would have the way of thinking of the high nobility prevail at the university; and hence his opinions on the duel, playing hazard, &c. In like manner he

* Meiners afterward adheres to the unanswerable judgment upon the duel, given by his colleague, the theologian Michaelis.

† Even his opinions on the duel clearly indicate this delicacy.

‡ Meiners, 280.

§ Meiners, 189. He mentions, also, other privileges of counts: such as the entering their names at coming in a separate book; having a seat before the court, &c.

expresses himself, with remarkable tenderness, in disagreement with the strictness of the Göttingen academical laws, not only against wild howling in the streets, but against singing; against cries both of *pereat* and *vivat*.

According to him, the whole university ought, like the single students, to be always careful of its manners, and never be disagreeable to any high personages passing through it.

I had, unfortunately, an opportunity to become well acquainted with the dark side of this varnished academical outside behavior, by means of a very dear school-fellow who went from the Gymnasium, a year before me, to Erlangen, and thence, the next year, to Göttingen. Through him I became acquainted with some students who, as indeed gradually became apparent to both of us, lived in a manner altogether vicious. Nothing was at first perceptible, except that they were passionate hazard-players. As to Meiners' remark, that it is not strange that the sons of good families, who have, from childhood, been used to see their fathers playing, should bring a fondness for it to the university with them, the case was exactly reversed with me. I was earnestly warned, by my parents, against dissipation; but they never thought of warning me against playing hazard, for the game never entered into their minds. Thus it happened that I was led into playing. The game did not seem to me a sin, but a matter of indifference. But what a life did it lead me into! The passion got entire possession of me, and made me indifferent to every thing which I had before loved most. It was as if my heart had frozen to ice within me. I thank God, that after a little, I had the great good fortune to have ill-fortune at play, which brought me to reflection upon this unholy and devilish occupation, and caused me to make a fixed resolution to give it up at once, and forever.

At the gaming-table I found out how terribly vicious were the lives of these men—most of them being loathsomely syphilitic. God preserved me from any dissipation in that direction, however, by means of the advice which my father had impressed strongly on me, and the fearful warnings which I saw before my eyes. And yet these men belonged to that "well-born" class who passed for refined people, who understood good manners, and who were everywhere invited to parties, and who shone in them.

My glance into this abyss of moral destruction made so profound an impression upon me that, for a time, I even shut myself up misanthropically from everybody. It still remains with me, and subsequent experience has strengthened it. It may be imagined how much pleasure I received when the *Burschenschaft* took ground earnestly and strongly against such abominations; and how decidedly I thought it my official duty, as professor, to speak everywhere in favor of that body. To my encouragement, I found an exceedingly true friend, altogether the opposite of these *roués;* an *anima candida*, the true son of his mother, remarkably interested in his profession, that of jurisprudence, and moreover, a competent mathematician. This was the present Senior of the University of Tübingen, Chief Councillor of Justice von Schrader.

Not to conclude the account of my Göttingen experiences with a discord, I will mention an occurrence which put me into the greatest excitement. This was the coming of Goethe, who, in the summer of 1801, went to Pyrmont by way of Göttingen. Scarcely had it become known that he had taken lodgings at the Crown Inn, when we, his enthusiastic admirers, determined to give him a *vivat*, at the risk of being taken up by the catch-poles.

We agreed to meet in the evening, before the Crown—Achim Arnim,* Kestner,† Blumenbach's son, with others, being the most active. We were all punctual at the moment. Arnim commenced the *vivat*, and we all joined in right heartily, but thought best instantly to scatter in every direction.‡

On his return from Pyrmont, Goethe spent a longer time in Göttingen, lodging at Krämer's house, where I myself lodged. Though this delighted me much, I was still too diffident to approach him, though I saw him often. One evening he took supper with some professors and students, at a club, presided over by Bouterwek and Reinhard,§ and which had been sportively named the Improvement Club. Some pedantic, stiff professors gave us to understand that it did not correspond with this name, that we gave Goethe's health, with cheers, at table, although it was done with great enthusiasm.‖

* In the summer term of 1801 I was much with Arnim and Brentano; both had been my friends at school.

† This, I believe, was the same who died at Rome two years ago, universally lamented. We called him Lottiades, for a reason which appears from his mother's correspondence, the publication of which, by my dear friend, Councillor R. Wagner, was so much disliked by many persons.

‡ I was much pleased to find this *vivat* mentioned by Goethe (*Works*, 1840, part 27, p. 81). He says, "Putting up at the Crown, in Göttingen, I observed, as twilight came on, a movement in the street: students came and went, disappeared in side streets, and appeared again in groups. At last there arose, all at once, a friendly *vivat!* and in a twinkling every thing was silent. I was informed that such demonstrations were prohibited, and was the more pleased because they had only dared to greet me from the street, in passing by." So little did the *curator perpetuus* of the University of Jena sympathize with this over-scrupulous prohibition!

§ Editor of Bürger's Poems.

‖ Goethe's Works, xxvii. 92. He gives a very ludicrous account of a night-scene at Krämer's house, when, between the barking of dogs and Miss Krämer's practicing trills, he fell almost into despair. I have often heard the singer, my fellow-lodger.

C.—Halle.

At Easter, 1803, I left Göttingen and went to Halle, the reputation of which was then very high, on account of the celebrated physician, Reil, and F. A. Wolf. I had labored excessively at Göttingen. The library, access to which was made very easy to me through Beneke's friendly interposition, had betrayed me into an immoderate amount of reading. Some recreation was absolutely necessary for me. This I found, by hiring a summer lodging along with friends, among whom were some previous school-fellows. We fixed ourselves in the house known as The Bunch of Grapes, beautifully situated, between Halle and Giebichenstein, whose garden looked down from a height upon the Saale. We occupied ourselves mostly with reading some of the great poets. We formed a society, which we called by the somewhat doubtful name of the Æsthetic Society; whose members applied themselves in part to philosophical studies, and in part to poetry. We met weekly, and contributed in turn, manuscript articles of the most various kinds—historical, æsthetic; some poems, translations, prose and poetical. We reckoned ourselves of the school of Schlegel. With him I had previously, while at the Gymnasium, come into contact in a singular way. Kotzebue had written his "Hyperborean Ass," a satire on the brothers Schlegel. One of our teachers, who hated the brothers, committed the mistake of reading this composition to us in the class. How this should have appeared to us as it did, when our teacher was so high an authority to us, I do not know. But as we did not like it, he himself permitted us, after it, to read A. W. Schlegel's answer to it, "The Triumphal Arch of Herr von Kotzebue," and then the various writings of the romantic school, of Tieck, Wackenroder, Novalis, &c. The opinions of these writers upon the heroes of ancient and modern times had great weight with us. Dante, Shakspeare, Cervantes, &c., whom they praised enthusiastically, were read by us with eagerness; while we neglected other authors, such as Wieland, for example, who had before been earnestly recommended to us.*

In the Whitsuntide vacation of 1803 I visited Dresden and the Saxon Switzerland. The Dresden gallery of paintings, in particular, attracted me. It would carry me too far, were I here to speak of the pictures which gave me always increasing pleasure; especially the

* Wieland had previously ranked as the representative of the golden age of German literature. especially his *Agathon* and *Oberon*. It is incredible how his authority was shaken by the few lines of the *Citacio Edictalis*, in the Athenæum, ii. 340. Our eyes were first opened, at a subsequent time, to many doubtful and exceptionable views of the romantic school.

Sistine Madonna—that apparition from a higher world—of the Correggios, Holbein's Madonna, the Christ of John Bellini, Von Ruysdael's and Claude Lorraine's landscapes.

At Michaelmas, 1803, I left my summer lodging and went to Halle, where again I lodged in the house with dear friends. One was the excellent Winterfeld, who was even then living entirely in the element of music. Unfortunately, we had some other fellow-lodgers, who lived in so shamefully debauched a manner, that at Easter, 1804, I gave up my boarding-place, and procured one in the house of the well-known eclectic philosopher, the aged Eberhard. He had formerly been a preacher at Charlottenburg, near Berlin, and was thence invited to become professor of philosophy at Halle. His bearing was that of a polished and educated Frenchman; such as used to be that of many educated Berliners. He belonged to the circle of Nicolai, that of the Universal German Library (*Allegemeine Deutscher Bibliothek*), which so long wielded the critical scepter of the German literary world. Hamann and F. H. Jacobi, at an earlier period, and afterward Fichte, Goethe, Schiller, and the romantic school, attacked the intellectual despotism of that periodical, and it is now obsolete.

I listened with the greatest interest to Wolf; attending all his lectures, from Easter, 1803, to September, 1804, except his course on Matthew, which I designedly omitted, not wishing to become familiar with his views in that direction. Those which I did attend were on the History of Greek Literature, the Satires and Epistles of Horace, the Menon of Plato, the Iliad, and the Clouds of Aristophanes. As I have, in the second part of this work, attempted to describe Wolf's character, I will here only mention with gratitude that he assisted me in a friendly manner, with advice and books.

A companion and dear friend at the university, Immanuel Bekker, was at that time my most faithful, pains-taking, reliable teacher. He will remember how, in the summer of 1804, we read Greek, with little intermission, from early in the day until late at night, often in the open air, in the most beautiful spot of the lofty bank of the Saale, at Giebichenstein. At the end of fifty years, his old scholar would once more offer him hearty thanks.

In the summer of 1804 Goethe came to Halle, and lodged, not as previously at Göttingen, in the same house with me, but opposite me, at Wolf's house. The street was not very wide, and I could, therefore, see him often, especially when he sat at the window with Wolf. But I did not speak to him even this time; not until the year 1808, when I was introduced to him in Carlsbad, as a pupil of Werner, from Freiberg. Goethe's deep interest in geognosy, especially in Werner's system, made him put himself on very friendly terms with me, and he questioned me very fully about life and instruction in Freiberg.

The baths of Lauchstedt are two miles from Halle. The Weimar stage company came thither every summer for several years. Goethe's biography tells how much he was interested in the artistic training of this troupe, and how much pains he took to substitute classical plays for the usual miserable ones. It may be imagined how much delight this theater afforded us. They represented Julius Cæsar, Othello, The Natural Daughter, The Bride of Messina, William Tell, and Jery and Bätely. When Friedrich Schlegel's Alarcos was produced, we thought it our duty to support the tragedy against the anti-Schlegelian party, although our admiration, being founded on principle, was somewhat cool. Wallenstein's Camp was excellently given. The numerous persons, notwithstanding the apparently confused and pell-mell movements of the piece, represented in a manner so wonderfully good, one artistic group after another, that we seemed to have before our eyes, in the little theater, the whole of the rude and troubled life of the Thirty Years' War. This picture of restless, homeless warfare, in the constant face of death, made a profoundly tragic impression upon the spectators.

Schiller came to Lauchstedt, being then near the end of his life. While Goethe, in the beauty and power of full health, wore an imperial geniality of aspect, Schiller had nothing extraordinary or imposing in his appearance, but seemed modest, reflective, and withdrawn within himself. We approached the great poet as much as civility permitted, and ate at the public table with him, where I had the good fortune to sit nearly opposite him. In the evening we gave him a *vivat*, with music. The wretched band of music had been directed to play melodies to songs by Schiller; but they only knew that threadbare and almost vulgarized one of "Pleasures, rays of beauteous gods." But the kind-hearted poet did not shame our good-will, and thanked us most heartily.

At Michaelmas, 1804, I had to leave the university and go from Halle to remain in my father's house at Dessau. This parting from the university was very painful to me. I had to give up so much in which my whole soul was interested, to lose sight of aims in life just coming into view, to resign all my wishes and hopes, and to enter a prosaic every-day life among law-papers.* While in this uncomfortable state of mind, I received a letter from an intimate friend at Halle. "You must," he said, "positively come back to Halle for one half-year. Steffens is come; only become acquainted with him; he is exactly

* Such was, with myself and many other of my student friends, the opposition of the ideas of student-life and Philister-life.

the man for you." This letter only expressed my own ardent desires, and I earnestly besought my father to permit me to return once more to Halle. Although my joy was great at his consent, still I had no idea how profound an influence that consent was to have upon my whole after-life.

To return to my university life.

Having returned to Halle, I attended Steffens' lectures on the internal history of the earth. These had a very remarkable influence upon me. Above all, I was impressed with Steffens' great idea that the earth has a history. This idea was neither brought out as an apparition of earth-giants, so as to prevent bold investigations by mere men, nor as a mere accident, without connection or basis. I learned, for the first time, that Werner had based a history of the development of the earth upon observations made at the present day; how the oldest mountains contain no traces of fossil animals and plants; how these are gradually found in the younger mountain formations, and stand out individually from the general mass of the stone. Man, according to Steffens, was the most individualized and independent creature; the crown and key-stone of the earthly creation.

Steffens' "*Contributions to the Internal History of Nature*," so full of genius, were the basis of his lectures. He himself considered these views as the masterpiece of his life. He wrote them at Freiberg, in 1801, under the inspiration of Werner's explanation of the epochs of mountain formations, but had based more deeply and developed more widely the views of his master. This he did in one treatise in them, entitled, "Proof that nitrogen and carbon are the representatives of magnetism in chemical processes." A second treatise is entitled, "Nature, by its whole organization, seeks only the most individual development." Here Steffens steps behind Werner's scientific circle, and characterizes, in sketches full of genius, the development of the classes of animals, from the lowest to the highest, as one graded individualization. He closes with the words, "He whom nature permits to find her harmonies within himself, who finds a whole infinite world within himself, is the most individualized creation; and is the consecrated priest of nature."

Goethe and Schelling had the greatest influence upon Steffens, he having become acquainted with them while a young man, in 1799. This occasioned the dedication of his contributions to Goethe; and the work itself shows a close adherence to Schelling.

But how thoroughly is Steffens' work forgotten! It is sad to see how eagerly, and with what restless haste the present generation drives forward, looking and aspiring forward only, without looking back at all upon the past. And yet very much could be learned from our predecessors. They did not divide and lose themselves in an infinite number of single things; indeed, compared with ourselves, they possessed but a small treasure of knowledge. But they were faithful in a few things, and put their money at usury; holding their intellectual powers compactly together, and living in great presentiments. They drew the sketches for mighty edifices. And even though they had not building materials enough to complete them, and sometimes used bad ones, still their successors cannot exalt themselves over them for it, merely on the ground of having had access to the richer and better materials which, in the course of time, have accumulated. Indeed, they have even the stronger claim to rank as masters, because, with such materials, they built in a firm, symmetrical, and workmanlike manner.

Before very long I came in closer contact with my beloved teacher, and visited him daily. He introduced me to the family of his father-in-law, Kapellmeister Reichardt in Giebichenstein, whose hospitable dwelling was visited, for longer or shorter periods, by the most eminent men, such as Goethe, Jean Paul, Voss, Fichte, Schelling, brothers Schlegel, Tieck, Novalis, Arnim, &c. The most prominent members of the University of Halle were also to be seen in the family circle of the Reichardts. Thus, Wolf was often at Giebichenstein. But the most intimate member of the circle was Schleiermacher, who had been invited to Halle together with Steffens, and was his most intimate friend. Their mutual relations will elucidate what Goethe says of his connection with Schiller. That is, they were of the most entirely opposite nature and character, and, for that very reason, were supplementary and attracted to each other. Steffens, then thirty-one years old, was a handsome, intellectual man, very lively, easily excited, often flying into a great passion, though of the utmost goodness of heart, imaginative, truly eloquent; indeed a born orator, hurried on by the fullness of his own feelings, and therefore carrying away his hearers by his enthusiastic speech. His lectures, in which, as in the ancient natural philosophy, science rose upon the wings of poetry, absorbed us wonderfully. His oration for war, delivered at Breslau, in February, 1813, had a most powerful influence; and a second, against the French, at the market in Marburg, in October, 1815, to the people gathered about him, so excited them that such partisans of the French as happened to be there were scarcely rescued from their hands by being locked up in the common prison.

Schleiermacher was entirely different from Steffens; being a small, quiet, and thoroughly discreet man. In society he never fell into harangues. He attended closely to what others said, understood it clearly, and agreed or opposed, with his well-known and peculiar dialectic keenness and skill. He never was seen excited into a passion; and even when his anger was aroused, he expressed it powerfully, but always calmly, and not without measure. He maintained constant control over himself, enough to enable him to fix his attention upon things for the full comprehension of which he had no gift; and thus always appeared judicious, even in respect to matters not familiar to him. The almost tyrannical dominion which he had and exerted over himself, was shown, even most strikingly, in little things. In a controversy, for example, whether the Low German pronunciation of sp, st., &c., was more correct and euphonious than the South German, which would say schp, scht, as in *schpitz* for *spitz*, he declared for the former. But, it was answered, why do you not pronounce accordingly in the desk? Instead of alleging in reply his habitude from youth up, he said "I will, beginning with next Sunday;" and I have been assured that he never afterward violated the promise.

Many students became followers of Steffens and Schleiermacher. These were divided according to their preferences for science or theory, or for the lectures of one or the other. But this never grew into the distinct development of two opposing schools, or even parties. As the two teachers were friends, who promoted each the good of the other, so the same was true of the pupils of each. It was also a characteristic fact that neither Steffens nor Schleiermacher was jealous of the pupils of the other. I never attended one lecture of Schleiermacher, and yet he was, in every respect, as friendly to me as he could have been to his most faithful and punctual hearer. He saw how profoundly I was interested in the results of geological investigations, and thought it entirely a matter of course that I should adhere especially to Steffens. I once had the confidence to say, in the presence of Steffens and Schleiermacher, that I was no friend to dialectical talking backward and forward, of long circuits about the truth, but that I preferred profound and compact aphorisms, which bring the truth directly before the eye, are simple in form, and need no such paraphrases. With the greatest reverence and love for our teachers, such was the freedom with which we might express ourselves before them. Accordingly, my presumptuous self-confidence in this case was wisely answered, and they gave me examples in Socratic dialectics, with friendly irony; but this without any the least disturbance of my relations with Schleiermacher.

It may, perhaps, be thought that the conversations and discussions in our circle were too exclusively on scientific subjects. But this was not at all the case. The most eager zeal of our scientific conversations was relieved by the participation of ladies in them; and the talking ceased whenever their very excellent singing commenced. They executed with pure and beautiful voices, and in a pure style, the best music from Palestrina, Leonardo Leo, Durante, Handel, and others.

This side of our academical life I felt obliged to glance at; indeed no one could omit it who should desire to characterize the influence of Steffens and Schleiermacher at that important period.*

I was so fortunate as to spend, also, the summer term of 1805 at the university.† In that summer Gall visited Halle, and lectured on his theory of the brain, which was then making a great excitement. According to him, definite local protuberances of the skull indicate definite endowments; organs of good and bad qualities. Thus, he found an organ for religion, and one for murder, and another for theft. Gall had more remarkable hearers in Halle than anywhere else; eminent men with eminent skulls, which we, the other hearers, during the lectures, used diligently for models. Above all, there was Goethe's magnificent head, whose lofty, mighty forehead showed no particular prominent organ; thus indicating a great, symmetrical, all-sided, calm organization. Near him sat Wolf, whose forehead, by the prominence over the eyes and at the root of the nose, indicated critical tendencies. Steffens, Schleiermacher, and Reil were also among the audience.

At the end of Gall's lectures, Steffens made known that he should come out against them. The new osteological theory of predestination had displeased him; and doubly, because it threatened to interfere with established things to an incredible extent. He delivered three lectures, which have appeared in print.

A faithful teacher should be interested, not only in his own special

---

* Steffens' *Autobiography*, Varnhagen's *Recollections* (vol. ii.), and Schleiermacher's letters of the period, all agree with me in this. But this is not the place to describe fully the pleasant garden life of Giebichenstein, or the never to be forgotten evenings with Steffens.

† In the beginning of the spring a very dear friend, Bartholin, and I, accompanied Steffens and Schleiermacher to the Petersberg, where we staid from Friday to early Sunday morning. On Saturday we saw a most beautiful sunset, whose silence was broken only by the sound of the bells of innumerable villages, ringing from the plain below us. We sat until after midnight, enjoying a most lively conversation between our teachers. This, however, ended early Sunday morning, for Schleiermacher was to preach the sermon on the death of the late queen dowager of Prussia, at nine o'clock, in Halle. In order to meditate the better, he walked twenty or thirty steps in advance of us. We arrived at Halle so late that he had barely time to dress in the utmost haste and ascend the pulpit; yet no one could see in the sermon any marks of his almost sleepless night and journey on foot; so clear and thoughtful was it. I felt obliged to mention this pleasure excursion, as it had so important an influence upon the mutual understanding, recognition, and friendship of Schleiermacher and Steffens; as appears from Steffens' account, and from a letter of Schleiermacher to Frau Herz. In one point I quite agree with Schleiermacher; namely, in his statement that he and Steffens were accompanied by two students.

followers, but in every thing which may promote the development of the individual gifts of each of his hearers. Such a faithful teacher was Steffens; who urged me earnestly to go to Freiberg and attend Werner's lectures.

I had been profoundly stimulated by Steffens, and even almost dazzled by his brilliant fireworks, compounded of varied pictures of nature, and vast predictions; and Werner's geognostic expositions affected me like a mild light; quieting and calming. He was not so mystical, nor poetically comprehensive as Steffens; but he gave me firmness and fixed views; and the sense of truth, founded directly upon the mountains, and comprehended by a clear and intelligent mind.

After the close of Werner's lectures I returned to Halle, remained there until September, 1816, and then returned to Freiberg. In October the terrible period of the French domination commenced. After the battle of Jena, Napoleon came to Halle and dissolved the university. Steffens returned to Denmark; and Wolf, Schleiermacher, and Reil were afterward invited to Berlin. Jerome, when king of Westphalia, re-established the university at Halle. Steffens returned, but complained, with a sad heart, of the entire destruction of the pleasant life formerly existing there. And how could it flourish and blossom under the hateful dominion of foreigners, so degrading to Germany ?

Before I now take leave of Halle for many years, I will name some few of those who studied there between 1799 and 1806: Achim Arnim, Von der Hagen, Nasse, and my brother Friedrich, among the earlier ones; and later, Boeckh, Immanuel Bekker, the theologians Theremin, David Schultz, Scheibel, Strauss, Kniewel, Neander; and also Varnhagen, Winterfeld, A. Marwitz, Dahlmann, the younger Scharnhorst, Przystanowski. Most of these belonged to the circle of Steffens and Schleiermacher,* and have since become known and celebrated as authors; and many more might be named, who have not written, but who have proved themselves, and still are proving themselves, in actual life, most valuable men.

The well-known and remarkable variety of character among those just mentioned is the best proof that there was in Halle, at that time, no such uniform school as was that of Hegel afterward. In Wolf, Schleiermacher, and Steffens, we had three teachers of character so different that it was impossible to be imitating them all. This directed us the more to the noble, free spirit of all three; who cared not at all for a troop of parroting and aping scholars.

---

* Part of them are described in Steffens' "*Autobiography,*" vol. v.; and by Varnhagen, in his "*Recollections.*"

It was asked whether, in a history of the German Universities, there would be nothing to be said of any students except such as belonged to the societies—*Landsmannschaften* and Orders? And the answer was, there were many students who belonged to no such society, but formed circles of friends, without any statutes whatever, but yet with a very definite character, with common ideals, a common work, and an endeavor after a common purpose. I said that I had known such circles, and had been a member of them.

It seemed to me very difficult, and indeed impossible to describe these circles by any abstract representations; and I therefore resolved to give, instead, some account of my own student life.

If any reader is dissatisfied at my giving so many details of my own pursuits, I may reply that this has served the purpose of exhibiting a picture of my own variously directed industry. Many others, of like views with myself, labored in like manner. Even in Göttingen, and much more strongly in Halle, we had, firmly fixed before us, a noble ideal of mental development, which we labored after with the most persevering effort.

In order to fill up the chasm between my student life and my academical professorship, I may mention briefly that I studied from 1806 to 1808 at Freiberg; made some geognostical journeys in company with a dear friend, State Councilor Von Engelhardt, lately deceased, in Dorpat; lived in Paris from September, 1808, to June, 1809;* went in October, 1809, to Pestalozzi, at Yverdun, remained there to the end of April, 1810; wrote my first book in the summer of 1810, at Nuremberg, at the house of my beloved friend Schubert, then went to Berlin, and there received an official appointment, in December of the same year.

D.—Breslau. (1810–1817.)

In December, 1810, I was appointed private secretary to Chief Mining Superintendant Gerhard, who was at the head of the Prussian department of mines. I accompanied him on his official journeys, and thus came to Breslau, in May, 1811. Here he directed me to make out instructions for a geologist who was to be sent to investigate the Silesian mountains. These, as I drew them, required a great deal from the geologist. When I handed them to the superintendent, he returned them to me, much to my astonishment. "The instructions are for yourself;" said he, "you are to make the examination."

I left immediately, and although it was in the heat of summer,

---

* An account of my life and studies at Freiberg and Paris is given in my "*Miscellaneous Works*," part ii. pp. 1–35.

made my trip through the mountains with great zeal. At this time the University of Breslau was organized. The appointees might be divided into three classes. The first were accomplished Catholic professors, some of them having formerly been Jesuits, and all having belonged to the Catholic University at Breslau, founded in 1708. The second were Protestant professors, members of the University of Frankfort, dissolved in 1810. Among these were the lexicographer and philologist, Schneider; the theologian, David Schultz; the physician, Berends, &c. In the third class were men invited from very various places: as Link, Steffens, Von der Hagen; the mathematician, Brandes; the old Sprickmann, formerly a member of the Göttingen Society; Passow, my brother Friedrich and myself; and, a little later, Wachler. My appointment was that of Professor of Mountain Mineralogy.

Having come to Breslau, I received, for use in my lectures on oryctognosy, an exceedingly meager collection of minerals. They came originally from the minister, Count Reden; but unfortunately, Chief Mining Superintendent Karsten had already selected out the best part of them for the Berlin collection. I was placed in a most uncomfortable condition, for the specimens given me were not sufficient for my use in teaching; and were, besides, so dirty that I had my hands full in cleaning them during the winter term of 1811–12.

Under these circumstances, I was almost glad to serve two masters—for besides my professorship, I was appointed Mining Councilor in the mining department of Breslau. In this capacity I continued my investigations of the Silesian mountains during the summer of 1812.

Teaching mineralogy, in the absence of the necessary means, could not, of course, give me much pleasure. I was in the case of a professor of exegesis without a Bible, a professor of the Roman law without the Pandects, an anatomist without a subject. I had, nevertheless, in the winter term of 1812–13, five hearers; who, as I very soon saw, imbibed a general impression that mineralogy could be taught without minerals.

I cannot tell how painful these lectures were to me, and how I tormented myself in trying to do what was impossible. The spring of 1813 freed me from my comfortless position. Of Napoleon's army, smitten by God, only a remnant returned from Russia. The time for freeing Germany was come; the King of Prussia had, by his proclamation of February, summoned volunteers to Breslau, where he himself, Blücher, Stein, Scharnhorst, Gneisenau, and the best blood of his people were gathered. Crowds of youth, gathering to the call of their king, burned with zeal to be led against the French, and to free their fatherland from the tyranny of Napoleon. But the king hesitated long before declaring war. Steffens, without waiting for this declaration, delivered that remarkable and enthusiastic oration to the students, in which he called upon them to take up arms for their country. This was a torch thrown upon powder; Steffens had spoken out what had long been in the hearts of the youths. All offered themselves for service, except those for whom it was an absolute impossibility. The academical lectures were discontinued at once; military drills took their place, and all Breslau was one great encampment.

Steffens was placed in the guard; and has himself related his experience during the war. I entered the Silesian militia, and was afterward appointed on Blücher's general staff. I have described my life, during that extraordinary period, in a little work entitled "*Recollections of the years* 1813 *and* 1814."

In June, 1814, I returned from Paris to Breslau. The university was still in disorder, and I had leisure to complete my researches in the mountains. During the winter of 1814–15, its members gradually reassembled. Having labored unremittingly, almost four years, to procure the purchase of a collection of minerals, I at last succeeded in having purchased the collection of the deceased mineralogist, Meuder; which was considered the best in Freiberg, after that of Werner.

My thoughts were now fully occupied with the hope of thenceforth fulfilling effectually my vocation as a teacher, when suddenly the news came, "He is out again—Napoleon has escaped from Elba;" and soon, "He is in Paris." Most of the volunteer youth were still with their standards; older volunteers agreed to serve again in case of need; although this did not appear to exist, all the allied forces being yet in readiness for immediate service.

The battle of Belle Alliance and the second taking of Paris brought the war to a close. While the thoughts of all had hitherto only extended to the rescue of Germany from the French tyranny, they now included the purpose of freeing and purifying her from evils which were in part ancient and deep-rooted, and in part only the consequence of the poisonous French influence.

The younger portion of Germany, especially, was seized with a noble enthusiasm. The influence of the war of freedom upon the universities was immeasurable. The young men, who at the summons of the king had entered the army by thousands, and had fought honorably in its great battles, returned to the universities in 1815 and 1816, to continue the studies which the war had interrupted. In the short space of three years, in which Europe lived through more than in three centuries before, was our youth metamorphosed. Enchanted, as it were, previously, in the chains of ignoble and even vulgar academical habits, they now felt themselves released, by the most lofty experiences. Thus they were delivered from the tyranny of false honor, and saw the *Comment* in its true form, as did Titania her beloved, when freed from her delusion. True honor and courage, devoted to the cause of their country alone, were substituted in the place of that imp, the frantic "point of honor," which was, by an unnatural, sickly sensibility, finding itself wounded everywhere, and seeking duels about nothing at all.* These contemptible customs, partly derived from the French, must have appeared in a sufficiently disgraceful light to young men who had fought at Dennewitz and Leipzig.

As in relation to honor, so, in the place of the former foolish academical looseness of morals, were substituted, in the students who returned from the war, purer moral ideas and principles. The reality of life and death had appeared to them, and had made an impression upon them. Many of the volunteers had been Turners before the war; and they returned to those exercises after it, with redoubled zeal.

The student songs, partly *renommist* and obscene, partly absurdly sentimental, were replaced by others, pure and powerful; and especially by patriotic ones.

The love of country, awakened and strengthened in the volunteers by the war, longed after the unity and unanimity of Germany. The *Landsmannschaften*, at enmity among themselves, appeared to them enemies of that unity and unanimity.

Together with patriotism was awakened in them a respect for Christianity; a feeling, though indistinct and undeveloped, that Germany, without Christianity, is helpless and lost. Their motto in the war was, "With God, for king and fatherland."

It is not to be wondered at that youths, who had fought like men for their country, should after the war have conceived the idea that that country, freed and consecrated by the blood of the martyrs who fell in battle, should now go forward, purified and renewed.

All these elements, springing from the war of freedom, found their expression in the Burschenschaft, which was intimately connected with the Turners. Of these we shall now proceed to speak.

---

* Most of the previous duels in Halle had originated "on account of the broad stone." If two students met upon this, neither would turn out; or if he did, he made just as little room as possible, so as not to appear a coward. If they touched, even in the least, the rule was that a challenge followed. This "broad stone" was the summit stone of a somewhat arched pavement. In order to put an end to these pitiful duels, the pavement was altered so that the "broad stone" disappeared. It is referred to in the somewhat vulgar student-song, "O Jerum, Jerum, Jerum.

a. *Founding of the Jena Burschenschaft, June* 18, 1816.—*Wartburg Festival, October* 18, 1817.

In various universities, the idea prevailed of founding a students' society, in which the new mental elements and ideals which we have mentioned, should take a form, and be called into activity. Jena was foremost, and established a *Burschenschaft*, June 18, 1816, the anniversary of the battle of Belle Alliance.* On the 11th of August, 1817, the Jena Burschenschaft sent the following circular to the Universities of Berlin, Breslau, Erlangen, Giessen, Göttingen, Greifswald, Heidelberg, Kiel, Königsberg, Leipzig, Marburg, Rostock, and Tübingen.

"JENA, August 11, 1817.

"GREETING :—

"DEAR FRIENDS :—As the jubilee of the Reformation is to be celebrated in this year, we wish, undoubtedly in common with all good German *Burschen*, since all men, everywhere, are intending to celebrate well this festival, to celebrate it also, in our own way. In order, however, not to come into collision with the other festivities, which might easily be disturbed by ours, and as the celebration of the victory of Leipzig will fall upon the 18th of October, 1817, we have agreed to observe this festival on that day, at the Wartburg, near Eisenach; firstly, because the fixing of that day will give sufficient time for attending the festival, without making it necessary to neglect any thing of importance; secondly, because those most distant would, perhaps, not attend for the sake of the festival; and lastly, that we may observe a festival in three interesting portions,—for the Reformation, for the victory of Leipzig, and for the first free and friendly gathering of German Burschen, from most of the German Universities, upon the third great jubilee of the Reformation.

"With reference to this triple purpose, the festival itself is so arranged that we shall assemble, in the market-place of Eisenach, on the 18th of October, as soon as it is light, proceed to the Wartburg, and listen to a prayer; then that we shall assemble again at about 10 A. M., either in the open air, or in the Minnesinger-hall if it rains, when an address will be delivered; then to take breakfast, and to put off dinner until after the divine service, appointed at 2 P. M., of the 18th of October, by the Consistory of the Grand Duchy of Weimar, in which most of us will wish to take part, in order then to partake of that meal together, in the Minnesinger-hall. In the evening we may conclude with a bonfire for the victory, and a joyous feast. To this festival day we invite you, in the most friendly manner, and request you to be present in as great number as possible; and in case this cannot be, at least, that you will take part by a delegation. It is hoped that all who are to be present will be in Eisenach on the 17th of October. Every comer is to go to the Wreath of Rue Inn, on the market-place, so that, in case there is not room for him there, he may be assigned lodgings; which arrangement is necessary, provided many come; and moreover, will assist in the forming of acquaintances. Further, we request each of you to invite to the composition of a song to celebrate the day; and that the same may be sent to us at least fourteen days before the festival, that we may be able to have it properly printed. And in particular, we request you to answer this, our friendly invitation, where possible, by the end of August; and to omit nothing which may cause this festival to be celebrated by a large number, and thus to become a gratifying example to all the world.

"Fare you well.

"In the name of the Burschenschaft at Jena,

"ROBERT WESSELHÖFT, *Stud. Jur.*"

To this letter very friendly answers were received from the various

* Section 243 of the Statutes of the Jena Burschenschaft.

universities; and all of them, with but one exception, accepted, with much pleasure, the invitation to the Wartburg. The distant students of Kiel answered, August 28, as follows:

"Your letter, dear friends, was to us a welcome confirmation of all the good and beautiful things which we have heard from Jena; and we congratulate you on your good fortune in having originated the invitation to the festival of the 18th, and the excellent arrangements for it. Your invitation has excited among us universal pleasure and enthusiasm for the undertaking; and it is due only to our great distance, and the consequent insurmountable difficulty, to many of us, of the journey, that we shall not be present in a number so great as we could wish. Of so much, however, we can assure you with certainty: that *Burschen* from this place will be present with you, and that their number will not be less than twenty. In respect to the song, we promise that it shall be sung in common at the Wartburg, as well as the others that shall be sent in; and we will not fail to send it to you in time.

"If this pleasant gathering of good *Burschen* at the Wartburg shall be numerous enough, the occasion will be an excellent one for considering many matters of general importance.

"Fare you well, until we shall ourselves greet you as friends, and celebrate, as Germans, the memory of our great countryman, who will always be our most perfect representative of German national excellence."

This letter, and the other answers given in the Appendix* were written without any concert whatever; which renders their agreement together remarkable, and a proof of the universality of the new spirit which had been awakened by the war of freedom. We will not criticise the style of some of these letters. When youth of strong and ardent character experience a profound moral change, this begins with feeling, and only afterward develops into a clear and conscious character. In its first stage, there is a sort of minority; a want of skill in verbal expression, which gives an air of affectation to their unripe and exaggerated style, without any real falseness.

The reply of the Rostockers, alone, is not liable to this charge; it sounds like jesting at the new period; but they "jested at themselves, and knew it not."

After the Jena Burschenschaft had received these answers, they presented to the prorector, September 21, the following paper:

"An earnest wish was simultaneously expressed, in various quarters, for the celebration, this year, at the Wartburg, of the great festival of the Reformation, with ceremonies at which delegates from all the German Universities are to be present; and it also seemed to be appropriate that the invitations should come from Jena. These universal wishes have been complied with, and all the German Universities notified to be present at the ceremony. The day appointed is the 18th of October, as the 31st must be observed by almost every student at his university, and this day, also, is almost everywhere not in the vacation.

"The common arrangements for the festivity will vary but little from those which have before been proposed. Care will be taken to secure brotherly behavior, such as is appropriate to such a festival.

"On the evening of the 17th, a committee, from members of the universi-

---

* See Appendix V.

ties, will be appointed to preserve peace and good order during the festival, and to arrange its details. The ceremonies are to be simple, but dignified.

"In the morning, all participants are to go in festive procession, with music, to the Wartburg, where, in the Knights'-hall, the hymn, 'Our God is a strong tower' (*Ein fester Burg ist unser Gott*), will be sung, with trumpets and kettle-drums. After this a *Bursch* from Jena will deliver an appropriate oration. Then will be sung the hymn, 'Lord God we praise thee.'

"The rest of the forenoon will be devoted to social conversation. At 12, a meal will be taken in common. After it there may, perhaps, be some gymnastic exercises.

"At half-past six a bonfire, for rejoicing and victory, will be lighted on the beacon of the Wartenberg, round which patriotic songs will be sung and addresses made.

"The festival will then be concluded with a pleasant hour of drinking and singing in the Knights'-hall.

"By order of the Jena Burschenschaft,

"DURR, SCHEIDLER, WESSELHÖFT."

The following "Order of the festival at the Wartburg, October 18, 1817," was now drawn up in Jena, and was approved by a committee of students at Eisenach :*

"1. At 8 A. M., assembly of all the *Burschen* in the market-place.

"2. At 8½, forming of the procession to the Wartburg. The order of the procession will be as follows: The Castellan; his four assistants, two and two; music; two color-guards; the colors; two color-guards; the committee from all the universities; all the *Burschen*, without precedence of universities, two and two.

"3. Order of services at the Minnesinger's Hall, in the Wartburg:

"Hymn, 'Our God is a strong tower.'

"Oration, by Riemann.

"Hymn, 'Now all thank God.'

"4. At 12, dinner in the Minnesinger's Hall.

"The healths will be given by the managers.

"5. At 2 P. M., return from the Wartburg to the city church in same order as in going up.

"6. After service, gymnastics in the market-place.

"7. At 6 P. M., general assembly of the Burschen for torch-light procession to the Wartenberg, where addresses will be delivered, and songs sung.

"EISENACH, October 17, 1817."

"This plan," says Kieser, "having been adopted as the basis of the festival, only those portions of the ceremonies which were performed according to it, ought to be considered as proceeding from the united assembly of *Burschen* from the twelve universities of Germany. Whatever further was done by individuals, . . . must not be charged upon the whole collectively."†

The Grand Duke of Weimar not only gave his permission for the festival, but directed the authorities of Eisenach to leave the arrangement of it to the students, and "not to take any measures of a police-

* We have three descriptions of the Wartburg festival. The first is by Court Councilor Kieser, who was present. Kieser, though enthusiastic in his recognition of the objects of the *Burschenschaft*, and yet moderate, declares himself strongly against the burning of the books. I follow, mainly, his clear account, and take his vouchers. Of a character opposite to Kieser's book is an anonymous one, much of which, both for contents and style, the author might well disavow. A third, by Fromman, is written in youthful sympathy with the festival but is hasty.

† Kieser, p. 15.

like character, and calculated to show lack of confidence in them;" inasmuch as of late years the students of Jena had "conducted themselves in a manner correct in a distinguished degree." The authorities complied, to the fullest extent, with this direction.

On the 17th of October the students gathered in from the twelve German Universities, to the number of about 500. Jena, alone, sent more than 200. The remainder were as follows: From Berlin, 30; Erlangen, 20 to 25; Giessen, 30; Göttingen, 70 or 80; Heidelberg, 20; Kiel, 30; Leipzig, 15; Marburg, 20 or 25; Rostock 3; Tübingen, 2; Würzburg, 2. A committee of 30 students were chosen, among whom were Sand, from Erlangen; Buri and Sartorius, from Giessen; Carové, from Heidelberg; and Binzer and Olshausen, from Kiel.

"The 18th of October opened. A bright autumn morning had silvered the peaks of the mountain with frost, and the Wartburg, illuminated by the rays of the ascending sun, and shining out with remarkable clearness from the vapors of the mountain, was saluted by every one as the sacred place of the day. At 6, the ringing of all the bells in the city proclaimed that the festival was commenced. A second ringing summoned the *Burschenschaft*, at 8, to the market-place. The dimensions of the Wartburg not admitting all the assembled multitude, it was necessary to issue admission tickets, of which about a thousand were given out. The procession was gradually formed, the *Burschen*, mostly clothed in black, taking the lead, decorated with oak leaves from the neighboring mountain, and going two and two. The standard of the Jena *Burschenschaft*, a gift from the ladies and young ladies of Jena, at the peace festival of 1816, and which had to-day the honor of ranging all the universities about it, was unfolded in the centre of the whole, and the procession moved toward the Wartburg at half-past 8, all the bells ringing, and with festive music."*

Scheidler, of Gotha, marched foremost; Count Keller, of Erfurt, carried the banner of the Jena *Burschenschaft;* and the students formed a procession extending a long distance, accompanied by innumerable citizens of Eisenach and strangers. Four professors from Jena, Schweizer, Oken, Fries, and Kieser, had gone to the Wartburg in advance of the procession, and were awaiting it in the Minnesinger's Hall.

"This hall, called also the Knights' Hall, and the chief beauty of the Wartburg, although lowered by nearly half its height, on account of the ruinous state of the walls, will hold, besides the gallery at one side, more than 1000 persons. Its antique, unchanged architecture, its small windows, the columns supporting the roof, the wainscoted and variously painted walls, strikingly decorated with a multitude of escutcheons and portraits of renowned princes of past times, and just tastefully ornamented for the festival, by the people of Eisenach, under the direction of Buildings-Inspector Sälzer, with oak wreaths, for the feast; by the partly faded wall decorations, and the dim light of the large hall, unoccupied for centuries, carried back the mind of every one who entered to times past, and especially to the century of the Reformation. In the middle of one side a modest speaker's desk was erected, and opposite to it were arranged several rows of seats, terrace-wise. Two students, sent on in advance, had charge of the arrangements, in order that the entrance of the procession might not be disordered. This made its appearance about 10,

* Kieser, pp. 22, 23.

following in serious silence the waving banner, which was planted at the right of the desk. The managers of the procession, with drawn swords and covered heads, formed a half-circle before the desk, and the remainder of the audience took their places in the body of the hall.

"After a brief, silent prayer, the singing-leader, Dürr, a student of theology at Jena, commenced, with a powerful voice, the chosen festival hymn, 'Our God is a strong tower,' which was sung by the whole assembly, to commence divine service. Afterward came forward the orator of the day, Riemann, of Ratzeburg, a student of theology at Jena, and knight of the Iron Cross, a distinction which he had gained on the bloody day of victory at Belle Alliance, and ascended the desk. In a well-arranged address, he began by greeting with modesty the highly respectable assembly ; turning to the purpose of the festival, he then referred to the chief occurrences of those remarkable times to the memory of which the festival was devoted. He then developed the needs of the present time ; showed that the young men, mindful of the past and the future, must hold fast to the good already attained, of German freedom ; and finally, in rising enthusiasm, invoking the shade of Luther, and of all the noble heroes who have fallen in the contest for freedom and right, to be invisible witnesses, he offered, with sacred zeal, in the name of the assembly, this vow : 'That which we have acknowledged we will maintain, as long as a drop of blood runs in our veins. The spirit which has gathered us hither—the spirit of truth and justice—shall so lead us through our whole life, that we, all brothers, all sons of one and the same fatherland, shall form a brazen wall against every outer and inner enemy of that fatherland ; that the roaring death of open battle shall not terrify us from standing in the heat of the fight, when the invader threatens ; that the splendor of the monarch's throne shall not dazzle us from speaking the strong, free word, when truth and right demand it ; that we will never pause in the endeavor after every human and patriotic virtue.' He ended with a simple but ardent prayer for the presence and blessing of the Most High. Sacred stillness pervaded the assembly.

"After this followed the hymn 'Now all thank God,' sung by the whole assembly. During the singing, Court Councilor Fries was besought, by some of his pupils, to make an address ; and, ascending the desk, he spoke, with deep feeling, a few heart-felt words.

"Singing-leader Dürr then invoked the divine blessing : 'The Lord bless us, and protect us ! The Lord let His countenance shine upon us, and be gracious unto us ! The Lord lift up His countenance upon us, and grant us His peace ! Amen !' And thus, in deep devotion and feeling, ended this portion of the festival, intended especially in remembrance of the Reformation."*

"A flourish of trumpets from the summit of the castle called to dinner at 12. Three rows of tables were set in the Minnesinger's Hall, and others in the adjoining rooms, at which the assembly took their places, the professors from Jena, invited for their friendly sympathy, in the midst. Gay songs enlivened still more the company, already inclined to pleasure ; and above all, the festive healths, given toward the end of the meal, by the managers of the ceremony, were received and repeated, as expressing the inmost feelings of their hearts, with endless acclamations, by the whole assembly. They were as follows :

"'The jewel of our lives, German freedom.'
"'The man of God, Doctor Martin Luther.'
"'The noble Grand Duke of Saxe Weimar and Eisenach, the protector of the day.'
"'The victors at Leipzig.'
"'All the German Universities and their *Burschen*.'

"Then were given by the professors present :

"By Court Councilor Kieser.—'The United German Burschenschaft, and the noble spirit which has united it.'
"By Privy Court Councilor Schweizer.—'To the joyful return of this anniversary.'
"By Court Councilor Fries.—'The volunteers of 1813 ; a model for you, German *Burschen*.

"Many more healths followed, given by various individuals, as they were suggested by the enthusiasm of the banquet, or the occurrences, relations, or memories of the time ; and the dinner ended after 2 P. M.

"Thus was concluded this dinner of about six hundred persons, who had

---

* Kieser, pp. 24–27.

assembled here, under the protection of a noble prince, in memory of a great occasion.''*

"The *Burschen* had proposed to precede by a public festival divine service in the city church of Eisenach; and an invitation from General Superintendent Nebe having confirmed their intention, the procession now, accordingly, took its way to the church. It would, naturally, seem a delicate matter to introduce to the house of God a company of lively youths, excited by a joyous meal, the clink of glasses, and music, as well as by the festivities of the day. But how profoundly the deep significance of the festival had penetrated the minds of all, was shown by the fact that even here, in the last part of the Wartburg festival, not the least disturbance interfered with the order and quiet of the day.

The procession, in the same order as at the beginning of the festival, descending the mountain, approached the church, in order to make room for the Eisenach militia, then just entering the church. Then the Burschenschaft followed, taking the places allotted to them, while their standard was placed next that of the militia, in the choir, and the managers placed themselves in brotherly-wise, together with the officers of the militia, within the choir. After church music, the clerical orator, General Superintendent Nebe, delivered an impressive address, appropriate to the day, filling with feeling, not only, as usual, the hearts of his congregation, but those of the students of the German Universities.

"As every happy juncture inspires happy thoughts, so here, also, did the festive union of the militia with the united *Burschenschaft*, in the temple of the Lord. After a brief consultation between the officers of the former and the managers of the latter, both, at the end of the service, repaired to the market-place, one in one half-circle and the other in the opposite one, with the standards and leaders in the middle. Such inhabitants of Eisenach as were unable to find admittance into the limited space of the Wartburg, were thus enabled to take part in the ceremonies. A hymn, written for the occasion, by General Superintendent Nebe, was distributed, in print, and sung to a full accompaniment, and the ceremony ended with cheers for various names proposed, of which the last from the militia, by their leader, Col. Von Egloffstein, was, 'Our beloved guests, the visitors;' and from the *Burschenschaft*, 'The militia and the noble citizens of Eisenach, the friendly hosts of the day.'

"The time until twilight, when the torchlight procession began to ascend the Wartenberg, was occupied with gymnastics, in the market-place, chiefly by the *Turners* of Jena and Berlin."†

The Jena professors remained until this time. "So far," says Kieser, "as concerns us, the academical instructors who were eye-witnesses and participants in the festival, I here give, in the name of my colleagues, our public testimony to what has already been said by the council and citizens of the city of Eisenach, as well as even the highest government authorities of the country, in various publications: That there was not one movement, not one expression or action, to which the most evil imagination could attribute a bad significance, or could be blamed by the strictest censor."‡

It might charitably be wished that the festival had ended here.

But in the evening, the students, with torches, went up to the Wartenberg, which is opposite the Wartburg, where they were received by the Eisenach militia. A song was sung, and the student Rödiger delivered an address, after which other songs were sung, and a collection made for the poor.

---

* Kieser, pp. 28, 29. † Ib. pp. 30, 31. ‡ Ib., p. 32.

But there now followed a proceeding not in itself to be excused, and still more lamentable on account of its consequences:

"Some *Burschen*, with a great basket full of books in their arms, a pitchfork in hand, and with great black tickets, on which were printed, in staring letters, the names of the condemned books, appeared by the most fiercely blazing of the wood-piles. This new and unexpected appearance attracted a multitude, who formed a compact ring around the actors. After a short address, in which Luther's burning of the papal bull, at Wittenberg, in 1520, was cited as an example, and the un-German sentiments of the authors condemned, the titles on the tickets were read aloud, and then, with the books, taken out of the basket, a few at a time, with the pitchfork, and committed to the flames.

"It was natural enough that the assembled crowd should applaud the act, if only from the suddenness of the show, and because un-German sentiments were being punished; although most of the books were unknown to them.

"There were put into the fire:

"1. F. Ancillon—On Sovereignty and Organization of States.
"2. Fr. Von Cölln—Confidential Letters.
"3. " " Candid Pages.
"4. Crome—Germany's Crisis and Rescue.
"5. Dabelow—The 13th Article of the Act of the German Union.
"6. K. L. Von Haller—Restoration of Political Science; or, Theory of the Natural Social Condition, opposed to the Chimæra of the Artificial-civic.
"7. The German Red and Black Mantles.
"8. J. P. Harl—On the Universally harmful Consequences of the Neglect of a Police corresponding to the Necessities of the Times, especially in University Towns, and particularly for the Supervision of the Students.
"9. Immerman—A Word of Encouragement.
"10. Janke—The Constitution-shrieking of the New Preachers of Freedom.
"11. Von Kotzebue—History of the German Empire, from its original to its destruction.
"12. L. Theob. Kosegarten—Address on Napoleon's day, 1809.
"13. Same—History of my 15th year.
"14. Same—Patriotic Songs.
"15. K. A. Von Kamptz—Code of Gensd'armerie.
"16. W. Reinhard—The Acts of the Union upon Whether, When, and How, German Deputies.
"17. Schmalz—Correction of a passage in the Bredow-Venturinian Chronicle for 1808.
"18, 19. Two later works of the same, on the same subject.
"20. Saul Ascher—Germanomania.
"21. Chr. Von Benzel-Sternau—Jason; a periodical.
"22. Zach. Werner—The Consecration of Power.
"23. " " The Sons of Thales.
"24. K. Von Wangenheim—The Idea of Constitutions; with reference to the ancient Constitution of Würtemberg.
"25. The Code Napoleon, and Zachariä upon it.
"26. Wadzeck, Scherer, and others, against the *Turners.*
"27. The Statutes of the Chain of Nobility.
"28. The Allemannia, and some other newspapers.

"After these books were burnt to ashes, there was added, a pair of stays, a cue of hair, and a corporal's cane.

"A song, sung by the assembly, terminated this addition to the ceremonies; and about midnight the militia and the *Burschenschaft* returned to Eisenach."*

It is incomprehensible how the founders of this *auto da fé* could have found those twenty-eight books in Eisenach. It was, therefore,

* Kieser, pp. 36–38.

believed that this burning was the execution of a measure long before resolved on; and that the books had been brought on purpose. But the riddle is very simply solved by the fact that what was burnt was a lot of imperfect sheets from an Eisenach book concern, upon which the titles of the books were superscribed.*

The students met once more at the Wartburg, on the 19th. Here consultation was had upon the relations of the *Burschenschaft* to the *Landsmannschaften*, which last found some defenders. The discussion was, at first, somewhat violent; but ended with thorough reconciliation of the contestants; they celebrated the "Brotherly League of Unity," and at noon, partook together of the holy sacrament.

On the 20th of October they separated.

The older among us can remember what an excitement the Wartburg festival made in Germany; how some were enthusiastically in favor of it, and others violently hostile. Among its adversaries was conspicuous, Privy High Government Councilor Von Kamptz, who presented to the Grand Duke of Weimar the following denunciation :†

"MOST SERENE GRAND DUKE :—Your Royal Highness is, doubtless, already informed that a crowd of unruly professors and abandoned students, on the 18th of the month, at the Wartburg, publicly burned various writings; thereby avowing their disapproval of them.

"Although true freedom of thought and of the press actually and successfully exists in your Royal Highness' states, yet it is certainly not consistent with a censure enforced with fire and dungforks by visionaries and minors, and a terrorist proceeding against the same freedom in other states. And it will always remain an enigma in history, how, under your Royal Highness' government, that classical fortress, from which, under your most noble ancestors, German freedom of thought and toleration proceeded ;—how the day of the festival for German liberty regained ;—how the memory of that great and tolerant man ;—how, indeed, our century, and German soil, could be so deeply dishonored and profaned by such a characteristic act of the vandalism of demagogical intolerance. It will not become me, most gracious sir, to enlarge upon the necessary consequences of such an outrage. Your Royal Highness' wisdom will clearly discern them ; even if the history of France did not teach us that the fire, which at last consumed the throne, proceeded from the funeral-piles which pardoned demagogues had before erected for writings in defense of that throne.

---

* I was so informed by one of the incendiaries; and the statement is confirmed in the "German Youth" (*Teutscher Jugend*), pp. 16, 17; where it is said, "The intention of injuring could hardly have existed, since scarcely one of those present knew either the names of the authors or the contents of their works." This is a principal fault of the burning. Among the books burned was one by the present Minister of Würtemberg, Von Wangenheim. This gentleman related to me, that he once met a young man in a public conveyance, who looked closely at him for a time, and then inquired if he were the author of the "Idea of Constitutions?" Upon his answering in the affirmative, the young man said that he had to accuse himself of having committed a great injustice toward Von Wangenheim. The latter replied, "But I do not know you, sir; how can you be chargeable with such an injustice?" "I burned your book," was the answer, "at the Wartburg festival." "If you did that," answered Von Wangenheim, "you are entitled to my heartiest thanks. I used, previously, to be charged with being a demagogue. But your burning my book relieved me so entirely from that charge that I have not since been obliged to answer it." But so much the more reason had the young man to blame himself. He had richly expiated his fault, however.

† Kieser, p. 185.

"It is the honor which was granted to one of my own works, of bearing a part in this *auto da fé*, the first in Germany, and thus far the only one in your Royal Highness' states, which is, as it ought to be, the single subject to which I shall confine myself, at least on this occasion.

"Among the books by the burning of which these heroes of the Wartburg have so well and distinctly proclaimed what freedom of the press it is that they and their adherents desire, was the *Code of Gensd'armerie*, published by me a few years ago, of which I most humb'y present your Royal Highness a copy herewith.

"Condescend to observe, from it, that it is nothing more nor less than a mere collection of the laws of various princes, including also your Royal Highness' self, on the subject of gensd'armes: to which end will your Royal Highness condescend to read the published law on that subject, as printed in full by yourself, pp. 359 to 369; and by your most noble and noble relatives, pp. 277 to 401.

"This Code contains, nowhere, my own thoughts, nor my own principles; and therefore, to my lively regret, I have not the honor of the disapproval of the collected unripe Solons of the Wartburg.

"But it was the laws and subscriptions of kings, and other princes, and also your Royal Highness' own laws, which have been publicly burnt in your Royal Highness' own states, by your Royal Highness' own servants and subjects; and which, in the intention of these censors by fire, were publicly insulted and disgraced.

"If I were not the subject and servant of a German prince—if I were not a German citizen—the honor and peace of Germany could not be important to me; I could see, with entire personal indifference, such a demagogical outrage; and indeed, merely as author of the Code of Gensd'armerie, I could only be pleased to see the urgent necessity of the institution whose laws I had collected, demonstrated, and confirmed.

"My supposition that in the court-martial of censors at the Wartburg, there were many to whom the peace and good order of our country was a great grief, and who would much prefer it to be in Germany as in Italy, where honest citizens have to buy safety from robbers, is fully confirmed by the fact that in the incendiary letters written from the Wartburg, insulting the police systems established in all the German states, and first in those of your Royal Highness, the reason alleged is, that no police is necessary in Germany.

"But is such a proceeding consistent with the respect for foreign powers, and for their laws, publicly proclaimed this very year? Is it an evidence of real freedom of thought, toleration, and public spirit? In what terms will history, particularly the history of German civilization, distinguish this outrage in her annals? What advantage will arise from it to culture, science, and social order? The most profound respect, which I feel I owe to your Royal Highness, forbids me from answering these and many other questions.

"It is proper for me to confine myself to the collection published by me, of the laws of your Royal Highness, and other princes; and inasmuch as I may not flatter myself that that collection is known to your Royal Highness, I venture to present it, accompanied with these most respectful observations, with the same unbounded respect in which I shall die.

"Your Royal Highness' most humble subject,

"KARL ALBERT VON KAMPTZ,

"Royal Acting Privy High Government Councilor and Chamberlain.

"BERLIN, 9th Nov., 1817."

The tone of this denunciation is such as to violate all respect due to the Grand Duke; and the more, as this prince had shown so favorable and friendly a disposition toward the festival. This was doubly unjust; for the burning of the books, as we have seen, was only an unfortunate accident, due to a few, and the rest did not even know of it. Herr Von Kamptz, however, holds all those present at the festival alike responsible for the excess of a few; and, it might be said, indirectly, the Grand Duke himself.

In opposition to this denunciation, and many other attacks upon the Wartburg festival, stands a dignified, earnest, and kind report from the Weimar Ministry of State, from which Kieser* gives the following extract:

"The assembly of our students from the various German Universities, at the Wartburg, on the 18th of October, for the celebration of that day, as well as for the jubilee festival for the Reformation, is the subject of so many uneasinesses, and of such various constructions, that a thorough acquaintance with the proceedings, the origin, and the spirit and significance of this assembly is unquestionably desirable and necessary. The undersigned considered it his bounden duty to collect the fullest information upon the occurrence, and to lay it before your Royal Highness. Your Royal Highness will be able to convince yourself, from it, that as this festival proceeded from an idea laudable in itself, and free from any political intention; it was, it is true, undertaken and carried out with youthful enthusiasm; but that whatever seems blamable in it was only accidental, and is to be charged only upon a few individuals. There has been no occasion so well calculated to remind the various German nationalities of the necessity of unity to their common welfare, as that of the 18th of October. From separation proceeded the wretched domination of Napoleon, whose grievous consequences, in the distracted condition of every country, almost every family has felt; and it was the re-establishment of their unity which glorified the victory whose recollection can never be lost from any German breast. All the German Universities yet have among their students youths who took an active part in that glorious victory. Some of these believed the festival of the 18th of October a most suitable occasion for removing also from the universities the divisions which had always been originated and maintained, during centuries, and in spite of numerous prohibitions by the various states and by the empire, by the *Landsmannschaften*, Orders, and other such societies; and which had been the sources of innumerable and unhappy divisions, not seldom extending to the states in whose service the youths afterward held public positions. With this view, and in this sense, the festival in memory of the great reformer, and in commemoration of the union of people and princes, on the 18th of October, at the Wartburg, was proposed to be used as a general *Burschen*-festival, and invitations were accordingly sent from Jena to all the universities. A short time before your Royal Highness' return from a journey, and a few weeks before the fulfillment of this before unknown design, the first information of it came here. It was clearly too late to prevent it, and it therefore only remained to prevent, as far as possible, all disorders and excesses. And, indeed, no good reason existed for opposing this praiseworthy beginning of the work of destroying the long-prohibited *Landsmannschaften* and Orders. With the permission of your Royal Highness, the police authorities of Eisenach were, for this purpose, advised of the expected coming of a number of students, and directed to take measures for their accommodation. It was believed the surest method of preserving good order and quiet, to place confidence in the honorable feelings and expressed intention of the young people, and to let them, themselves, take charge for that purpose. This confidence was not abused. All the eye-witnesses, including the higher authorities of the circle of Eisenach, testify to the religious solemnity, the dignified bearing, and the feeling, with which, on the whole, the festival of the 18th of October was celebrated. It is certainly not a blameworthy spirit which is expressed in the whole order of exercises; for the festival of October 18th, at the Wartburg, afterward in the church, at the second assembly, on the 19th, at the Wartburg, and at the partaking together of the Lord's Supper, the young men vowed to each other brotherly love and unity, and removal of all divisions and orders among themselves; and, as an immediate consequence of

---

* Kieser, p. 188.

this agreement, there now prevails among the students at Jena a grade of morality, and a strict observance of the laws of the land, the enforcement of which has heretofore been vainly striven for by the authorities. While this praiseworthy design, and the inspiring idea of a beautiful unbroken unity influenced the body of the assembly, it could not but happen that there would be some present who would fail to comprehend the true significance of the occasion, and who, not controlled by their more intelligent fellows, would be guilty of wanton acts. And thus it did, in fact, happen, that in the latter part of the evening, when the minds of all the young people were excited by the flames of the festival bonfire, that a few strangers, apparently not all of them students, were guilty of the wanton act of burning certain books, with many unseemly expressions. It is certain that but very few of the students had any previous knowledge of this *auto da fé*, so called; and that most of the books burned were unknown to them, from which facts many misconceptions arose, which spread rapidly, and as usual, have become much magnified. It is altogether false that the Acts of the Congress of Vienna, and of the Holy Alliance were among the works burnt. It must be confessed, with concern, that Professor Court Councilor Fries has printed an address to the students, which, although his personal character forbids any suspicion of wrong intentions, by its entire want of good taste, as well as by its unseasonable mystical ambiguities, is reprehensible, and has deserved the disapprobation of your Royal Highness; and that the same gentleman, carried away by love of his pupils, and intending to oppose a damaging calumny, has expressed himself, in the public papers, upon the occurrence, with less than the proper calmness and dignity. He has well expiated the hastiness of his unwise proceedings, by having received an intimation of your Royal Highness' displeasure, and by having been subjected, from various quarters, to the lash of satire. The statement is, however, due to him and to the other instructors who were at Eisenach, that they were not present at the bonfire on the mountain; an unfortunate occurrence, for it may be added that their presence would, perhaps, have restrained the petulance of the young people. This was the plain course of the affair, which, through misunderstandings and lack of official accounts, which have only now been received of a reliable character, has been much distorted, and represented in the public papers as of importance. Your Royal Highness will herefrom be enabled to conclude that the anxieties which have sprung up are without a foundation; and it remains with your Royal Highness' wisdom to determine, whether, besides the investigation already ordered for the originators and participants in the burning of Von Kamptz' collection of police ordinances, the prohibition already issued against the proposed *Burschen* Gazette, and the renewed severe admonition to the editors of the Opposition paper and the People's Friend, any further measures to prevent ill consequences are needed. As several of those present at the ceremony at the Wartburg were from Berlin and the Royal Prussian States, and were not students, it would not be improper to request the co-operation of the Royal Prussian Government, so far as is compatible with the Constitution of the Duchy, as fixed and guaranteed by the guarantee of the German Union.

"KARL WILHELM, BARON VON FRITZ.

"WEIMAR, Nov. 10, 1817."

However bad these immediate consequences of the festival, the storm was appeased by the publication of this dignified and truthful report, as is more especially evident from the following circular, of December 19, 1817, issued by Count Von Edling, to all the residents and agents of the Grand Duke:

"I hasten to inform you that his Highness the Prince Von Hardenberg and his Excellency Count Von Zichy have been here, and have performed the commission intrusted to them. As I desire to anticipate all false conjectures, I have the honor of sending you the details of the same, of which I beg you will make immediate use. The Prince Von Hardenberg and the Count Von Zichy presented to his Royal Highness the Grand Duke the letters of their respective sovereigns. These letters have, throughout, called for the grateful acknowledgments of his Royal Highness, as giving him indubitable proofs of the confidence and good wishes with which he is honored by his Majesty the Emperor of Austria and his Majesty the King of Prussia. The request that he will adhere to the measures which may be taken at the Diet of the Union, for the purpose of establishing a just and liberal freedom of the press, entirely coincides with the wishes of his Royal Highness the Grand Duke, who has always considered that a general regulation of this matter was necessary and indispensable for the maintenance of order, and the commercial weal in Germany.

"As Count Von Zichy desired to convince himself, personally, of the spirit prevailing in Jena, I had the pleasure of accompanying him thither; and although the writings of a few extravagant individuals, in reference to the festival of the 18th October, have with justice attracted the animadversions of the better part of Germany, yet, on the other hand, the order, discipline, and good feeling which prevail among the students at Jena, and particularly among the subjects of his Majesty the Emperor of Austria there, have convinced his excellency that matters are not there as they have been reported.

"This result must be gratifying to all those who take a lively interest in the occurrence; and we may congratulate ourselves that the affair was intrusted to the experience and wisdom of Prince Von Hardenberg, and the well-known rectitude of Count Von Zichy. Their mission must, if possible, knit still more closely the bonds which have so long united his Royal Highness with their sovereigns.

"With the assurances of my distinguished consideration, &c., &c."

This paper shows both how much excitement was caused by the Wartburg festival, and how important it appeared to the governments of Prussia and Austria.

b. *Founding of the General German Burschenschaft.*

On the anniversary of the Wartburg festival, October 18, 1818, delegates from fourteen universities met at Jena,* and founded the General German Burschenschaft, whose statutes are given in the Appendix.†

They determined (§ 2), upon equality of right and duties, in all *Burschen*, and that their purpose was, "Christian German education of every mental and bodily faculty for the service of the fatherland." No duels were to be fought between members of the *Burschenschaft* (§ 20). Foreigners could not become voting members.

The Constitution of the Jena *Burschenschaft* goes more fully into principles and details.‡ It gives full definitions of the executive and legislative powers, for each separate office in the Burschenschaft, and for the order of business in their meetings. The place of exercising (*Turnplatz*), is taken under their protection (§§ 15 and 229). Those admitted into the *Burschenschaft* must be Christians, Germans, and honorable (§ 168). The *Burschenschaft* is called "Christian German."

No difference of birth is recognized among the members of the *Burschenschaft*, and they call each other "thou" (§§ 194, 195). Only "greater or less experience" is a basis of distinction (§ 197); and it is on this principle only that students are eligible to the committee after their second term at the university, and to the managing board

---

* Haupt, p. 52. † Ib., p. 257. Appendix IV.—(A.) ‡ Ib., p. 264. Appendix IV.—(B.)

after their third (§ 198). "But these distinctions shall not occasion any younger member to be reckoned inferior to an older; for it is only individual excellence, not years' standing which can be alleged in favor of members" (§ 199). This paragraph is a most distinct declaration against Pennalism, which, as we have seen, extended down to our own times.

The statutes* of the General Burschenschaft, and of that of Jena, seem to have been drafted by students at law, and with a judgment and breadth almost unyouthful. But any one who knew the youths who, in the first innocent period of the Burschenschaft, lived in freedom and unrestrained vigorous exercises within the limits of these laws, will make no objections to this characteristic. And if any person is disposed to criticise them sharply, and find them too mature and strict, he will, upon a comparison of them with the Comment (also in the Appendix), find reason to change his opinion, and to look favorably upon them.

E.—Breslau. (1817–1819.)

The influence of the Wartburg festival and of the foundation of the Burschenschaft spread like wildfire to all the Protestant universities of Germany, and to Breslau among the rest. Here, the members of the Burschenschaft were also the most active Turners.† The history of the Breslau Turning-ground, already given, is actually that of the *Burschenschaft* of that place, except that the former, as recognized by the government, comes more into the foreground. The opponents of the Burschenschaft, and of the Turning system, accused the young men, especially, of premature and ill-regulated political action. The reader will learn the nature of the various accusations made from the following dialogue, in which I endeavored to delineate them:‡

Turning and the State. (Otto—Georg.)

O. Dear Turners'-defender, will you answer me again to-day?

G. It will be sure to be once more "Complaints, nothing but complaints!"

O. What we are to become very fond of, a profound writer says, we have first to fight stoutly against.

G. A beautiful sentiment! You will give me good hopes that you will become a true adherent of the Turning system. But what are your new objections?

---

* As found in Haupt. I do not know that they have been printed elsewhere.

† Gymnasts.

‡ This dialogue first appeared in 1818, in the Silesian Provincial Gazette. I reprint it *verbatim*, as a contribution to a picture of the patriotic ideas, aspirations, and struggles of the period.

O. One man said to me that the system was only a coarse system of bodily exercise, which neglected the mind. Are children to be made tumblers and rope-dancers? And a little afterward, another complained that the Turning was well enough, if it were only confined to bodily exercises; but that all manner of mental instruction was connected with these; a useless plan. What is your answer to these?

G. As an advocate, I ought not to have to make any answer at all to two objections so diametrically opposite; but I will endeavor to illustrate the point to which both relate. Jahn by no means confined himself to a comprehensive description of and instruction in the various bodily exercises, their mutual relations, and influence in the development of the body. He felt, very clearly, that what the ordinary masters of fencing, swinging, riding, &c., had taught, as matters of bodily application only, must be illustrated by an intellectual element.

O. Can you not describe this element more fully?

G. It is difficult, at the beginning of a great development, to fix upon the germ of a powerful principle which is to live and work in manifold forms and deeds for coming centuries. It can only be imagined. Its efficiency through Jahn and others was not its only efficiency. Its most marked development was in the recent Turners, in whose hearts it dwelt and worked, chaining them to the Turning-ground with an attraction more powerful than could have been that of merely bodily exercises.

O. But its adversaries say that this was a revolutionary spirit.

G. As was Luther's; as are all to whose renovating power humanity owes eternal youth.

O. That is not what they mean. They refer to a Jacobinical revolutionary spirit.

G. Many things may be misunderstood. But this misunderstanding could not happen to any one earnestly seeking to comprehend the Turning system or the future of Germany. But for this is necessary the unprejudiced reading of works on Turning and related subjects; and still more, thorough observation of the system itself, friendly intercourse with the Turners, and, most of all, a comprehension of the errors and sins of the times, and a heartfelt desire to help them.

O. Can you, then, really disprove this accusation of Jacobinism?

G. Jacobinism! These opponents should consider what words they use. Even if they believed that the friends of Turning were in an error, they would have to do them the justice of admitting that they meant honorably. And they compare them with the Jacobins, those most abominable productions of hell that ever appeared in human form!

O. But the Turners must have given some occasion for the charge?

G. I have never heard any expressions at the Turning-ground which would bear, even remotely, such a construction. But, lest you should believe it, I will refer you to matter in Jahn's "German Nationality," and "German Gymnastics."

O. Let us hear.

G. Take the Turners' motto, "Bold, free, gay, and pious."* Is that a Jacobinical motto?

O. No, indeed.

G. Or this appeal: † "German people, let not discouragement lead you into contempt for the ancient houses of your princes; open the history of the world, and seek for better." Is that Jacobinical?

O. Certainly not.

G. Or Jahn's remarks, that ‡ "It is an injustice to old families, as old as the state, and often among its first founders, to permit the dogma of a moment to have as much influence as the hard labor of whole centuries. If every Jack can, by the prefix *von*, do as much as the traditions of early deeds, then can a mortal syllable (which will be no creative word in eternity), do as much as the long-ripening fruits of time. An ancient oak of a thousand years, and still green, is honorable; and so is an old man who has lived usefully. We remember how many things they have lived through and endured; to how many wanderers they have given shade and coolness. No one stands long before a mushroom," &c. Is this Jacobinical?

O. Most completely the opposite.

G. Or when he says that § "Political revolutions have seldom done good, and what little they have was but the companion of an army of miseries;" or that,‖ "Even in the worst time of the French period, love to king and fatherland was instilled into the hearts of the Turners." Is all that Jacobinical?

O. His opponents must certainly never have read Jahn's works.

G. And they contradict each other, too; for they sometimes make the charge of Jacobinism, and sometimes find fault with Jahn and his friends, the advocates of Turning, for desiring a constitution. When did these anarchical king-murderers desire a constitution?

O. But I have heard it said that Jahn and his friends did not, themselves, know what they meant by a constitution.

G. But that is what both everybody and nobody knows. Every one that is, desires security in his sphere of life, undisturbed from without,

* *Frisch, frei, fröhlich und fromm.* Gymnastics, p. 233.

† Nationality, p. 233.

‡ Ib., p. 286.

§ Ib., p. 283.

‖ Gymnastics, p. 234.

and entire freedom within it; and by a constitution he means an instrument which will secure this to himself and to all; which will leave to the authorities the utmost freedom for good, but will restrain them from evil. But how such a one can be obtained, certainly very few and perhaps none can show.

O. That may be. But I imagine it might be for the best if our youth were not troubled with any civic concerns whatever.

G. Would you have it so now? The Turning system was organized in 1811. And not only did it contemplate the training of youth to general acquirements, but the misery in which the German fatherland was sunk was at hand, to be held up before their eyes as a consequence of civic dissensions and intestine quarrels. It was necessary to train them promptly to maturity as citizens, for the prompt salvation of their fatherland was necessary. The war of its rescue is ended; and what wonder is it that its first sounds are yet echoing?

O. I am pleased to see that you think an excuse necessary here.

G. Not too fast. The sounds uttered then shall re-echo through all time.

O. What sounds?

G. "One Germany!"

O. That is your chief point, then? But is it not clear that the greatness of Germany consists in the very multitude of its nations and princes, and that its very life is aimed at by these preachers of unity?

G. You unreasonable man! If you were advocating One Prussia, or One Austria, or One Bavaria, would you be in favor of compressing together all Germany into that one? If yea, you are right. But who has any such design? The One Germany which is desired is, free and friendly confederate existence of all the German nationalities, in all their numerous individualities, in mutual recognition, respect, and love; and, when necessary, in united strength against external enemies. For centuries the Germans have been lamenting over the grievous internal divisions of their fatherland; and now, when the first serious intention of healing them is shown, a howl goes up, from all sides, as if the utmost danger were at hand.

O. But the preaching of hatred to the French, long after the end of the war, is certainly most useless!

G. Useless? That is as you take it. I know of nothing more unworthy than insults to a subdued enemy. Has it not been repeated, even to weariness, yet not often enough for some people, that French influence remains successfully operative in the inmost mind and heart of numberless Germans; that even yet, a French education in manners and language is the highest ambition with an innumerable number;

especially with a large part of the German nobility, who ought to set a better example. The war is yet active against this French power within the limits of Germany.

O. But contempt for foreigners, such stringent restriction to the national and popular, seems to me entirely unnatural to Germans, and entirely opposed to their cosmopolitan character.

G. Your charges stand in each other's light.

O. How so?

G. If you had just now expressed apprehensions lest Saxony, Prussia, or Hesse, should, by strictly limiting themselves to what is national, or relates to their national descent, lose their general German character, this last charge of yours would seem an extension of the former. But you expressed an apprehension precisely opposite; lest the individuality of the German races should be lost in a general characterless Germanization; as a consequence of which you must naturally fear lest the German traits should be lost in an entirely characterless cosmopolitanism. And this would be a much better grounded fear than that of its opposite, from too strict a limitation of Germany within itself.

O. I must admit that you are right.

G. No one imagines that, in order to live a life of entire devotion to his country, a good citizen must have no house of his own; nor should it be supposed necessary that a German, in order to live for the good of all nations, must have no fatherland. Is it meant that the devil should play on the Germans, as those fools do on the violin who take so much pains to imitate all manner of instruments on it, but cannot bring out the real proper violin tone? A skillful leader would ask such a player, What is the use of that poor and incompetent imitation of the flute and the hautboy, when we have the flute and the hautboy themselves? Do you expect, with your ape-fiddling, to surpass the originals? You ought to be ashamed for so dishonoring your noble instrument, which ought to lead all the rest of the orchestra!

O. Your application is clear; that an imitator of all the world is by no means a cosmopolitan.

G. Precisely; just there is the misunderstanding. "The devil is the imitator of God;" said the Jesuits, who were good judges of such a case. A few great and gifted Germans, like Goethe and Tieck, for instance, have profoundly penetrated and lived in the spirit of foreign nations, with love and sympathy. They were trained for this by understanding and loving the glory of their own country. And with these great minds are confounded those who become Frenchified apes, because they are too God-forgottenly strengthless to become German men. It is imagined to be one and the same thing, whether a great merchant become rich at home, by honest trade, invests capital at the ends of the earth, or whether a bankrupt peddler, with no home anywhere, borrows wherever he goes and makes a great display with the money!

O. But I should fear that this preaching to Germans against becoming Gallicized, might be unintelligently perverted into a truly unchristian hate of the French.

G. If you put the matter upon conscientious grounds you shall be answered accordingly. What German is ready to love the French? If he is a Prussian, let him love the Austrians and Bavarians first; if a Bavarian, the Prussians. Will one who does not love his child, love a stranger? Do you suppose that the Good Samaritan loved strangers only, and had no love for his wife and child and his fellow-Samaritans? Shall these empty cosmopolitans boast of their Christian perfections and their love of universal humanity, while they show themselves heartlessly indifferent to fellow citizens and countrymen within the narrow sphere of their own actual lives? No. Only the German who loves all Germans with a comprehensive, heartfelt love, is ripe for the love of foreigners; and as long as he retains one spark of hatred against any German nationality, let him not claim credit for the greater until he has fulfilled the less.

O. You may be right. But I must return to a previous inquiry, which you did not answer; that is, where is the good of orations, about civic affairs, at the Turning-ground?

G. I said before, that the pressing period of 1811 demanded a stringent education. But have you lately heard any such orations?

O. You know that I have never been upon the Turning-ground.

G. I have been there, and have heard no such; still less have I delivered any. And I agree with you entirely; they are no place for such. As the Turning exercises contemplate the development of the human body, not civil training for a definite future occupation, for smiths, carpenters, or miners; so, in like manner, the mind should not be trained in a civic direction, but in a general development—to truth, faith, candor, moderation, chastity, hatred of lies and deceit, of drunkenness and licentiousness. Let such a mind be implanted in the Turners, and it will of itself develop, in the after relations of life, into the civil virtues, without any artificial direction toward them, or any untimely hot-house forcing, which seeks to anticipate the natural time of ripening.

O. But this does not seem to me consistent with the premature instruction of the Turners, on all occasions, in love of country.

G. But do you consider the fatherland a civic organization? In order to love it, must one first have received the privilege of German burghership? Do you not believe that a German country—a German heaven—bind even the youngest German hearts with a thousand bonds of love before they ever hear the words "German State,"—and that it is this very love which is the very heart of all the later civic virtues?

O. "German heaven—German country;" how do these enchain the child and the youth? His place of abode, his immediate neighborhood, enchain him. "Germany" is only an idea, which he is not even able to comprehend!

G. How your charges refute each other! At one time you say the German fatherland is far too narrow and confined for the cosmopolitan tendencies of the Germans. And this is believed by thousands, not only of German men, but of children; and the sphere of observation of infants is to be enlarged beyond the limits of Germany, by instruction in foreign tongues, and knowledge of foreign lands and history. And these very same men who think this kind of instruction quite natural, because it is usual, are displeased to have love of country impressed upon the hearts of youth, as if it were something beyond their capacity.

O. But only tell me this: What shall our youth understand by the term "German fatherland?"

G. Understand? Our pious forefathers made their children pray, and taught them edifying texts and hymns. The childish heart found in devotion the life of its life; the deep impression never perished, but consecrated their whole existence, to their death. Illuminati asked, What can a child understand by the names of God and Christ? and prayer, Bible, and hymns were thrown away. This was worse than church sacrilege; it was sacrilege of the inward inborn holiness of the heart. Shall we, in like manner, rob our children of the name of fatherland, to preserve it until their understanding is ripened? The name will make no impression upon men—they will not understand it—unless they have loved it instinctively from their earliest youth; unless, in the clod of earth on which they are born, they love, symbolically, their whole country. And fathers and teachers who would impress upon the young a love of country, must love it sincerely themselves.

O. And also, at least, incline to revolution.

G. I think I have thoroughly refuted the charge of Jacobinism made against the Turners. But if you should hear an expression which has a revolutionary sound, reflect that it is an echo of 1813, the year when all Prussia, from king to peasant, rose up; and remember those who then uttered such words. That period of violence is, thank God, past; and what is now needed is quiet and peaceful development. But the argument has another side, also. Every germinating truth is revolutionary against prevailing errors; every germinating virtue, revolutionary against prevailing vices opposed to it. And, therefore, there is always an outcry at the rising up of new youthful truths and virtues. The current errors and vices scent the coming of a powerful enemy, and the end of their power.

O. But you surely do not mean that errors and vices should be rooted out in the bloody French revolutionary fashion?

G. How can you ask so foolish a question? Most people have learned enough by the French revolution, not to believe decapitation a sure remedy for disorders in the head. Heaven protect us against such a casting out of the devils through a Beelzebub as that, where the evil spirit would return with seven others worse than himself! But in Prussia there is no call for any remedy of the kind.

O. And what protects Prussia herself against a reformation?

G. If a government opposes the development of the divinely ordained spirit of the times, and persists in forcibly maintaining antiquated and obsolete forms, in propping a rotten house with rotten timbers, it has no business to be surprised if the roof tumbles down on its head. But the course of the Prussian government is directly the opposite. It attentively observes, follows, and promotes the development of that spirit;* and thus will a renovation be peacefully accomplished, for the sake of which, in France, millions of bloody sacrifices were offered. Consider the extinction of the convents, of many of the privileges of the nobility, of the guild-restrictions; the institution of the militia.

O. Against all those steps I have heard much outcry, especially of late.

G. And no wonder. I have cried out against them myself. Every process of renovation causes, for a time, an uncomfortable state of affairs; like that when one removes from an old and failing house, but in which he has lived happily, into a new one, handsomer, but not yet put in order. The old house is empty and waste; and in the new one every thing is in confusion; if we would sit, there are no chairs, and if we would lie down, no bed. We may, naturally, be a little impatient; but who would lament as if he had no house at all, and return

* "The spirit of the times" has, unfortunately, come to mean a wicked spirit, opposed to the eternal kingdom of God. The divine—rather the God-fearing—spirit of the times is the very opposite of this, inasmuch as it is observant of, and obedient to, the indications from above. (Remark in 1854.)

to the beloved old ruin in which he had lived so many years? He should rather be quiet, and help set things in order.

O. Exactly such desires to return to past times have I heard from many sources; and particular praises were given to the strict forms of Friedrich II.

G. They would be just as harmful now as they were valuable then. The great task for our present government seems to me to be, so to loosen up all relations that each and every germ of development can grow freely and unrepressed; and yet, notwithstanding this freedom, to hold all surely together.*

O. But what is to be the result of all this?

G. The government will discontinue what discontinues itself, by not possessing inward force enough to maintain itself. This is the principle of the Prussian *suum cuique*, that great principle of justice which asks not, When were you established? but, Are you what you claim to be? Every wicked clergyman must be displaced who believes that his office shall consecrate him; every nobleman who thinks that his rank will raise him, when he is ignoble, both in thought and deed; every artisan, who is untrained and unskillful, but still would keep himself from being dismissed out of the company of skillful masters, by means of guild privileges. The man is himself, is the new maxim; the man is no longer to be consecrated by his station; but desecrated stations are to be consecrated and restored to their place by the men who shall fill them. Every man must be fit for his position in the nation; and the consciousness of this fitness must give him inward peace and outward safety. Thus will justice abide in the earth.†

O. But, my dear friend, is your paradise to develop itself by nothing except mere negation of what is obsolete? Do you mean that your equality will be secured, after the leaving and pulling down of the old house, by a new one, which shall build itself? If you do, things can not be in a more promising condition than they are in France; for the pulling down business has never been more thoroughly done than there.

---

* By this is not, of course, meant the dismal and devastating labor of moles, who root and undermine the most beautiful meadows in such a manner that not a blade of grass can be seen; but the benignant influence of the spring sun, which warms and stirs up the earth, gray and stiffened with frost, until all the seeds, resting in their death-like winter sleep, awaken and spring up, and adorn the fields and meadows with their youthful greenness. (1854)

† Office and social station lay upon men a responsibility to God, which not even the best completely discharge. (Luke xvii. 10.) But we refer, not to conscientious workers and champions but to those who, so far from striving to fulfill the duties imposed upon them, even go in the opposite direction, and are, morally, minus quantities. In reference to clergymen particularly, church authorities are to replace, as far as possible, such as are manifestly unworthy. As far as possible, I say; for that a complete purification of the church is not possible is acknowledged by the eighth article of the Augsburg Confession; with a wise view to the consolation of congregations afflicted with unworthy pastors. (1854.)

G. Do not think me so foolish. It is true that Prussia has peacefully pulled down, where France did it with violence and blood; but, God be praised, she has done more than to pull down. Parallel with that process, there went one of building up, of which no one in France even thought; and which gloriously distinguishes the Germans from the French.

O. To what do you refer?

G. To education. What Frenchman thought of that in the time of the Revolution? The schools were dispersed, the best clergymen were banished, and the youth sank into barbarism. But woe to the revolution whose actors forget posterity! What is the disuse of old forms and the introduction of new? If the men, and especially youth, are not renovated, the new forms are, and remain, empty delusions. Such a hopeless revolution was never laid to the charge of Germany, and could only happen to short-sighted and most degraded people. Remember what Luther, whom the Germans may cite to the shame of the French revolutionists, did for schools; how he made them even a chief object of attention. In like manner, the Germans, even in the most perilous period, from 1806 to 1813, in that time of trial, when a divine revolution in their minds strengthened them for a new birth, never lost sight of education. The abandoned French revolutionists, drunk with victory, went to the opposite extreme, and forgot their own times, thinking only of posterity. I read, not without feeling, a little while since, Fichte's remarks on this subject, in his Address to the German Nation, in 1808: "Every one sees what is clearly before our eyes, that we can make no active resistance. How can we, therefore, vindicate our title to continual existence, forfeited by this fact, against the charge of cowardice and an unworthy love of life? No otherwise than by determining not to live for ourselves; and to prove this determination by planting seeds of honor for our posterity, and patiently enduring until this object shall have been safely accomplished."

O. It is in accordance with these excellent sentiments that the government, during that evil time, founded two universities.

G. It did more than that—not of so obvious a kind, however.

O. To what do you refer?

G. I spoke of the ancient forms which they discontinued. They were not under obligations to proceed in the same manner in respect to the many antiquated educational forms in the schools and universities. Only raving French revolutionists would "throw away the child with the bathing-tub,"—would exterminate the schools entirely. The necessary process was a renewal, slow and imperceptible—a renewal which could not be forced, but such as comes to pass of itself, when the spirit of the age causes to be born men with new needs, new loves, and new talents.

O. Among whom you doubtless include Pestalozzi and Jahn.

G. Undoubtedly. The government has, up to this time, so ordered affairs that the old and new elements have not come into opposition. The classical schools and universities have, on the whole, adhered to the ancient principles; Pestalozzi rules in the teachers' seminaries and lower schools, and the Turning-grounds, again, stand by themselves, in contrast with all. The new elements are thus enabled to develop themselves symmetrically and appropriately; and already the beginning may be seen of a mutual influence and strengthening between the old and the new.

Old principles become definite in an existence of centuries, modify crude and ill-adapted novelties, and are in turn reinvigorated and rejuvenated by them. Blessing and grace may be hoped for, when all are bent only upon the good of the young; when none believes himself alone to be possessed of the truth, but allows others to correct and warn him, and lovingly does the like for them; when all, as the noble Fichte said, determine "not to live for themselves alone, and to prove their determination by planting the seeds of honor for their posterity,"—a posterity, I may add, whose growth, and development in the divine spirit of the age, the German fatherland will protect against all revolutions.

The contest between the Burschenschaft and the Turners came to such a height, in Breslau, as to cause an entire separation into friends and opponents of the latter. The account of the Wartburg festival gave additional vigor to this contest. But it reached its height in March, 1819. I cannot forget the fearful impression made upon me when my late friend Passow, quite out of his senses, came to me with the words, "What do you think! A student has murdered Kotzebue!" It was as if the foresight of all the evil consequences of this wicked and most unfortunate deed, had terrified me, all at the moment.

We gradually learned all the particulars. The excitement caused by Sand's crime, not only among members of the university, but among all classes, was excessive, and was stimulated by the falsest reports. It was said that a great and wide-extended conspiracy had been discovered, to which Sand belonged, and that the duty of murdering Kotzebue had fallen to him by lot; that a list of the names of sixty-six persons had been found, who were yet to be stabbed by members of this association. This made many opponents of the Burschenschaft uneasy, as their names might also be upon the list, and this naturally made their enmity more bitter, and caused their attacks to assume a character of self-defense against these imaginary dangers. Opponents of the Burschenschaft among the students put forth a statement, in which they expressed their disapproval of Sand's crime; whether this was put into the hands of the authorities, I do not know. We who were friends of the Burschenschaft were placed in a very uncomfortable position. As we—*i. e.*, Passow, Harnich, the younger Schneider, Schaub, and others—were going to the public Turning-ground, we were recognized, and it would be remarked that we belonged to the conspiracy. This excitement was increased by a set public educational address, by Adolf Menzel, against the Turning system, and by the report that, in Berlin, various persons, and especially Jahn himself, had been imprisoned.

But enough of the results of Sand's act at Breslau. Let us proceed to an account of Sand himself, based chiefly upon his own diary.

a.—SAND.

Karl Ludwig Sand* was born at Wunsiedel, 5th October, 1795. He was the youngest son of Councilor Justice Sand. A dangerous attack of smallpox and a severe fever impeded his studies, and he could receive no instruction until his eighth year. His teacher, Rector Saalfrank, removed, in 1810, from Wunsiedel to Hof; and thence, in 1812, to the Gymnasium at Ratisbon, to both of which places Sand followed him.

From his teachers at Ratisbon he received a testimonial of mental endowments, expressed in high terms. "If he continues in the same course," it said, "he will one day exercise a happy and powerful influence for the good of his fellow-men, both by thorough learning and moral excellence." (!) In like manner, his graduating certificate at Ratisbon, of September 10, 1814, praises his mental gifts and natural traits, his industry and progress in "philosophical and philological subjects;" and it was only in mathematics that he was somewhat deficient.

---

* "Karl Ludwig Sand, described from his diaries and letters from his friends. Altenberg, 1821." I have also made use of the following works:

"Complete Account of the Proceedings against C. L. Sand for Assassination. By State Councilor Von Hohnhorst, presiding member of the communion appointed for that purpose. Tübingen, Cotta, 1820."

"C. L. Sand, by Jarcke. Berlin, Dümmler, 1830." A new edition, enlarged from unpublished sources. This appeared first in the 11th, 12th, and 13th parts of Hitzig's "Annals of Criminal Law."

"The German Youth in the late Burschenschafts and Turning Associations. Magdeburg, Heinrichshofen, 1828."

I have received much oral information respecting Sand from credible persons.

In November, 1814, he was matriculated at Tübingen; and in April, 1815, he enlisted, at Mannheim, as a volunteer in the corps of Jägers of the Rezat; which step he announced to his parents in a letter full of fiery patriotism. The account of the battle of Belle Alliance arrived while the Jägers were still in Hamburg. They, however, marched into France as far as to Auxerre, and on the 2d December, 1815, returned to Ansbach. On the 15th of the same month, Sand was matriculated at Erlangen.

Before going further, we must consider the influence of Sand's mother upon him, which was a most powerful one throughout his life.

In a letter to her, May 26, 1818, he says: "Yes, dear mother, all the love which I have in my heart for religion, for truth, for my country, for beneficent actions, was, for the most part, excited in me by you; and however I consider myself, you have been all to me, in almost every respect." (p. 159.)*

Thus it becomes important to know the mother who had such an influence upon the son. Their correspondence affords the necessary materials, and I give the following extracts from her letters as especially characteristic.

While he was a student at the Gymnasium, and only sixteen, she writes him:

"There are three sorts of education for man. The first is that which he receives from his parents; the second, that which is derived from circumstances; and the third, that which the individual gives himself."†

These extracts, and another, hereafter to be given, leave scarcely a doubt that she had read Rousseau's "*Emile*."

"Man," she writes, in another letter. "can, of himself, be very much, and almost any thing, if only he *will*." This is in a more detailed statement of the third kind of education.

"May the Ruler of heaven and earth let his spirit rest upon you." (p. 103.)

"Though it be a part of Christian duty, and necessary for living happily, to consider men as having been good when they came from the Creator's hand,‡ yet every man is his own nearest neighbor; and if one daily endeavors to be-

---

* This and subsequent references in the text are to Sand's diary.

† See *Emile*, Book I. "This education we derive from nature, or from men, or from things. But of these three different educations, that of nature does not depend upon us at all; that of things depends only upon certain relations; and that of men is the only one of which we are really masters." "Men" were mainly represented by Rousseau, who sets parents aside, by tutors; but the mother naturally says, instead, "parents." For "things," she writes, perhaps after a German translation, "circumstances;" and for the education of nature not depending on us, she says, "the education which the individual gives himself;" placing the will, with Fichte, in authority over the natural endowments.

‡ "All is good when it comes from the hands of the Maker of all things; all degenerates in the hands of man." Thus begins Rousseau's "*Emile*." For "base human goodness," Rousseau says "the rabble."

come better, and to rank with the best and selectest men, the lofty worth that pertains to such a character will, of itself, save him from the low snares of a base human goodness.'' (p. 105.)

Frau Sand had enjoyed the religious instruction of the excellent pastor Esper;* and many beautiful Christian expressions in her letters remind us of him. These are, however, predominated over by others, proceeding from want of self-knowledge and the excess of proud self-esteem thence arising. Her ideal, and that of her son, is moral development by individual power and effort—moral pre-eminence. Christian holiness is but seldom alluded to.

As a means toward moral perfection, Sand practiced a painful and morbid self-observation and self-education. This appears in his diary, where he entered moral observations, discussions, and conclusions. The book reminds us, in part, of Franklin's diary, in its moral account-keeping and entries of debit and credit of one and another virtue; it is only occasionally that a spirit or sentiment truly Christian appears.† And, accordingly, there appears throughout Sand's life, a struggle between Christian elements and those unchristian, or pseudo-Christian. We shall see how doubtful it was, during his studies at Erlangen, which way the victory would incline; at Jena he was in perplexity about Christianity, which prevented him from controversies with its adversaries; and at last he came under the influence of a man who had formed for himself a higher pseudo-Christian morality, which proudly overlooked the simple morality of the catechism. He thus followed a will-o'-the-wisp instead of the true light which truly enlightens all men, and followed it until, at Mannheim, it led him into the path to death.

To return to the history of his life. He was matriculated, as we have seen, at Erlangen, December 15, 1815. Here he soon found friends, with whom he had much intercourse upon morality, Christianity, the country, and academical life.

From his diary and letters we become acquainted with the varying tendencies of his moral efforts, and with his dogmatic views. In 1813 he had written to his mother:

"I shall now recommence my diary, and thus daily seek to investigate myself. Oh, how happy must he be, who gives up to the control of his divine guide, Reason, all his inclinations, desires, impulses, powers, appetites, and dislikes; and who has so far attained as not to have the least thought of that

* For Esper, see Schubert's "*Old and New*," vol. ii. pp. 155–164.

† Sand's diary extends to the last of December, 1818, and contains entries made every evening, of "what he had done well or ill." One of Gellert's hymns may have suggested both this self-examination and the diary. It is entitled "Evening Examination," and begins, "The day is gone again, another part of life; how have I employed it? is it gone in vain?" In some respects it may have been imitated, also, from Lavater's well-known diary.

(evil ?) by means of which he may confirm the authority of his conscience." (p. 21.)

"The All-good will indicate the means and the way by which I may, perhaps, very soon maintain a glorious strife, as a young moral hero, against external dangers." (p. 20.)

And in the letter already quoted, from Tübingen, April 22, 1815, announcing to his parents his intention of serving against the French, he writes: "With the help of God, I shall pass safely through the many trials to which I am exposed in this new situation, pure, and at peace with myself."

The likeness of the morality of the son with that of his mother, above described, is only too clear; and it is also clear, that in the quotations given, no reference is made to *Christian* morality.

During his life at Erlangen, there is, indeed, to be found the recognition of the divinity of Christianity; but very seldom any obedience to the Christian commandments, if they stand in the way of his views or his actions. Such recognition is to be found in the following extracts. After having read the inspired praises of love in the thirteenth chapter of 1st Corinthians, Sand writes:

"Ah! we must confess that we feel ourselves impressed and inspired with a new life by these divine lessons; and that our own merely human minds would never, of themselves, have arrived at these teachings of revelation." (p. 39.)

Upon a sermon of Church Councillor Vogel, he remarks: "Vogel is not ashamed of the pure Gospel; he believes in Christ, who alone is able to free us from our great guilt, to strengthen us, and make us upright. Ah, gracious God! let me, in like manner, penetrate thy word and thy spirit; grant me the unending bliss of being soon able, with like power, to preach all thy sanctifying truth; and grant me, also, what he prays for, thy blessing and holiness." (p. 86.)

May 30, 1817, before communion: "Awaken me, to-day, O gracious God! to just self-inspection; awaken me to the lofty pleasure of being permitted to partake of thy holy supper. In order to close my account with thee up to this time, nothing is more necessary for me than with an honest heart to pray for thy grace, and that, for the sake of the death of thy son Jesus, thou wilt forgive my many secret and open sins, and put me at peace with thee, and with my fellow-men." (p. 90.)

September 15, 1817, he writes: "I have never felt and believed so strongly that it is Christ alone that justifies, and that man possesses a safe foundation for goodness, only through him, and through humble acknowledgment of him." (p. 110.)

With these expressions of Christian morality are mingled others, showing a strange confusion of Christian and unchristian sentiments. Thus, he writes, "Thy paternal love, O God! *O Absolute!* is promised me by thy son Jesus; and I will, and do believe in it." (p. 53.)

On the 28th April, 1816, Sand partook of the communion. He writes: "Eternal power sustains all, through eternal love; to which system, (?) however, we could only be raised by Christ and his sacrificial death. Oh, what a happy occasion, when man lives with God and thee, Christ! Could I not, at this moment, even give myself to death, for noble purposes?" "In the evening" (of the same day), "I attended, at the Harmony Theater, the representation of Kotzebue's '*Silver Age*,' a very beautiful thing. It inspired me with not contemptible thoughts." (p. 48.)

July 23, 1817, while waiting for an antagonist with whom he was about to fight a duel, he prays: "I believe wholly in thee; and implore thee, for the sake of thy son Jesus, to be gracious unto me, and permit me, at this time, to be at peace with thy holy spirit, and to receive what shall happen to me with the true spirit of the one strong and powerful love, and with the courage and face of truth."

To these words he adds, at evening, "We waited two hours, but the rascal N. did not come." (p. 115.)

He offered a similar prayer before a duel which was in contemplation on the 18th of August, 1817.

"Shouldst thou, eternal Judge, summon me before thy throne, I know that I have deserved eternal punishment; but, O Lord! I build not upon my own merits, but those of Jesus, and hope in thy paternal love, because he, thy Son, has suffered for me also." (p. 117.)

And on the same day when he wrote this, he preached his first sermon, in the Neustadt church, at Erlangen.

It is easy to observe, in these extracts, how the conscience of poor Sand was already clouded, and how he was beginning to be surrounded with the perplexities of dangerous fantasies.

To his painstaking endeavors after his own moral perfection, was added a second undertaking, viz.: the purification of the body of students at Erlangen from vice. He and a number of friends established, for this purpose, in 1817, the Erlangen Burschenschaft, and they imposed upon him the task of drawing up "Ideas for the organization of the future Burschenschaft." They had scarcely organized, before, as at other universities, they made vain endeavors to connect the *Landsmannschaften* with themselves. This ill success led to bitter quarrels.*

On the first evening of the year 1817, Sand prays God for more power of self-observation. "Strengthen the decisions of my reason, and strengthen my will, so that it may rule my flesh and bridle my fancy; so that it may not sink below the sphere of holiness, and may drive away the devil." (p. 77.) And afterward (September 4, 1817), he writes: "Strengthen me, O God! with thy Spirit, that I may begin right powerfully to contend against the assaults of the devil, against

* The references to these quarrels in the diary are too scattered to make it possible to construct a connected account from them.

every insidious attack, from the very beginning, in thy justifying name, O Jesus!"

Before the Wartburg festival, Sand composed a short paper, which he distributed there. It agreed, substantially, with the statutes of the General and Jena Burschenschaft. Virtue, learning, fatherland, is its motto, and freedom its chief object. "In pious simplicity and strength, with upright courage, let us follow in the traces of the holy revelation of God." Every effort is to be consecrated to the German fatherland. A General Burschenschaft, but without any oath of association. Such were some of its leading thoughts.

The chief idea of the Wartburg festival was, "We are all, by baptism, consecrated to the priesthood. (1 Peter, ii. 9: 'Ye are a royal priesthood, a holy nation.') That is, through our high consecration, by baptism, gospel, and faith, we are all placed in the ministerial office; and so long as we are consecrated to our divine Master as valiant and active servants, there is no other distinction among us than that of our offices and labors; we are all spiritually free and equal." (pp. 126–132.)

We have seen that Sand was on the committee of management of the Wartburg festival. From that place he went to the university of Jena.

Here his inward strifes came to an end. The theologian would call them strifes between nature and grace; for man cannot serve both—one master must be supreme.

These struggles, though ending, ended in a very sad manner. The diary shows clearly his gradual circumvention and conquest by evil. Gradually—for at first, the rude and reckless unchristian life, which he had not before encountered, seems rather to have strengthened than weakened his faith. At first he is only surprised. "Jena," he writes, November 9th, "has its wise men." He found friends who contended, with much zeal, "against the understanding of the Bible maintained by the orthodox theologians." November 16, he writes:

"I heard from N. a stupid, malicious sermon. . . . He spoke so shamefully against the awakened faith of late grown up, and in favor of a cold rationalism, that I was enraged." (p. 135.)

In the same month he writes intelligently to a friend,* "You seem to me . . . to have departed from your former plain, and pious, and powerful faith, and to have taken up, instead of it, the sentimental and credulous opinions, if I may so describe them, of the priests. Do you not, yourself, find that you vary more and more from the firm and strong beliefs which were those of our Luther, and are gliding into this unchristian pietist way, who neglect that dearest of all earthly objects, our country, and who scoff at *German* Christians, including us in our country? I pray you, do not, on this point, believe any longer the 'inner voice' that you profess to have, if it is to withdraw you from

* Von Plehwe, a captain in the Prussian service.

the powerful faith which makes us free, and which our Luther possessed. Try this voice, whether it is agreeable to the Holy Scriptures; for the devil seeks to rob us entirely of the kingdom of heaven; and most, when we are susceptible of believing." (pp. 136–138.)

A comparison of these sentiments, so lucid, and so modest, in the best sense of the term, with many of those previously quoted, so confused, and visionary in the worst sense, leaves us to the belief that scarcely any young man can be cited of such inconsistent views.

It seems as if poor Sand, in the last words just quoted, had expressed a presentiment of the evil that threatened him; although it came upon him from a direction opposite to pietism. He writes again, on the 18th of November: "The devil knows how he would despoil me again of my *Christianity*." (p. 139.)

On the 31st December, Sand prays:

"O gracious God! permit me to begin this year with prayer. At the end of the last year I was more thoughtless and out of temper than before. On looking back, I find myself, to my sorrow, not to have become better or more perfect, but have only lived through so much more time, and had so much more experience. O Lord! thou wert always with me, even while I was not with thee! It almost seems as if thou hadst, during the storms of these latter years of the spring of my life, changed all my previous love to faith; at least, in all my needs, I feel Jesus Christ right near to me, and build upon him; and he alone is to me always a sufficient and constant encouragement, a place of refuge for my fears, and a central point for free and powerful efforts. Through him I feel myself, above all things, made right free; and I have learned to know freedom as the highest good of humanity, of nations, and of my fatherland; and I shall hold fast to it." (p. 144.)

At the beginning of the year 1818, he prays, again, "O God! let me hold fast to thy salvation of the human race through Jesus Christ; let me be a German Christian, and let me, through Jesus, become free, peaceful, confident, and also persevering and strong." (p. 147.)

But, at the same time, he writes: "It is all over with devotees. What is needed now is action."

A letter of the end of March, 1818, to Cl——, indicates a still greater departure from Christian simplicity. In this he says:

"I cannot charge myself with being a doubter. It would be to me the most fearful of all things, to be feeble or indeterminate.

"And yet there is one thing which distresses me; which has, for a long time, had power to cool my warmth, and with which you must be made acquainted; in regard to which I may, perhaps, receive from you an impulse toward a more fixed belief.

"During last summer I attained a real fixity in my convictions upon the subjects of highest importance to us. My faith became more firmly grounded; I desired, even if I could do nothing more, at least to be a real Christian and a real German. Trusting confidently, in all things, to the grace of Our Father, I was free in my belief, always courageous, and could go with firm steps in the road which my will and my reason had chosen. Love excited me to action, prevented me from becoming stupefied, and rendered me decided, firm, and peaceful in all matters that concerned me. Thus I experienced, in reality, the blessedness of faith, expressed it in my sermons, and could, with truthfulness, encourage others to faith.

"Since my coming hither, into a world wider, and quite different in all its peculiarities and chief traits; since I have seen, in many whom I love, too much of the northern modesty, and have heard the sphere of my own beliefs described as visionary by others, who yet discourse upon faith; and since, besides other books, I have, chiefly by your means, become acquainted with Herder's views, it has gradually come to be with me otherwise than before. At first, my attention was excited only; after, what I heard was repugnant to me; sometimes I was confused within myself, and on the whole, I am at least colder and less courageous than heretofore.

"In truth, so much is my firm determination; that reason shall be my supreme rule; I would possess not a visionary, but a pure and sound faith; and even if I hold to my former beliefs, I must be able to make them out as clearly sure and sound. I have always reverenced in Jesus the highest and most beautiful picture of our manhood; but to consider him a mere ordinary man, seems to me, now, too desolate and harsh.

"I will not willingly renounce reason and understanding; but it makes me cheerful and happy, and certainly does not impede me in action, to reverence in the great Teacher of the eternal God, a constant helper, a divine brother, who kindly makes up for the deficiencies of the world and humanity, who raises us above a system of legality. Did he now die for himself alone, a hero for the sake only of his own opinion? Did he merely bear witness to the truth of his instruction, without intending to purchase a great benefit for men?" (p. 148.)

In a second letter to the same friend, he says: "But you know that, by little and little, my whole system of beliefs grew continually darker, and that I was almost entirely fallen into a blind dependence upon ancient formulas of belief, giving up my own independent faith; and you know how I have come into this condition mainly by your means." (p. 154.)

But on the 5th of May, the unhappy fruit of the refinements which drew him further and further from a pure Christianity, comes clearly out in these words of his diary: "Lord, to-day again this so miserable unhappiness has sometimes attacked me; but a steady will and steady occupation solves all, and helps through all, and the fatherland becomes a source of pleasure and virtue. Our God-man Christ, our Lord, is a picture of humanity that must always remain beautiful and peaceful. When I reflect, I often think that some one, courageous beyond himself, will undertake to drive a sword into the vitals of Kotzebue, or some other such traitor to the country." (p. 150.)

In the same month of May, 1818, Sand became acquainted with one K——r, a pupil of Hegel, who made a deep impression on him by his cunning frenzy, and carried him quite beyond control. To understand this K——r, and his influence on Sand, it will be abundantly sufficient to quote what the latter writes in his diary, October 20, 1818:

"K——r came in in the evening, and was healthy, noble, and free, clear and firm, immovable, and consistent in his views. He told me how he had formerly had such misgivings, but how he was now completely free from them, and how he was consistent and clear on the question of religion. Heaven must be boldly taken by storm; all stain of sin, all distinction of good and evil, must completely disappear from before the soul, as an empty and false show; and then will the soul vanquish men, earth, and the mansions of heaven! Only in unity is there blessedness, to him, in equal and everlasting rest. But he respects every brother as near himself, and recognizes him, as a complement of himself. Yet he is free above freedom, and has another home besides the fatherland. He knows how to seek it, and is firmly determined to do so. I seem to him pious, as well as near to him, and recognized as such; I was pious in the sight of God, and would remain so; and I desire to be holy only in comparison with the world; not in my own eyes. If he can seem holy in his own eyes, let him do so—I must remain behind. But he vowed freely that he would undertake to maintain such a character continually, or that he would disappear, a wretched mass of dross. Thus he acts not for himself, but for all of us, since we are all one spirit,—a pure spirit. And all this he said so clearly, so loftily, with a peacefulness so powerful as I never saw. I lost all feeling of strangeness, and was drawn to him as a brother in freedom. God help!" (pp. 168, 169.)

The contrast between Sand and K——r comes out more strongly in the following important extract from his diary:

"November 2. Victory, unending victory! To will to live according to my own convictions, in my own way, with an unrestricted will, beyond which nothing in the world pertains to me before God; to maintain, with life and death, among the people a state of pure uprightness (that is, the only condition consistent with God's commands), against all human sentiments; to desire to introduce, by preaching and dying, a pure humanity among my German nation. This seems to me altogether another thing from living in renunciation of the people. I thank thee, O God! for thy grace. What infinite power and blessing do I discover in my own will; I doubt no more! This is the condition of true likeness to God." (p. 170.)

A letter to his mother contains expressions quite similar. In this he says:

"K——r, as you correctly judge, seems to me an acute and powerful mind; for he has deep and firm convictions, and an individualized and powerful will; and thus has the impress upon him which we derive from God. But his conviction is a distinct disgust at every thing that exists; at all being, life, and effort; he endeavors boldly to destroy the form of every thing, and even himself, as he now exists; he has no pleasure in his existence, in the world, or in his nation. Humanity, which should be to him a pure and holy picture, such as we know it to be displayed in Jesus, our Saviour, counts with him for nothing; is to him nothing but a delay in individuality—in evil.

"And therefore, dear mother, I must say to you, that among our people I know bolder and nobler heroes; and that in the path in which K——r thrusts me backward, and kills me, I feel myself drawn toward them with inexpressible power. Like him, they recognize no human attainment more holy than the good of the highest divine grace, likeness to God; the possession, by man, of an individual conviction and will for himself. In this belief they are wholly without doubt, and as strong in their wills as K——r; but their convictions look toward active life and pleasure in striving; and if they could have their own way, they would insist on introducing among our German people that pure condition of humanity in which every one can train himself to every thing for which God has ordained him; they would glorify humanity in our nation! And since they have attained to this condition, not one doubt has assaulted their souls; they have not even trembled.

"Of this mental pleasure, and this victory, I experience some indications; and therefore I quite give up K——r. My inherited feelings had already disinclined me to his views; but now I possess a faith, the loftiest belief upon this earth; and this alone I will enjoy." (pp. 171, 172.)

Who were these bolder heroes to whom Sand felt himself attracted with such inexpressible power, and from whom he expected such transcendent benefits to his fatherland?

Late researches, and especially a work entitled "*The German Youth in the Late Burschenschafts and Turning Societies*," indicate, with the utmost clearness, that Sand alluded to Karl Follenius and his followers.

The author of the above-named work (Robert Wesselhöft), thus describes his first visit to Follenius:

"He received us like old acquaintances. We called each other *thou;* he was hearty and easy, open and confiding, without requiring that any one should at once unconditionally reciprocate all this. But there was in his demeanor, his attitude, the tone of his voice, his emotions, and looks, in short, in the whole man, something noble; peace, power, clearness, a seriousness almost proud; an individuality, which insensibly secured a remarkable degree of respect from all near him. And in his morals he was as strict, as pure, and as chaste as in his language; and we have found no one like him, or certainly no one equal to him, in purity and vigor of morals and manners."*

Follenius lectured on the Pandects. His "philosophy was, throughout, practical. He required all that is recognized by the human reason as good, beautiful, and true, to be accomplished by means of the moral will. . . . The State must be organized correspondently with the reason of the members of it."†

In this manner, proceeds our author, Follenius developed a degree of self-consciousness that was astonishing:

"He was bold enough to assert that his own life was such as reason required. With an indescribable expression of contempt in his features, he accused those of cowardice and weakness who imagine that the knowledge of truth and beauty, and especially of their highest ideals, could be disjoined from living them out, practicing them, realizing them in their widest extent. For he asserted that man's knowledge of good and right never exceeds his power and his will; and that the latter are limited only by the former.

"It will be readily understood that these proud sentiments gave the more offense in proportion as Follenius' own life furnished fewer opportunities for disputing his positions. All that could be alleged against him amounted to the charge, that he was deficient in a certain humility and modesty. But this accusation could not provoke, from one who saw his superiority recognized, any thing more than a compassionate laugh, which said, clearly enough, 'Ye weaklings! Your envious vanity and vile weaknesses are remarkably shrewd!'"‡

Follenius required unconditional acquiescence in, or difference from his views.

"While in Giessen, he had driven his opponents to this position, and maintained his own ascendency, because he had control of the existence of the Giessen Friends known by the title of Black. But at Jena he had not this control."§

"As soon as Follenius defined this unconditionality in its whole extent, all seemed to bow before the boldness of his conceptions. The conviction that showed itself so profoundly and strongly, commanded respect, but it was felt that it was respected only as it existed in Follenius, and could not be separated from him. But his hearers did not yet understand themselves thoroughly enough to be able at once to be clear in this feeling. But they were sensible of some opposition of thoughts within themselves which prevented them from resisting, with Follenius, all history, and all things, both past and future, and from asserting, with him, that whatever had happened had been brought about by men, and that it might just as well have been otherwise, had men followed a better knowledge, and been willing to put the reason in possession of all its rights. But Follenius claimed that he possessed this better knowledge. Politically, he was purely republican; for he would construct the State as it should be, from the individual man as he should be; and he thought himself competent to represent the latter, and, therefore, authorized to require as much from others. And this he required unconditionally; concluding that any one who would accept this unconditionally, would also accept unconditionally the republican frame of government. Any one accepting his system became 'uncon-

* "*German Youth*," &c., p. 65. † Ib., p. 71. ‡ Ib., p. 72. § Ib., p. 73.

ditioned.' As his whole system had a practical purpose, and looked to the realization of its principles, thus the receiving of his views—*i. e.*, 'unconditionality'—was really a very serious matter; and it can readily and clearly be apprehended that the unconditional recipients of Follenius' opinions were as earnest in them as he, from the moment of their accepting them.

"Fortunately for the world, of about thirty Friends who formed the narrow circle around Dr. Follenius, only three were entirely 'unconditional,' and there were about five more in a doubtful state. One of these three was Sand. All the rest were in favor of moderate views; many were only seeking instruction and interchange of ideas in their circle, and were neutral; and a few desired Follenius' conversion. It was supposed that Court Councilor Fries would best accomplish this work of information and conversion, and shortly the whole society met once a week with him, and disputed vigorously. But as both Fries and Follenius had a fixed and completed system, this led to no result. Neither convinced the other."*

But among the students there was no thought of an agreement, and in March, 1819, the whole society was broken up into a completely inimical separation, only three adhering to Follenius, among whom, as we have said, was Sand. Our author goes into some detail as to the reasons why Follenius was not acceptable to the other students. He says: "All authoritative proceedings were much hated at Jena; the students only loved their teachers and valued their intellects. Follenius, with his moral-political ideas, could not succeed in Jena. People had learned and received too much from previous teachers to give it up for what Follenius offered. They criticised him, and advised others to do so—why should Follenius not be criticised? The harshness with which he would have propagated his beliefs and opinions, and with which he asserted that only cowardice and weakness refrained from adhering to them, and carrying them into practice, drove his friends into such an opposition as made it out of the question for his instructions to have any influence on the students. Even those who could not refuse their respect to Follenius, opposed him strenuously at the same time; asserting that no one, unless he were Christ, was entitled to claim that he was possessed of the truth. Only Christ held that position; and in him intellectual freedom is to be enjoyed. In a moral and religious sense, there is a Saviour; but nobody is going to believe in a moral-political Messiah."†

This reference to Christ relates to a hymn which Follenius wrote for the communion. It began:

"A Christ thou must become."‡

The last stanza is:

"The man is flown away;
A Christ canst thou become.
Like thee, a child on earth
Was he, the Son of man.

---

* "*German Youth*," &c., pp. 74-76. † Ib., p. 83. ‡ Ib., p. 84.

Within thy being nothing is destroyed.
God guideth thee as thou dost guide thyself.
Through thee, by love, God doth become
A man, that he may still be end and aim into us."*

Another poem of Follenius', a turbulent summons to insurrection, Sand had printed and distributed as widely as possible. It begins:

"Human crowd, O thou great human desert!
Who of late the mental spring-time greetedst,
Break at last—crash up, O ancient ice!"†

As an additional description of Follenius, I add the following:

"When we asked him if he believed that his system could be put into practice without blood, he answered, calmly, 'No. In the worst event, all must be sacrificed who entertain different opinions.' And when we replied that our feelings revolted at such a terrorism, and that, as Christians and men, we thought it wrong to murder men, otherwise, perhaps, good and upright, because they ventured to think and believe differently from us; and even that we did not claim the right of condemning the moral convictions of others, he answered that 'the feelings have nothing to do with this case, but necessity. And if you have the conviction in you that your beliefs are true, the feeling of the necessity of acting out this truth cannot be strange to you, unless by reason of cowardice. The means are not to be considered when the case is one of moral necessity.'

"When we observed, that this was the Jesuitical principle, that the end sanctifies the means, he calmly replied, that 'a moral necessity is not an end at all; and in reference to that, all means are alike.'

"Fortunately, we could find no such moral necessity within us; and had to admit that we did not believe it existed, except in him.

"'Good;' he answered 'that is enough, however.'"

We shall, hereafter, refer once more to Follenius; and, therefore, shall only describe him so far as is necessary to show how predominant an influence he exercised upon Sand. Although this is plain, from many of Sand's expressions, already quoted, it appears still more clearly in portions of the latter part of his diary. He writes, on 5th December, 1818:

"I will have but one grace—the everlasting grace of God—which, therefore, can never turn back from me, but is inwoven with the rudiments of my being. I renounce the feeble belief in the occasional interposition of God's hand behind the scenes of the play of nature and humanity, and proportionably more shall I, on the other hand, elevate my own spirit, and praise thy primeval grace, O God! by my whole active existence and life. And these immediate relations with thee, O God! my soul shall never mistake, nor destroy, nor forget. Here, thy grace shall endure forever, with every day—here, in thy love. I will rightly understand my will, the loftiest gift of God, the only real possession; and with it will possess all the infinity of material which thou hast placed about me for trial and for self-creation. I reject all grace which I do not acquire from myself; such undesired grace is none at all for me; it destroys itself. Not to live distinctly up to one's convictions, to vary from them for fear and human opinions, not to be willing to die for them, is brutal—is the vileness of millions for thousands of years. Flee, with circumspection, the snares of Satan." (p. 173.)

On the 31st of December, he writes: "Thus I celebrate the last day of this year, 1818, seriously and joyfully, and am sure that the last Christmas is past which I shall have kept. If any thing is to come of our efforts; if humanity

* Hohnhorst, vol. i. p. 50. † Ib., vol. ii. p. 193.

is to prosper in our fatherland; if, at this important time, all is not to be forgotten again, and enthusiasm to perish out of the land, that wretch, that traitor, that corrupter of youth, A. v. K., must go down—that I see. Until I have accomplished this I shall have no rest; and what shall console me until I know that, with honorable boldness, I have set my life upon the deed? God, I ask nothing of thee, except upright purity and courage of soul, lest, in that most lofty hour, I may lose my life." (p. 174.)

Sand carried about with him this firm resolve upon murder for months. Nevertheless, his friends report that there was observable in him no change, no disquiet, no uneasy abstraction. He even attended lectures most regularly, as if preparing himself for many future years of life.

But in this unhappy and fearful silence the scheme of murder was becoming riper and more fixed.

* On the 9th of March, 1819, he left Jena and went to the Wartburg, where he wrote in the book at the inn:

"Into the true heart strike the lance,
A road for German freedom!"

On the 17th he reached Frankfort, and thence proceeded, by Darmstadt, to Mannheim, where he arrived at half-past nine A. M.

His first step was to call on Kotzebue, who was not at home; but he was admitted to see him about five in the afternoon. After some little conversation, Sand drew his dagger and struck down the "whimpering" Kotzebue, with the words, "Here, thou traitor to the fatherland!" He stabbed him three times, though the first blow was fatal, having severed the main artery of the lungs. Kotzebue died in a few minutes. Sand then rushed out of the house and cried, with a loud voice, to the gathering crowd, "Long live my German fatherland, and all of the German people—all who strive to better the condition of pure humanity!" Then, kneeling down, he prayed, "God, I thank thee for this victory;" thrust a short sword into his left breast until it stuck fast, and fell down.

He was brought into the hospital at six P. M. He lay there, "stretched out on his back, his face deadly pale, his lips blue, his hands and feet cold and stiff, scarcely breathing, his pulse hardly perceptible." He was revived by warm wine, so that at half-past seven the question could be put to him, whether he had murdered Kotzebue. He raised his head, opened his eyes, and nodded quickly and strongly. He then asked for paper, and wrote, in pencil, "A. v. Kotzebue is the corrupter of our youth, the defamer of our national history, and the Russian spy upon our fatherland."

During the night he caused the account of the battle of Sempach to be read to him, from Kohlrausch's History of Germany.

* The following account is from Hohnhorst, vol. i. pp. 48–82.

His wounds healed after fourteen days, but an extravasation in the cavity of the left chest made a painful operation necessary. This left a wound which remained open some months, and the dressing twice a day, and the constant position on his back, caused him, often, the severest pain. On the 5th of April he was removed from the hospital to prison.

"His demeanor, during his whole imprisonment, was praiseworthy; without making demands, he thankfully received whatever was done for alleviating his sufferings; and toward the members of the commission of investigation he was mostly obedient and modest. But this did not prevent him from purposely endeavoring to delay the investigation by numerous untruths."*

The result of a long investigation was, that the high court of justice in Mannheim decreed, on the 5th May, 1820, that Sand, "having been guilty of the murder of Imperial Russian State Councilor Von Kotzebue, and having confessed the same, should, therefore, for his own punishment, and for the example and warning of others, be put to death with the sword."

This decision was approved by the Grand Duke on the 12th of May.

On the 17th of May, at half-past ten A. M., in the presence of two witnesses, the sentence of death, confirmed by the supreme authority, was read to Sand, who, by permission, dictated the following paper:

> "This hour, and the honorable judge, with the final sentence, are welcome to him; he will strengthen himself in the strength of his God; since he has often and clearly proclaimed, that of human miseries, none seem to him equal to that of living without being able to live for the fatherland, and for the highest purposes of humanity; that he dies willingly, where he cannot labor, according to his love, for his ideas; where he cannot be free.
>
> "Thus he approaches the gate of eternity with free courage; and since he has ever been inwardly oppressed by the fact, that, on earth, true good only comes out in the strife of opposed miseries; that any one who desires to work for the highest, the divine, must be leader and member of a party. . . .† He cherishes the hope of satisfying, by his death, those who hate him; and, likewise, those with whom he sympathizes, and whose love is one with his earthly happiness. Death is welcome to him, for he feels himself to possess the requisite strength, with the help of God, as a man should."

The 20th of May was the day of execution; and until that time the officers of the prison were ordered to admit proper persons into it, on the requisition of the prisoner, especially Protestant clergymen, and to comply with all his reasonable wishes.

During the period up to the execution, the commissary in charge of the arrangements visited the criminal at various times, and observed, in a report of May 19th, that at all these visits Sand maintained the

* This testimony is from the chief of the investigating commission.

† Something, says Hohnhorst, seems wanting here.

same steadiness of demeanor as at the time of hearing his sentence. On the same day, Sand requested that he might be allowed to go to the place of execution without any clergyman, alleging, as a reason, that such attendance was a dishonor to the clergyman and to religion. The last must exist in the heart; and cannot come in from without, certainly not during the excitement of such an occasion. As all exhortations, even of the clergymen in attendance, had been fruitless, there was no hesitation in granting this request.

On the 20th of May, at five in the morning, Sand was placed in a low, open carriage, within the closed doors of the prison, having with him the head-jailer, who was, by his request, to support him, and to conduct him to the place of execution; and two under-jailers were appointed to walk behind the carriage. He wore a dark green overcoat (not an old-German black coat, as various papers stated), linen pantaloons, and laced boots, without any covering on his head. The carriage and its personal attendants were received, before the prison, by a squadron of cavalry, drawn up in readiness. The procession advanced to a meadow, lying not far from the city gate, where was the scaffold, surrounded with a square of infantry. Sand was lifted from the wagon, and mounted the scaffold himself, leaning on the shoulders of the two under-jailers. Having arrived at the top, he turned himself about, with rolling eyes, threw quickly down upon the ground a handkerchief which he carried in his hand, lifted up his right hand, as if pronouncing an oath, lifting his eyes to heaven at the same time, and then permitted himself to be led to the block, where he remained standing, by his express desire, until the time of preparing for execution. The sentence of death was now read aloud by an actuary, and the hands and body of the prisoner bound fast to the block, Sand saying, to the executioner's servant, in a low voice, "Do not tie me too tight, or you will hurt me." His eyes having been bound up, the execution was finished, the head being severed from the shoulders with one blow.

The execution was conducted with the utmost order, and in the deepest silence on the part of the spectators, except, at the moment of the decapitation, some expressions of sympathy were heard.

A little before the stroke, he said, in an audible voice, "God gives me much pleasure in my death—it is finished—I die in the grace of my God."

He died, with much firmness, and entire presence of mind, about half-past five. His body and the separated head were soon placed in a coffin, which was in readiness, and which was immediately fastened down. The military escorted the body back to the prison.

At eleven o'clock on the following night, Sand's body was buried in the Lutheran church, near the prison.

It remains to add, from the documents relating to the trial, as given by Hohnhorst, some matter which may serve to fill out the sketch of Sand's character, and to explain his connection with the society of the "Blacks," and with the *Burschenschaft*, and with particular reference to the murder.

His expressions as to religion, patriotism, politics, are quite consistent with those in his diary and his letters, and remarkably with the views of Karl Follenius.

On Christianity, Sand expressed himself thus:

"1. The divine laws are not so much positive commands as an advisory code, by which man may govern his actions according to his own convictions.

"2. The man who endeavors to seek the divine, so far as is within his power, who never finds pleasure in evil, but seeks to keep it as distant from him as possible; and, on the other hand, adheres, to the utmost of his ability, to what is good,—he represents the image of God upon earth.

"3. But this knowledge proceeds only from the man himself; it consists in his determination that, as soon as he has recognized any thing as true and clear, he will openly confess it for the good of all. When a man has, according to his powers, so recognized a truth, that he can say, before God, 'This is true,' it is a truth also when he *does* it. When one can comprehend his whole being, and can then say, before God, 'This is true,' he easily becomes concordant with himself. For whither would it lead, if men should assume to see, investigate, and condemn, as to be rejected, their own endowments? Every one must stand for himself before God.

"4. But one who seeks to repress the divine in man, is trebly deserving of murder and the stroke of death.

"5. Any one not of this opinion, or who would apply texts of the Bible to the actions of a criminal, is a theological blockhead."*

For such did Sand pronounce the author of a letter to him from an unknown hand, otherwise a very well-meant letter, as he himself said, in which he was admonished to receive a sense of his crime, with a reference to various places in the Scriptures.

He prayed God, daily, for knowledge and enlightenment. If he should learn, by divine suggestion, that his act was wrong, he would repent it from that hour; but, so far, this has not happened.

As to the laws of the State, and the State itself, he said: "A reasonable faith, properly based upon the understanding, is to me a law. I must live according to my free will; and that which my convictions have determined, I must live up to. In case of collision with earthly laws, no man should be restrained by these, if any thing is to be done for the fatherland." In a true human state, every man must be able

---

* Hohnhorst, vol. i. pp. 109–111.

to govern himself as far as is possible. Germany must be free, and under one government.

"The logical result of these views," says Hohnhorst, correctly, "seems to be this: My own conviction is my law; I do right when I follow it; it is, for me, above human or divine precepts."

With an incredible inconsistency with these views, Sand took a New Testament with him on his journey to Mannheim, and strengthened and edified himself, particularly by reading the Gospel of John.* But he also took with him Follenius' hymn, "A Christ must thou become!"

"*The end sanctifies the means.* This principle found in Sand a strenuous supporter. It was, he said, neither dangerous nor shameful; for it was made abominable by the Jesuits only because they applied their means to shameful ends. All means for a good end must always be good."† His adherence to this frightful principle explains only too well Sand's constant and hateful lying at his trial, which stood in the strongest contrast with his proud endeavors after moral perfection and moral heroism.

Nearly all Sand's sentiments agree entirely with those of Follenius, above quoted; and show, obviously, that the latter had completely got control of poor Sand, who had, intellectually, come to be quite near him; had, in truth, unconditionally enslaved him to whom free and self-confirmed conviction was to be the highest law of all action. There is only One who makes truly free those who give themselves unconditionally to him.

The question has often been asked, What was the reason of Sand's murder of Kotzebue? Sand gave the answer, the night after the murder, as I have given it. Whether Sand was acquainted with the details of Kotzebue's life and writings, cannot be certainly ascertained.‡

After all the matter which I have quoted from and relating to Sand, no one will wonder that the most various judgments were formed upon his deed.

Such persons as based their opinions upon a strict subjection to the Holy Scriptures, saw nothing except a positive violation of the divine command, Thou shalt not kill; and no defense, however subtle and sophistical, could drive them from this belief. And yet even the

---

* "In the world," says Sand (Hohnhorst, i. 127), "men have sorrow, wherever they go." He had applied to himself, as will appear from his letter to his parents, the words of Christ, "In this world ye shall have tribulation; but be of good cheer, I have overcome the world." John, xvi. 33.

† Hohnhorst, i. 119.

‡ Those not informed as to Kotzebue's character are referred to Appendix VI. for a passage on his work, "*Bahrdt with the iron forehead*," from the General German Library, vol. cxii. pt. 1, p. 213, &c.

simplest Christian felt that this murder was not similar to murders by criminals whose motives were personal revenge, robbery, and the like. Thus, a profound sympathy with Sand was united with the fullest condemnation of his crime.

This connection of sentiments was the basis of De Wette's much-quoted letter to Sand's mother;* which, it must always be remembered, was written only eight days after the murder. A copy of this letter, which was sent to the King of Prussia, occasioned De Wette's dismission. In the beginning of this letter he says: "The deed which he has committed is, it is true, not only unlawful, and punishable by earthly judges, but also, speaking universally, is immoral, and contrary to the moral code. No right can be established by wrong, fraud, or violence; and a good end does not sanctify wrong means. As a teacher of morals, I cannot countenance such actions; and should advise that evil is not to be overcome by evil, but only by good." (Romans xii. 21.) De Wette wrote with confidence to the Berlin theological faculty, "The foregoing general moral principles laid down in the letter, according to which I declare the act a wrong one, will be found unblamable by the faculty; they are those of the Gospel." He afterward said to the same faculty, "Only within the narrow circle of those who knew and loved him (Sand) well, and to his relatives, can it be pointed out, that there should be accorded to him a large measure of excuse; not an unconditional justification. It was within this circle that I wrote the letter of comfort to the mother; I did not obtrude myself for the purpose, but circumstances drew me into it."† . . . "It would never have occurred to me to publish that letter in that form."‡ And accordingly, De Wette writes to the mother, that he was writing to her a "defense" of her son; and this is so true, that his letter corresponds, in many respects, to the defense made for Sand by the counsel appointed for him by the court.

The double character of Sand's action, and the consequent two views to be taken of it, appear most clearly in the following extract of De Wette's letter to the theological faculty. "Calixtus says, correctly, 'Even a mistaken conscience is binding; and one who acts contrary

---

* "*Collection of documents upon the dismission of Professor Dr. De Wette, published by himself.*" Leipzig, 1820. Vogel.

† De Wette had met Sand in Jena, on the 15th of August, 1818, and had been hospitably received, at Wunsiedel, by his parents. ("*C. L. Sand*," p. 164.)

‡ De Wette refers to this extract from Luther: "There is a great difference between a private and a public letter; and he who publishes a private letter, against the will and wish of its writer, falsifies not four or five words of it, but the whole letter; so that it is no longer the same letter, and does not convey its right meaning; because the complexion and character of the whole letter, and the meaning of the writer, are completely perverted and altered." "This," says De Wette, "bears strongly upon my case."

to his mistaken conscience, sins.' The corresponding proposition," continues De Wette, "is true, that one who obeys his mistaken conscience acts conscientiously, and therefore does right. By his truth to himself he maintains his own internal consistency, and therefore fulfills, within his sphere, the law of the moral world. Nevertheless, however, it certainly remains true that he does wrong when he thus errs."*

This opinion of Calixtus would justify all the crimes of such fanatics as Clement and Ravaillac. But the question is, Has not this mistaken conscience always a definite sin at the root of it? The prophet says: "It is told thee, O man, what is good, and what the Lord requireth of thee; to obey the word of God, to love thy neighbor, and to be humble before thy God." And St. Paul refers to "those who say, 'Let us do evil that good may come:' whose condemnation is just."

Thus the apostle most distinctly rejects the Jesuitical principle upheld by Sand, that the end sanctifies the means; and the prophet requires, simply and unmistakably, that we obey God's word and be humble before God. Sand having lost this humility, his aims became perverted by persons who acted only after their own choice. Them he followed, and in pride and delusion imagined that his subjective, godless ideal of moral perfection stood high above all which real Christians recognize as a holy and undoubted duty. He was like a shipmaster who should hoist a light at his masthead, and steer his course by that instead of the unvarying polar star in the heavens. To realize his distorted ideal, at whatever cost, appeared to him the loftiest moral heroism. Betrayed by his pride, and his conscience deluded, he fell, in violation of the clearest command of God, into a great crime.

The preacher says: "God made man upright, but he found out many inventions." He therefore gave him a right conscience; but by his many inventions—by the sophistry of his pride—man is resolved to free himself from his obligations to obey God and his word, and to establish his own righteousness. Thus he becomes deaf to the voice of God within him, at last drives away his good angel, and incurs the penalties of delusion and hardness of heart. In this delusion Sand remained, even to the scaffold.

But it is not my task to discuss further the question of conscience and conscientiousness. If what I have said seems too harsh, reason may

* De Wette, p. 28. Even the strongest opponent of Sand's moral principles, Jarcke, says, "Sand was one of those deep and uncommon natures who are not merely superficially influenced by an idea, a theory, or an opinion; but who, subjecting their whole wills to it, make it the highest and only rule for their life." Thus we admire the bravery even of foemen; and only lament that they are not contending on the right side; and, on the other hand, despise a cowardly braggart. It seems to me clear that Jarcke's view coincides with that of Calixtus and De Wette.

be found to moderate it in the following letter, written by Sand to his friends before going upon his fearful errand to Mannheim:

"To all mine:—

"True and ever dear souls:—I have thought and hesitated as to writing to you, lest I should much increase your grief. For sudden information of my deed might cause your severe sorrow to pass by more easily and quickly; but the truth of love would thus be violated, and deep sorrow can only be removed by our emptying the whole full cup of affliction, and thus remaining piously subject to our friend, the true and eternal Father in heaven. Out, therefore, from the closed and unhappy breast; forth, thou long, great agony of my last words; the only proper alleviation of the grief of parting!

"This letter brings you the last greeting of your son and your brother!

"I have always said and wished much: it is time for me to leave off dreaming, and to proceed to act for the needs of our fatherland.

"This is, doubtless, the greatest sorrow of living on the earth, that God's affairs should, by our fault, come to a stand-still in their proper development; and this the most dishonorable reproach to us, that all the noble objects for which thousands have boldly striven, and thousands have gladly sacrificed themselves, should now sleep again in sad discouragement, like a dream, without lasting results; that the reformation of the old, lifeless ways should become ossified, half-way to success. Our grandchildren will have to suffer for this remissness. The beginning of the reformation of our German life was commenced with spirits encouraged by God, within the last twenty years, especially during the sacred year 1813; and our ancestral residence is shaken from the foundations. Forward! Let us rebuild it, new and beautiful, a right temple of God, such as our hearts long to see it. It is only a few who oppose themselves, like a dam, against the current of development of a higher humanity in the German people. Why should multitudes bow themselves again under the yoke of these wretches? Shall the good that was awakening for us die again?

"Many of the most reckless of these traitors are unpunished, pursuing their designs even toward the complete destruction of our people. Among these, Kotzebue is the acutest and vilest; the true mouthpiece for all evil in our day; and his voice is well fitted entirely to remove from us Germans all opposition and dislike of the most unrighteous measures, and to lull us again into the old slothful slumber. He daily practices vile treason against the fatherland, and yet stands, protected by his hypocritical speeches and flattering arts, and covered by a mantle of great poetical fame, in spite of his wickedness, an idol to half of Germany, which, deluded by him, willingly receives the poison which he administers through his periodical. If the worst misfortunes are not to come upon us—for these outposts announce the coming of something not free nor good; and which, on occasion of an outbreak, would rage among us together with the French—if the history of our times is not to be laden with eternal disgrace—he must go down!

"I have always said, if any thing beneficent is to be accomplished, we must not shrink from contests and labor; and the real freedom and enthusiasm of the German people will awaken for us only when good citizens shall dare and endeavor—when the son of his fatherland, in the struggle for right, and for the highest good, shall set aside all other love, and love only death! Who shall attack this miserable wretch—this bribed traitor? In distress and bitter tears, praying to the Highest, I have long waited for one who should go before me, and relieve me, not made for murder; who should free me from my grief, and allow me to proceed in the friendly path which I had chosen for myself. Notwithstanding all my prayers, no such person appeared; and, indeed, every one had as good a right as myself to wait for another. Delay makes our condition worse and more pitiable; and who shall relieve us of our shame, if Kotzebue shall, unpunished, leave the soil of Germany, and expend in Russia the treasures he has earned? Who shall help us, and save us from this unhappy condition, unless some person—and first of all, I, myself—shall feel called upon to administer justice, and to execute what shall be determined on for the fatherland? Therefore, courageously, forward! I will attack him with confidence, trusting in God (be not frightened), and strike down the disgracer and perverter of our people, the abominable traitor, that he may cease to turn us away from God and from history, and to deliver us over into the hands of our most cunning adversaries. To this an earnest sense of duty impels me. Since I have known how lofty an object there now is for our nation to strive after, and since I have known him, the false, cowardly knave, a strong necessity lies upon me—as upon every German who considers the good of all. May I, by this national vengeance, turn all impulses, and all public spirit toward the point where falsehood and violence threaten us, and in reason direct to the right quarter the fears of all and the vigor of our youth, in order to rescue from its near and great peril our common fatherland of Germany, the divided and dishonored union of its states—may I inspire fear among the vile and cowardly, and courage among the good! Writing and speaking are inefficient—only deeds can secure this union. May I at least throw a brand which shall kindle up the present indolence, and help to maintain and increase the flame of popular feeling, the honorable endeavor of humanity after the things of God!

"Therefore am I, although frightened out of all my beautiful dreams for my future life, still peaceful, and full of confidence in God—even happy—for I know that the way lies before me, through night and death, to pay all the debt which I owe to my fatherland.

"Farewell, therefore, true souls! This sudden separation is grievous, and your expectations and my own desires are disappointed. But may this matter be a preparation, and encourage us to require, first from ourselves, what the needs of the fatherland require:—which has, with me, become an inviolable principle.

"You will ask each other: But has he, by our sacrifices, become acquainted with all of life upon this earth, the pleasures of human society, and had he learned deeply to love this land and his chosen vocation? Yes, I have. It was under your protection, by your innumerable sacrifices, that country and life became so profoundly dear to me. You introduced me to learning; I have lived in free mental activity; have examined history, and then turned again to my own nature, to twine myself firmly around the strong pillar of faith forever, and by free researches into the understanding, to attain a clear knowledge of myself, and of the greatness of things around me. I have pursued, according to my ability, the usual course of learned studies; have been put in a position to examine the field of human learning, and have discoursed upon it with friends and men; and I have, to become better fitted for actual life, examined the manners and pursuits of men in various parts of Germany.

"As a preacher of the Gospel, I could, with pleasure, live such a life; and in the future destruction of our present society and learning, God would help me, if I were true to my office, to protect myself! But shall all this prevent me from averting the imminent danger to my fatherland? Should not your inexpressible love stimulate me to risk death for the common good, and for the desires common to us all? Have so many of the Greeks of our day already fallen for the sake of rescuing their nation from the rod of the Turk, and died almost in vain, and without hope for the future; and are hundreds of them, even now, consecrating themselves for the work by education, not permitting their courage to fail, but are ready to give their lives again at once for the good of their country; and shall I hesitate to die? Shall we, whose rescue and reformation are so near to the highest good, not venture any thing for it?

"But do I undervalue your love, or am I thoughtless of it? Believe it not! What could encourage me to death, if it were not the love to you and to my fatherland, which impels me to inform you of it?

"Mother, you will say, Why have I brought up a son to adult years, whom I have loved, and who has loved me, for whom I have endured a thousand cares and constant solicitude; who, through my prayers, became capable of usefulness, and from whom I was entitled, in the last days of my weary life, to receive filial love? Why does he forsake me now? Dear mother, might not the mother of any one else say the same if he had sacrificed himself for the fatherland; and if no one should make the sacrifice, where would the fatherland remain? But complaints are far from you, and you know no such speech, noble woman! I have before received your charge; and if no one will step forward on behalf of Germany, you would yourself send me to the contest. I have still two brothers and sisters, all honorable and noble ; these remain to you ;—I follow my duty ; and in my stead, all young men who think honorably for their fatherland, will be true children to you.

"My vocation was for this. If I should live fifty years longer I could not live a more active or real life than that of these later years. This is our vocation ; that we acknowledge the only true God, strive against evil, and praise the Father with our whole lives. In the world we have sorrow, but, like Christ, in God we can overcome it. Oh, that we could possess his peace in full measure! Left to that path alone, which I shall follow, I have no other resource but to him, my gracious Father ; but in him I shall find courage and strength to vanquish the last sorrow, and man-like to complete my important task.

"To his protection, his encouragement, I recommend you ; and may he keep you in a joy which no misfortunes can interrupt. Overcome your sorrow by the enduring joy which is in him ; and think not of my sad farewell, but of the love which is between us, and which can never end. And remain true to the fatherland, in whatever storms. Lead your little ones, to whom I would so gladly have become a loving friend, speedily out upon our mighty mountains, and let them there, upon a lofty altar in the midst of Germany, consecrate themselves to humanity, and vow never to rest nor to lay down the sword until we, brother races, united in freedom—until all the Germans, as one people, under one free constitution, in one realm, shall be indissolubly bound together, great before God, and powerful among the surrounding nations!

"May my fatherland remain joyfully looking up to thee, O God! May thy blessing come richly upon that bold band among the German people, who, acknowledging thy great grace, are courageously determined to promote the interests of pure humanity, thine image upon earth!

"'The latest cure, the highest, is the sword!
Within the true heart drive the lance,
A road for German freedom!'

"JENA, beginning of March, 1819.

"Your son, and brother, and friend, bound to you in everlasting love,

"CARL LUDWIG SAND."

Who can read this letter without the deepest emotion—without feeling a profound sympathy for the unhappy man who, with a sore heart, turned away from the path of peace, led astray by a delusion?

His last words, before his death, were, "I die in the grace of God." May God be gracious to him, and to all of us!

b.—CONSEQUENCES OF SAND'S ACT.—INVESTIGATIONS.—RESOLUTIONS OF THE UNION.—DISSOLUTION OF THE BURSCHENSCHAFT.

We have been long occupied with Sand and his act, but for this will not be blamed, considering the immeasurable consequences of it to the German universities. These consequences were most unhappy. The Wartburg festival had caused a great excitement, especially the burning of the books. This extravagant execution upon works which most of the actors in it did not know, was declared to be high treason by the enemies of the Burschenschaft. But, as we have seen, by the judicious action of the government of Weimar, this excitement was quieted, and an intelligent and just estimate made of the good and evil of the festival,—even the Austrian and Prussian governments were put at ease.

But no one had any idea that one of those concerned at the festival, as if driven by an evil demon, was to break up and destroy the peace and all the quiet and beneficial developments which sprang from it.

Scarcely had Sand's deed become known, when the adversaries of the Burschenschaft arose again everywhere, and boasted that they had formed the only just judgment of the Wartburg festival. This, they said, originated with a general revolutionary conspiracy of academical students; and others would soon follow it. This time the views of these opponents prevailed. Even those favorable to the students were of opinion, that although foolish and extravagant speeches, and even fantastic actions, could be pardoned to the students, because judgment and moderation will soon come to them with years, yet, after such an action, their doings assumed an appearance so seriously criminal that all measures must be resorted to for eradicating the evil. No man believed that Sand had been entirely isolated, and had so acted without accessories and fellow-conspirators.

The evil demon who had betrayed him to the murder, and had put into his heart his abominable maxim, might seem to be laughing in scorn at the consequences of his action. This brought to pass the precise opposite of all that Sand held for most desirable, and for the attainment of which he had thought even a murder not only permissible, but sanctified. For instance, the king of Prussia, upon hearing of it, rejected, upon the spot, a plan which had been laid before him for connecting Turning-departments with the schools.

The murder also caused endless investigations. Especially, it was naturally sought to be discovered whether any others, and particularly members of the Burschenschaft, had known of Sand's design. Hohnhorst, the president of the investigating commission, states, on this point, "that the investigation discovered no trace whatever of any particular conspiracy against Kotzebue's life." And again, he says: "Besides that, the investigation found no reliable trace of any conspiracy whatever against Von Kotzebue's life; it moreover failed to discover any certain indications that there were any accessories to the act, who took either an active or passive part in it, by encouragement or concealment."

The investigation was next directed against the association of "Unconditionals" or "Blacks," at whose head Karl Follenius was considered to be. His principles, and his influence upon Sand have been described; and it has been mentioned that he had followers in Giessen, but that in Jena only three students had submitted themselves "unconditionally" to his instructions, one of them being Sand. But that, even in Giessen, Follenius' influence had not extended to a great number, appears from a letter of a Giessen student to Sand, dated May 12, 1818, in which he says, "We young men are almost alone in the fatherland; scarcely ten older persons are *unconditional* followers of the truth."

Jarcke gives some details respecting this association of the Blacks, mostly from the judicial documents. Among others is "Outlines of a future Constitution for an Empire of Germany, by the brothers Follenius;" Jarcke's opinion upon which is as follows: "This piece of patchwork is not unworthy of attention, as being the last of those paper constitutions which the revolutionary system brought forth by the dozen. At its basis, as at that of Follenius' 'Sketch of a Constitution for a German Republic,' lies a complete disregard of every existing right; the delusive notion that it is possible to develop a living constitution from an abstract theory; and lastly, the political dogma of the sovereignty of the people."

But this constitution differs from others of the same kind in an important point, namely: in that Christianity is an element in it. Thus, it says, "Every German is an elector, and may be chosen to any office, provided he has been admitted to partake of the holy sacrament." And § 10 reads:

"Since the Christian faith is free from dogmas, which restrict the growth of the human intellect, and as a faith of freedom, truth, and love, is in agreement with the whole mind of man; it is therefore adopted as the religion of the empire. Its source—to which every citizen has free access—is the New Testament, and separate sects are to be consolidated in one Christian German church. Other faiths, which are uncongenial to the aims of humanity, such as the Jewish, which is only a *form* of faith, shall not be allowed in the empire.* All take part in public worship who feel the need of it. There is no compulsory belief whatever; and family devotions are not interfered with."

By § 11, the clergy are officers of the church, and are to be models and teachers of pure Christianity.

One German Republic was aimed at, and one German Christian church; and as the first was looked for from a consolidation of all the small German states, so there was to be a consolidation of all the confessions—or sects, as they called them—into one church. So Sand wrote: "We Germans—one empire and one church."† His political views, indeed, corresponded entirely with those of Follenius.

---

* This is like Rousseau, who put together the religions of the Jews, Turks, and Christians, and abstracted from them, jointly, a universal religion, adding, that if any one should teach contrary to this, he should be banished from the community, as an enemy to its fundamental laws. (See this work, vol. ii. pp. 215, 216.)

† Hohnhorst, vol. i. p. 190, in Sand's composition entitled "Death Blow."

For the further description of these "Blacks," Jarcke cites poems from the "Free Voices of Bold Youth," by the brothers Follenius.*

To make this description complete, however, we must allude to a second collection of hymns, published by Adolph Follenius, with the title "Ancient Christian Hymns and Songs of the Church, in German and Latin, with an Appendix. By A. L. Follenius."

These appeared in 1819, at the same time with the "Free Voices." Their preface was as follows:

"These hymns and songs mostly date back to that mighty time when faith removed mountains; that is, when by free power of will in faith, wonders were believed, and therefore could happen, such as the weakness of our times scoffs at; when the power of the purely divine in the human mind showed itself in operating upon and moving material matter.

"The author is convinced that these hymns and songs are among the noblest fruits which have ever been gathered in the fields of poetry by any age or nation;—believing that the oak is not more beautiful than the lily.

"It is sad that, notwithstanding the recommendations of Herder, Schlegel, and others, these Christian poems are almost unknown in the Protestant German Christian congregations, are not so much known as they deserve in the Catholic German ones, and have never passed from the Latin hymn-book into German life. We unfortunately have, except of a few hymns, not even an endurable German translation; while the genial Horace and the great Virgil, with whom, as heathens tending to cultivate the mind, young Christians cannot too early be made acquainted, are spread all over the learned portion of our beloved fatherland, and lie on every table, in innumerable German versions, hexameter and others. Our ancient popular songs and Christian hymns seem nearly related to our ancient cathedrals and council-houses, both in the spirit of their construction and in their fate. In spirit,—for these poems, like the cathedrals, while most richly and artistically finished, even to the smallest particular, never lose the loftiness of belonging to their consecration as a whole; and in fate,—because the subsequent French, Italian, or Greek architecture and poetry have covered in and hidden our Christian cathedrals and Christian poetry, to such a degree, that even a sight of them can only be had after diligent tracing and scouring."

A. Follenius selected the best Latin church hymns, and translated

* A second edition of this appeared in 1820.

them, mostly in his own spirit, and with an adaptation to his own purposes.*

In this collection, church hymns and worldly political songs stand in a contrast like that of the church and the temporal republic, in the prosaic and dry scheme of Follenius' Constitution for the Empire. There is often a mingling of both elements; the political one, however, running into a frightful revolutionary extreme.

The Latin church hymns translated by A. Follenius are purely ecclesiastical; and being mostly distinctly Catholic, they are directly opposed to the one national church of his Constitution.

As an example of his politico-religious hymns, I give one of Buri's poems, placed by A. Follenius in the appendix to his "Church Hymns." It bears the singular title of "Scharnhorst's Last Prayer;" and is as follows:

"Thou call'st, O God!
Thy flaming image stands on high uprear'd
Within proud hearts that thee have never fear'd.
O sea of grace!
Thou art our place
Of strength in need; and thou our mighty tower,
Whence the alarm shall sound in needful hour.

Through want and death,
Through joy and grief, stands ever open wide
The fane of freedom. As we long have sigh'd
To see fall down
Beneath thy frown
The hold of tyranny, so let it be,
That freedom's standard we unfurl'd shall see!

O Jesus Christ!
Thy words are plain:—Freedom alike to all.
And from God's love and oneness he doth fall
Who to this word
Of grace thus heard,
And thus confess'd, doth not in heart hold fast—
For this word doth not live, and die for it at last.

My heart, how low,
Before thy God in meekness art thou flung,
Since freedom's spark for thee to flame hath sprung!
Such strength is won
By love alone;
Such doctrine did the Saviour still dispense,
And such hath long been proved the best defense.

O light of God!
How lords and knaves, in hate and envy, still
Strive after thee; while I, my faith, my will,
Proudly and bold
By thy cross hold,
Where thou thy word all-powerful, sealest sure,
Which shapes thy people o'er, for freedom pure.

* Among these hymns are, "*Quem pastores laudavere,*" "*Stabat mater dolorosa,*" "*Dies iræ,*" &c.

My people, hear!
To thee I call, in joyful dying strife;
Thy Saviour comes! Awake anew to life!
The mockers fly!
The tyrants die!
Thy standard moves—the victor's cross before!
Onward! for open'd wide is Freedom's door!"

The same hymn is given in the "Free Voices," but remarkably altered. The title here is "Kosciusko's Prayer;" and Buri inserted, after the fifth stanza, another, which, to be sure, would not have been more inappropriately placed in the mouth of the dying Scharnhorst than the others.*

As in this poem, pride and humility,† love and hate, Christianity and revolution, the most discordant elements appear in conflict with each other; so, in like manner, especially in many of Karl Follenius' poems, the demon of revolution, entirely unchecked by Christianity, appears in his most frightful shape. An unbridled and unbounded hate of kings inspires and preaches rebellion and murder.‡ It is not to be wondered at, that after Sand's crime, such poems should no longer be endured with patience, and that the demoniac violence which inspired them, and stimulated to similar actions, should be feared.

Jarcke gives many results of the investigations which followed Sand's deed, particularly oral and written expressions by students of Giessen, Heidelberg, Freiburg, and Jena. They agree, in general, with Sand's views. On the question, whether the end justifies the means, they were not agreed; at Giessen, a majority were in the affirmative.§ It also appeared that the murder of Kotzebue was approved, and even praised, by many.

This is not the place to go further into the details of these investigations, to mention the punishments which were inflicted on some of the young men, &c. But the following four resolutions are of very great importance to the universities, which were passed by the German Union (*Bundestag*), September 20, 1819, and published in Prussia, on the 18th October, the sixth anniversary of the battle of Leipzig. They are as follows:‖

"§ 1. There shall be appointed, at each university, an extraordinary royal overseer, with proper instructions, and wide authority; to be a resident at the university city, and to be either the present curator,

* There was, also, a characteristic alteration in the third stanza. Instead of the words above translated, "Freedom alike for all," were inserted, "*Freiheit, Gleichheit Allen*"—"Freedom and equality for all." Evidently the well-known *shibboleth* of the Revolution.

† Compare the first three lines of the first stanza with the same of the last.

‡ See the poem already mentioned as distributed by Sand, "Human crowd, O thou great human desert;" and the so-called "Hymn of Union of the United Netherlanders," in the "*Free Voices.*" Jarcke cites others.

§ Jarcke, 138.

‖ See Koch, i. 15.

or some other person recognized as fit for the place by the government. The office of this overseer shall be, to provide for the fullest compliance with existing laws and disciplinary regulations; carefully to observe the spirit in which the academical teachers deliver their public and private instructions, and to exercise over them a healthful control, without immediately interfering in their scientific duties, or methods of instruction, and with reference to the future destinies of the students; and, in general, to devote his uninterrupted attention to every thing which can promote good order and external propriety among the students. The relations of this extraordinary overseer to the academical senate, and all matters connected with the details of his field of labor, and his occupations, are to be set forth, as fully as possible, in the instructions which he is to receive from his government, having reference to the circumstances which have occasioned the appointment of such overseer.

"§ 2. The governments of the German Union pledge themselves to each other, that if any teacher in a university, or other public teacher, shall be guilty of proved dereliction of duty, or transgression of the limits of his duty, by misusing his proper influence on the young, or promulgating instructions of an injurious nature, as at enmity with public order and quiet, or subversive of the principles of existing governments; and shall thus give unmistakable evidence of unfitness for the important office confided to him, they will exclude him from the universities and other public institutions for education; no impediments being by this intended to be opposed to the progress of such institutions, as long as this resolution shall remain in force, and until definite regulations shall have been made on the subject. But no such measure shall be resolved upon, except after a proposition by the government overseer of the university, thoroughly explained by him, or upon a report sent in previously by him. An instructor dismissed in this manner cannot receive an appointment in any public educational institution whatever, of any of the States of the Union.

"§ 3. The laws which have long existed against secret or unauthorized associations in the universities shall be enforced in their whole extent and significance, especially against that society established within a few years, under the name of the General Burschenschaft, and the more strictly against this society, inasmuch as it is based upon an altogether inadmissible permanent connection and correspondence between different universities. It shall be the duty of the government overseers to exercise especial watchfulness on this point. The governments agree with each other, that individuals who, after the publication of this resolution, shall be proved to have remained in, or entered a secret or unauthorized association, shall be appointed to no public office.

"§ 4. No student who shall have been dismissed from a university by decree of a government overseer, or of a university senate, upon his motion, or who shall leave the university to avoid the result of such a decree, shall be admitted into any other; and, in general, no student shall be received from one university into another, without a satisfactory testimonial of his good standing at the former.

"Done and given at Berlin, October 18, 1819."

The third of these sections required, unconditionally, the dissolution of the General Burschenschaft.

Thus far, we have discussed only the investigations in the matter of Sand, and respecting the association of the "Blacks," or "Unconditionals," of which Sand was a member, and whose views he not only believed in, but had proposed to carry out into practice, and enlighten all by his example.

But it was not thought sufficient to punish him only who was found guilty. Evil-disposed men stirred up an incessant excitement about the vile murder of Sand, and disturbed peaceful people. By means of the phantom of an extensive revolutionary conspiracy, they were enabled to cause upright princes to execute the most unjust measures, and to disgrace the most honorable men. How unrighteous, for instance, were the measures pursued against Arndt, the truest of patriots, who has done such infinite service to Germany!*

The inquiry was now made, whether the Burschenschaft, though neither an accomplice in, nor cognizant of Sand's deed, was, nevertheless, based upon the same religious, moral, and political dreams and principles from which that action had followed. By no means.

The result of the criminal investigations showed that no member of the Burschenschaft knew of Sand's crime, nor was, in any way whatever, accessory to it.

To what we have already given, may be added the following remark of the investigating judge, who says:† "While the academical senate at Jena asseverated that the Burschenschaft there had not the least connection with Sand's act, the Mannheim investigations left no reason for doubting this, and there was no reason for claiming that Sand's relations to the Jena German Burschenschaft had even the most indirect influence upon his crime."

But what were the relations of the Burschenschaft and the society of the "Unconditionals?"

* See Arndt's "*Forced Account of my Life.*" 1847.

† Hohnhorst, ii. 49.

By § 8 of the Jena statutes, "The Burschenschaft can exist only in a free and *public* social life suitable to students;" while that society was obliged to conceal its views and purposes, and thus assumed a character entirely opposed to that of the Burschenschaft. "The Burschenschaft rejected the character of a secret association," wrote one who knew it thoroughly.* We have seen that Karl Follenius, the leader of the "Unconditionals," had only three followers in Jena, and that among the numerous other members of the Burschenschaft he met with no success. "The Jena Burschenschaft," says another author,† "received not the least influence from all the efforts which the friends of Karl Follenius made in various ways."

Jarcke's statements, and the letters and statements of the "Unconditionals" which he gives, agree exactly on this point.

A., a student from Heidelberg, declared‡ that "The Burschenschaft had merely established a general union for the cause of Germany; but nothing more than this could be expected from an association which was at least twenty times larger than the society (of Unconditionals), for nothing judicious could come from it. For this reason, those of the Burschenschaft who trusted in each other to pursue, with earnestness and perseverance, the often contemplated plan (of a republican form of government), united themselves into a smaller association: that is, into the society."

L., a member of this smaller society at Jena, wrote, July 24, 1818, to A——, "The students in general disgust me; it is a miserable, pitiful brood; God preserve the world and the fatherland from any salvation which is to come through them! I do nothing for the Burschenschaft with pleasure and pride, but only out of duty. I have long given up the idea that our salvation is to come from the universities. There are at least nineteen rascals to one good fellow. That sounds hard, but it is true. God preserve us from such salvation as can come through such fellows!"

G., also a member of the same smaller society at Jena, wrote at or about the some time to A——, "It is out of the question to accomplish what we aim at merely through the Burschenschaft. I see, daily, that through their means alone we shall never arrive at the point at which we aim."

That this society would gladly have perverted the whole Burschenschaft to a concurrence in its own principles and foolish plans is clear; but how little was accomplished in this direction at Jena we have seen. This appears from the above letter of L., who was a member of

---

* "*German Youth*," &c., p. 82. † Ib., p. 83. ‡ Jarcke, p. 196.

the society at Jena, and who was profoundly in enmity with the Burschenschaft, which opposed the tendencies of the "Unconditionals." G. speaks to the same effect, but more mildly.

The Burschenschaft, therefore, came unscathed from all the investigations of 1819. But in the apprehension that they might afterward fall into error, it was not thought sufficient to punish the guilty, but the whole society was abolished. We shall see that this dissolution was the direct cause of the subsequent real faults of the Burschenschaft.

Upon the publication of the decree of dissolution to the Jena Burschenschaft, they wrote to their protector at that time, the Grand Duke of Weimar, as follows:

"Most Serene Grand Duke!

"Most Gracious Lord and Prince!—The confidence which we have learned to feel in your Royal Highness causes us to believe that we need apprehend no difficulty in expressing, once more, our feelings toward your Royal Highness, now that we are separated and torn away from the beautiful hopes which had grown up in our young hearts, in the unity and harmony of an allowed and virtuous social life.

"It was the will of your Royal Highness that the Burschenschaft should be dissolved. That will has been carried into effect. We hereby declare, solemnly and publicly, that we have paid strict obedience to the command, and have ourselves dissolved our association, as was ordered; we have torn down what we had built up after our best knowledge, upon mature experiment, with upright and blameless good faith, and with the genuine belief that we were doing a good thing. The consequences have answered our expectation, and there grew up a virtuous and free mode of life. Trustful publicity took the place of creeping secrecy; and we could, without shame, and with a good conscience, display to the eyes of the world what we had meditated in our inmost hearts, and had carried out into actual existence. The spirit of love and of uprightness led us, and the voices of the better part of the public have sanctioned our efforts down to a very late period.

"The spirit which has united us has sunk deep into the bosoms of each one of us. Each of us understands what should be the relations of one German youth to another. The right of standing by one another, in its ancient form, was discontinued. Good morals were the first and last motives of our united action. Our life was intended to be a preparatory school for future citizens. This fact has not escaped your Royal Highness; and the two searches of our papers have not, according to our best knowledge, led to any different conclusion.

"This school is now closed. Each of its members will depart with what he has learned. This he will retain, and in him it will live. What they all have recognized as true, will continue true to each. The spirit of the Burschenschaft, the spirit of virtuous freedom and equality in our student life, the spirit of justice, and of love to our common country, the highest of which man can be conscious—this spirit will dwell in each of us, and will lead him forward for good, according to his capabilities.

"These things, however, grieve us deeply: first, our influence upon those who shall come after us; and second, that our efforts have been misunderstood, and misunderstood publicly. In truth, we could not have been wounded more deeply. Only the good conscience within our bosoms can teach us that no one can destroy our own honor, and can show us the means of consolation for this injustice.

"As it regards this decree, we leave it to time to justify us, and willingly admit the belief that at least there has been a time when our efforts were not misunderstood, even by our noble prince and lord. Nothing shall change our love to him; and perhaps some better day shall, in future, permit us gratefully to prove it to him.

"With warm wishes for our fatherland, and for the prosperity of your Royal Highness, we subscribe ourselves, in unchangeable love, your Royal Highness' most faithful servants,

"THE MEMBERS OF THE LATE BURSCHENSCHAFT."

A hundred and sixty signed the document.

Binzer, one of them, composed the following song, afterward extensively sung:

"A house we had builded,
So stately and fair;
There trusting to be shielded,
In God, from storm and care.

"We lived there so gayly,
So friendly, so free;
It grieved the wicked daily,
Our true accord to see.

"That fair house may perish,
When greatest our need—
Its spirit still we cherish—
But God's our strength indeed."

Both letter and song testify to a good conscience.

After the dissolution of the Burschenschaft, the strictest measures were taken to prevent its re-establishment. These remind us of those employed in the seventeenth century to uproot the abominable system of Pennalism. Yet no two things could be more completely opposed than were Pennalism and the Burschenschaft. The latter had an especial contest with the associations corresponding to the earlier "Nations," in which Pennalism had its home.

We have given Klüpfel's description of the Landsmannschaften, and have seen how, at the time of the War of Freedom, there had been a profound moral change and reformation in a large part of the academical youth. The same students who then followed the standards as volunteers, and fought in those ever-memorable battles, now fought a second time, as volunteers against the profound demoralization of the universities. We call them volunteers, for they did not act at the command of the authorities, nor did their movements proceed from a new code of laws; but from the young men's hearts, which God had drawn toward himself, and renewed. The advantages which followed were such as neither commands nor prohibitions had availed to secure. I will mention but a few.

"Almost all the Burschenschafts very early banished the hazard-table from their precincts."*

"Above all, the duel was disapproved for various reasons, and often altogether rejected; and this without any injury to those who adhered to this opinion. By means of the courts of honor, the disuse of the duel was carried to a point beyond all expectation. In the summer of 1815, there were once, at Jena, thirty-five duels in one day, and a hundred and forty-seven in one week, among about three hundred and fifty students. In the summer of 1819, the court of honor decided for the fighting out of eleven duels among seven hundred and fifty students; and about forty were brought before it. No duel was allowed until after reference to the court of honor. No witness, second, or surgeon, was to attend a duel without such reference; and it may be confidently asserted that no duel took place without the previous reference to the court of honor, as long as that court could inflict the penalty of exclusion from the association. The proportion of duels to those of previous periods was similar in other Burschenschafts."†

Within my own knowledge, a society had been formed in Berlin, which wholly excluded the duel, and was upheld in so doing by the Burschenschaft.

"Among the virtues of their ancestors, that of chastity was set very high. It was no longer considered witty to make sport of innocence or ignorance of play; and it was thought a shame to resort to licensed houses of ill-fame."‡

"Conscious of such an endeavor after an inward moral reform, the

---

* "*German Youth*," &c., p. 34. I was assured that this was the fact as to the members of the Burschenschaft at Halle. † Ib., pp. 29, 30.

‡ Ib., p. 35. The same was true at Halle, by the testimony of students there.

Burschenschaft could neither seek secrecy, nor be indifferent to a recognition of the authorities. Thus, they acquired an open, straightforward, and downright character. They endeavored, everywhere, to secure the approbation of the authorities, both by their conduct as a society, and by attempts to secure direct recognition. They had no idea that they could be considered dangerous to the state; and when this character was given to them, there crept in, with the secrecy which then obtained in their organization, an unreasonable fancy respecting it, which led them, like boys, not to fear a contest with the authorities, and even with the law itself. They could scarcely have foreseen, that with this secrecy, and this delusive opinion, the first condition of their good character—moral uprightness—would be destroyed."*

While the earlier innocent years of the Burschenschaft are truly delineated, the origin and the development of their downfall is also correctly pointed out. This will appear from the following account.

F.—Halle. (1819–1823.)

I was transferred from Breslau to Halle in the year 1819. I had passed through many severe struggles; and still severer ones lay before me.†

As to my own office as an instructor, I was, for the second time, put in charge of an academical collection of minerals, which was not nearly adequate to the purposes of thorough instruction; and I sought in vain for assistance, in this respect, during four years. I was obliged to content myself with the use of a tolerable private collection, which its proprietor very kindly allowed me to use for my lectures. I occupied myself, also, with practical instructions in geognosy, making geognostic excursions during two afternoons of the week, in which the Prussian mining students, more especially, joined. I lectured here on pedagogy, for the first time, in 1822.

I occupied, with my family, the house and garden formerly Reichardt's, at Giebichenstein, half a mile from Halle, and where I had enjoyed such happy days when a student there. A young theological student, whom I had known at Breslau, was the first who came to live with me, but others soon followed him.

The Burschenschaft was dissolved at Halle, as well as at the other universities. A singular condition of affairs was the result. The same students who had lived together as the Burschenschaft, remained at Halle. They were no longer to associate together. Let their conduct

---

* "*German Youth*," &c., p. 36. † See "*History of Pedagogy*," part 3, § 2, pp. 236–239.

be as honorable and open as possible, this did not avail to prevent them from becoming suspected by the authorities, and from being most incessantly watched over by them. They had, up to the publication of the decree of September—up to October 18, 1819—been not only associated together as members of the Burschenschaft, but had been, personally, the most intimate friends; and it was, therefore, a strange requirement that they should, from that day, become indifferent to each other, and that all social intercourse among them should be interdicted.

The Prussian government, agreeably to the decree of September, appointed a government overseer to each of its universities. The office of these was, not only to watch over the students, but, as section 1 of the decree requires, over the instructors also. All dignity and influence was thus taken from the academical senate; and instead of a paternal academical discipline, was introduced a completely police-like practice, which was harsher for the reason that only evil was presumed from those previously members of the Burschenschaft. And, on the other hand, even the most immoral students were countenanced and protected, because they were considered adversaries to the Burschenschaft; persons to whom the ideals of that body were only a jest.

A similar distinction was made among the professors, accordingly as they were considered partisans or opponents of the reaction which was introduced.

At Berlin, Privy High Government Councilor Schultz was appointed over the university; a harsh, self-conceited, and intensely reactionary man. "Irritated at the senate and the professors, of whom he regarded Schleiermacher and Savigny as the chief friends of the Burschenschaft, he required the senate, in January, 1820, to justify themselves in relation to their connection with the Burschenschaft."* On the 21st March, 1820, Schleiermacher wrote to Arndt, "While Schultz persecuted the Burschenschaft, he extravagantly favored the Landsmannschaften, who are eminently the destruction of the university." On the 18th of August, 1822, Schultz declared that "He was now convinced that he could no longer reckon upon truth and good faith in his dealings with the ministry; and that it is to those officials themselves that the faults of the members of the secret societies are to be imputed."†

But this dignitary had already seen how fruitless were all his stringent regulations. In a letter of October 29, 1821, he wrote, "It is astonishing to what an extent those disorders in the university, for whose removal I have now labored for two years with the greatest

* "*Correspondence between Goethe and State Councilor Schultz,*" p. 76. † Ib. p. 76.

zeal, increase from day to day; and the circumstances attending my labors are such, that I see, with sorrow, the moment approaching when I must resign my post with reproach and shame, even if vexation and useless labor do not sooner entirely destroy my health and put me out of the world."*

The example of Schultz shows how much difficulty and harm may be caused by misuse of his functions, on the part of a harsh, reckless, short-sighted, and proud overseer. Vice-president of Mines Von Witzleben, appointed over the university of Halle, was diametrically the opposite of Schultz. He was mild, always benevolent, and a supporter of every thing good.† But the nature of the office which had been conferred upon him was any thing rather than mild. He was obliged to obey the orders of others. What he saw at Halle, and the results of his investigations there, was not permitted to determine his views or his actions. It was said that the proceedings at the separate universities could only be correctly judged of at the central point of the investigations; only at Mainz, the seat of the investigating commission appointed by the Union, which could overlook the whole conspiracy.

We have seen that the Burschenschaft was made to suffer for the transgressions which Sand had committed, both in word and deed, but the association of the Unconditionals in revolutionary prose and poetry.

No pains whatever were taken to distinguish between the innocent and the guilty, but the whole Burschenschaft was declared guilty, and its dissolution was as sternly followed up as if it had been judicially convicted of the accusations against it. It is, therefore, not to be wondered at, that a man otherwise so upright and mild as Witzleben, came to see wicked secrets and intrigues everywhere, and at last, even to think the very honestest of the students the most cunning, and utterly unworthy of any confidence.

I myself enjoyed the fullest confidence of those students at Halle who had belonged to the Burschenschaft. They complained to me that, notwithstanding their punctual obedience to the laws, they were treated

---

* Schultz was upon the very point of breaking up the Altenstein ministry, and of being placed at the head of the departments of Church and Instruction; the necessary cabinet order having been made out, but never having been published. He was, at last, removed from his overseership by a cabinet order, dated July 6, 1824.

† He had shown himself such during many years' most benevolent and active service as administrator of the school at Rosleben. The able Rector Wilhelm remained at the head of this school for fifty years, notwithstanding many honorable invitations elsewhere. He said that "he could not find a Witzleben for his official superior anywhere else." ("*Golden Jubilee of Rector Wilhelm*," Weimar, 1836; pp. 16, 17.)

as if guilty. To remove all misunderstanding and distrust, they twice handed in to the authorities fair and truly written reports of their doings. They did this voluntarily; and had no difficulty in being public in doing so, because they were conscious of no fault.

Among those who often visited me was an excellent young physician, X., whose strong character rendered him highly esteemed by his acquaintances. He induced them, on the 12th of January, 1821, to celebrate the anniversary of the foundation of their Burschenschaft. This celebration was wholly unpremeditated. But the authorities saw in it, not a memorial of a suppressed association, but that very association continuing to exist. During the investigation which followed, I drew up the following testimonial for X.:

"*Testimonial for X., student of medicine, on occasion of his receiving the admonition to depart* (consilium abeundi), *from the academical senate, on account of the festival of January* 12, 1821 (*the festival of the foundation of the Burschenschaft in this place*).

"I have been acquainted with the student X. for more than a year. He has visited me once almost every week since, and even oftener; and has spoken with me frequently, and fully, respecting his own circumstances as a student, and those of the whole body of students; not as to a superior, but as to an old friend. He had no reason to deceive me in any thing, and I am firmly convinced that he would have been precisely as truthful if questioned before the most rigorous judge.

"I have, in particular, spoken often with him respecting the Burschenschaft, of which he was a member during its existence. I know distinctly, from him, that he adheres strictly to the word of honor which he gave, not to re-establish the Burschenschaft, nor to aid in so doing. He, and many of like views, it is true, lament that unhappy political occurrences should have caused the suppression of that body. But these do not indulge the dream that they are fitted to exert any influence upon civil society. How little X., in particular, concerned himself with politics, is indicated by a remark which he made in my presence, that he was too busy with his medical studies to have time to read the newspapers.

"But if these young men, while fully admitting the bad tendencies of a portion of the Burschenschaft, desired to hold fast to the true benefits which had resulted from it in the universities, can they be blamed for this? But when ardent love of truth, chastity, temperance, patriotism, and so many holy Christian virtues have sprung up, of late, in the universities; when young men associate together in order to confirm themselves in these virtues, and when they do every thing to reform those who are in evil ways, in that case those universities in which such a spirit prevails, should think themselves fortunate. And this doubly, when they compare this spirit with that formerly prevailing, of dissoluteness, and of emulation in many vices. Nor is this latter spirit, unfortunately, yet extinguished; those of better intentions are daily annoyed by their attacks.

"I know how much X. has done to uphold this good feeling, and how strenuously he resisted those evils. The best swordsman in Halle, he has not fought one duel, but has adjusted innumerable misunderstandings. As an example of strict morality, he was superior to the rest. In originating the celebration of the 12th of January, as a memorial of so much that was praiseworthy in the designs of the Burschenschaft, his purposes were pure; and it is only to be lamented that a false construction was put upon youthful, though even blamable carelessness.

"My official oath, as professor, bound me 'to use all my exertions to increase the glory of God, and the safety of the church, and of the republic; to lead the students away from vice, and to influence them to integrity of life and purity of manners.' This oath, and my own impulses oblige me, on this occasion, to speak distinctly. While it is, on one hand, the conscientious and official duty of a teacher to warn and protect young men from the vicious errors which were made the cause for suppressing the Burschenschaft, it is equally his sacred duty to protect the new and pure influence—the spirit of Christian virtue—which grew up with the Burschenschaft. I know of no greater fault with which an instructor of youth could charge himself, than that of opposing such an influence.

"I call my oath to witness, that I have written the foregoing according to my best inward conviction."

In the academical senate, I added to this testimonial the following remarks: "I shall add, after this paper, only a few words. Since writing it, I have had additional reason for believing myself right in the views therein expressed respecting the condition of the students. The jurisprudence of the university seems to me to differ from that of the usual courts, especially in this: that in its decisions it may not only consider each case by itself, and compare it with the body of the laws, but more especially in that it may decide according to a personal knowledge of the accused, and rather on moral than on judicial grounds. Thus, for the same act, a good-for-nothing fellow may be treated severely, and one otherwise of good reputation, moderately. The present case is one where the accused, according to the law, by the opinion of the overseer of the university, should be acquitted. Since they are, moreover, known to be, especially the medical student X., unblamable, virtuous, and industrious men, there is double reason, considering the case as one of discipline, to acquit them."

About this time my intercourse with the students seemed worthy of attention in high quarters. I received a letter from the Chancellor of State, Prince Hardenberg, in which he spoke, though mildly, yet with displeasure, of my relations to three certain young men. I answered:

"The more I recognize the kindness expressed toward me in your grace's letter, the more I feel it my duty to justify against misunderstanding, to your grace as my immediate superior, my civic and official life. I was a member of a Turning association, when it was not only permitted, but favored and recommended by the Prussian government in many ways. It was my belief that in this I not only was not violating my official duty, but was doing it better than was required.

"When, some two years ago, I expressed my profound conviction of the great value of the Turning system for youth, in a printed publication, I declared myself, at the same time, distinctly opposed to any political tendencies in it. This I did of my own free will, under no influence from without; and I spoke accordingly to young persons, against any premature grasping after the station of a citizen.

"Various of the Turners in Breslau were also my scholars in mineralogy; among them M. and W.

"When these two were subjected to an investigation, I thought it my duty to warn and admonish them, to the best of my ability, where they were in fault; but not to give them up; to protect, more carefully than ever, the good element which I recognized in them. I considered myself their teacher, in whom they placed confidence, not their judge; as bound to improve and instruct them, not to condemn them; and I was the less ready to condemn them, because I had, myself, experienced how difficult it is, in a season of excitement, always to act prudently and moderately.

"A year ago I became acquainted with L., in Berlin. I found out afterward, to my sorrow, that he had certain faults. At the last Whitsuntide vacation he made a short trip from Jena, and came to Halle. I conversed with him, and satisfied myself that nothing was more important for him than at once to get into some honorable occupation, and never to leave it. He showed a particular inclination and aptness for land-surveying and engineering. As there are excellent opportunities at Dresden to study these, I made application to a friend there, to learn from Herr Fischer, professor at the Military Academy, what steps a young man should take in order to be admitted to instruction in land-surveying, what expenses would be, &c.

"Your grace will see, from this correct account, how far I have been connected with L. It has never occurred to me to desire to bring him under my influence, as a teacher, in any way. This would have been a most improper design, for L. was by no means a suitable person for it, and I am convinced that your grace will certainly never blame me for having endeavored to set L. in a way to cultivate his talents to his own pleasure and quiet, and to the benefit of his fatherland.

"It is a cause for mourning before God, that a large part of our youth are, at present, in an unprecedented misunderstanding with the generation preceding them. I consider it, accordingly, the sacred duty of the teacher, whom his official duties bring into close contact with them, to treat them in every respect paternally, and to use all means of restoring a good understanding, and of preparing the way for a pleasanter future. This they can especially do by having regard to the peculiar talent of each young man, and by assisting, with counsel and action, in cultivating it, and thus helping to educate men who will be both skilled and satisfied in their destined sphere of life.

"I have endeavored, according to my powers, to contribute my mite toward this object.

"Thus your grace will not misunderstand my intercourse and correspondence with young men accused; since it is the endeavor to fulfill my duty as an instructor of youth, that has been the occasion of them.

"I am, of myself, most decidedly opposed to political revolutions, and an adherent to what promises real and enduring peace, and all the benefits of prosperous times. I feel myself happy in my sphere of life; why should I not abhor all violence and destruction, and desire calm and peaceful progress?

"I would gladly acquaint your grace with the experiences which have been occasioned me by means of the full confidence which has been reposed in me by those young men who have been accused. I would gladly, as their advocate, produce the conviction that, notwithstanding the undeniable improprieties and unjustifiable views which they have, youth-like, thoughtlessly written, still they are so disposed that they would gladly offer up their lives for king and fatherland, should a second year 1813 require that highest evidence of their truth.

"I most humbly request your grace to receive this letter with favor, and remain, &c., VON RAUMER."

The unhappy impression now gained ground among the students, that, notwithstanding all their propriety of conduct, no confidence whatever was placed in them. It was easy to foresee the unhappy consequences which must, of necessity, sooner or later, arise from this opinion. Want of confidence, on the part of the government overseer and the senate, produced the like on the part of the students. There would be an end of all good influence by the former on the latter, if the breach between them should widen. Every thing was to be feared, should the students be driven from their previous openness and truthfulness to secresy and lies. I was in great trouble on this account. Under these circumstances, there came into my hands the Tübingen "Statutes for forming a Students' Committee,"* which were sanctioned by a royal ordinance of January 2, 1821, and whose contents are given by Klüpfel. I conceived the hope, that by means of a similar committee, the open and proper conduct of the students at Halle might be maintained, and unhappy secret doings avoided.

To this end I drew up the following paper, to be read at the session of the senate, on January 5, 1822:†

"It is to be considered what are the best means of healing the evil of associations among the students, which are more strictly prohibited than ever by government.

"It cannot naturally be required that each student shall live entirely isolated in his room, like a monk in his cell. He will associate with congenial friends; and one will have many, and another few. Indeed it would be a sad mark of entire lack of friendly feelings, if none should inquire about another, and therefore it cannot be the design of the government to put an end to social friendship. This was intended only of all formal (or prohibited) associations, which are very different from informal social intercourse. From such prohibited associations, many of the students here are entirely disjoined, though they have, against their wills and contrary to truth, often been included in the appellation of Burschenschaft. They have no constitution, no officers; nothing is said among them of commanding or obeying. They have so little of secresy, that they have, entirely of their own free will, twice drawn up a complete account of their modes of life and doings, and handed it in to the curator. That mode of life—as, indeed, was to have been expected from his character—received his friendly approbation, as regards its morals. It was the just confidence in their good intentions, which they saw to be felt by a high official, which occasioned this course. But if this confidence of theirs has not

* P. 318, &c. See Appendix VIII. A ministerial decree, of Nov. 30, 1820, had already stated that the king was not opposed to such a committee.

† Some less important portions are omitted, but what is left is given *verbatim*.

caused a corresponding one, and if there yet prevails an apprehension that present circumstances may secretly bring about an entirely different formal association, I know of only one means of relieving this apprehension—which I have already referred to.

"We all know that the most watchful police cannot entirely discover the schemes and views of the students, if they resort to falsehood and deceit. Something may occasionally come to light, and one or another individual may be punished; but to what end? Punishment may be inflicted to-day, but the hydra head grows again to-morrow.

"May God preserve those students, who presented the writing I have cited, from giving up their confidence and love of truth, and from addicting themselves to secresy and falsehood! And, above all, may God prevent the honorable senate from becoming the cause of such a revolution! What excuse could be made for such a result?

"But to prevent this result, I can, as I have said, see only one means. Instead of ourselves destroying the confidence in us of the young men, by police regulations—by the establishment of a completely police-like relation between ourselves and them—instead of depending upon shrewdness as police-officers, which cannot accomplish our objects, we ought, according to my opinion and experience, to repay their confidence with a full return of it. A full return, I say, for half confidence is no confidence. We should soon see with what sincerity of heart, how freely and openly, the students would respond to such treatment. Above all, it would then be in our power to counteract all erroneous tendencies in them, because we should know them thoroughly; and all the phantoms which terrify us in the dark, would disappear in the bright daylight of such a condition of things.

"Such a clear and open relation between ourselves and the students can, in my judgment, not be more beneficently and honorably brought about than has been done by his majesty, the King of Würtemberg, by an ordinance to the university of Tübingen, of the 2d January of last year. This enacted that the students should choose, from among themselves, fifteen persons, whose duty it should be to communicate the wishes of the senate to the rest of the students, and to assist in accomplishing the same. This committee is also empowered to bring before the senate the wishes of the body of students. Each member of this committee is bound, by section 27 of the ordinance, to warn his fellow-students against every secret association, or one shunning publicity, and so far as in him lies, to exert his influence to deter them from joining any such. I refrain from giving here any details of this excellent ordinance, inasmuch as I venture to submit a copy of it to be examined by my colleagues; and only observe that I have good information that the university of Tübingen already experiences good results from this ordinance. Von Raumer.

"Giebichenstein, Jan. 6, 1822."

Unless I am mistaken, there is but one man now living who was present at the sitting where this proposition was read, namely, my friend Prof. Schweigger. He will remember in how incredibly tumultuous a manner my reading was interrupted. He repeatedly begged that I might at least be allowed to read to the end. I can not, after thirty years, trace this opposition to individuals. But I remember vividly how some protested most strenuously against this Students' Committee, as if it would be a profound injury to their official dignity, and to their relations with the students; and how others exclaimed that they were not in the habit of learning from the Würtembergers how the students were to be managed, and so on. As this opposition was so violent that I was actually unable to read to the end, I sent the paper next day to Royal Commissioner von Witzleben, writing to him at the same time as follows:

"I take the liberty to send your excellency my proposition of yesterday in the senate. Its design was to acquaint that body with the Würtemberg ordinance, with which your excellency is familiar. wrote it down, because, in case of certain occurrences, I will adhere to it, word for word, and neither more nor less. My official duty forbids me to conceal my honest convictions. Accordingly, I was yesterday desirous of expressing my conviction that nothing of the nature of police regulations would succeed in the case then in hand, but that paternal and confiding measures, like that of Würtemberg, would be of incalculable service. Many of my colleagues agree with my views respecting police measures.

"I am sufficiently acquainted with your excellency's views to know that your own feelings prefer a paternal, rather than a police-like mode of administration; I hope that you may not be prevented from acting in accordance with those feelings. Von Raumer."

I now saw the evil daily coming nearer, and was convinced that no help was to be looked for from the senate. Every day the ill feeling of the students increased, and was especially stimulated by some young men of talent, who, about that time, came from Jena to Halle. These individuals used every influence to induce the dissatisfied to join a secret Burschenschaft which they had founded at Jena. One, named C.

was particularly active, advocating the establishment of such a Burschenschaft with the utmost eloquence and sophistry. He unfortunately found the ground so well prepared during two years, that the seed sown by him and his fellows quickly sprang up and grew. C. afterward confessed before a court, that "his exertions, during his stay at Halle, were intended to establish there, also, the secret Burschenschaft, and to propagate among its members the political views of the organization at Jena." * He avowed that he, with three others, had "earnestly endeavored to re-establish, among the partisans of the Burschenschaft in Halle, that organization, dissolved by the authorities." He declared, in so many words, that "the step from this Burschenschaft to our smaller political association was not difficult, as the members of the former, by having broken their word of honor, given to the authorities, were thus placed in opposition to them, and also to the existing government."

I became acquainted with C. Without (as will easily be conceived) introducing me to his demagogical plans and endeavors, he made no secret of his theory. This was, in truth, exceedingly radical, although he was under the delusion that it was based upon the most correct moral principles. The Burschenschaft, for instance, he said, aimed at the purest morality in life; the governments which had broken it up had, therefore, put themselves in direct opposition to the purest morality; and, therefore, there remained no other course for young men than to obey God rather than man, and to take an active part for morality.

He also cited political reasons; and especially the fact, that the well-known thirteenth article agreed on by the Congress of Vienna had not been carried into operation by Prussia and other governments.

C., whom I loved much, and who has long ago escaped from the errors of his youth, and who is a very useful man, will remember well how I discussed all these matters with him. An enemy to sophistry and dialectic fencing, I adhered to the Christian code of morals, which had always, from my youth, been to me holy and perfect; rejected all Jesuitism, and enforced strongly this principle: that the holy God would never require us to assist in supporting and extending his kingdom by unholy and wicked means. The unhappy consequences of Sand's action were also placed in a strong light before his eyes.

A strife now arose between those who, led away by this newly discovered code of morals, which appeared to them of supreme authority,

---

* "*Information against the Members of the so-called Youth's Union*" (*Jugendbund*). Halle. 1826. P. 49.

advocated joining the secret Burschenschaft and the "Young Men's Union," and those who, restrained by the word of honor which they had given, opposed such adhesion. The latter were overcome. The "Young Men's Union" was the chief temptation to them, and with its foundation a new period may be commenced; the previous one having been distinguished by the association of the "Unconditionals." But Karl Follenius had now also a hand in the game.

The detailed history of the "Young Men's Union" is given in the "*Information*," already quoted, by the Royal High Court of Breslau.* I shall refer the reader to this; and shall here only give the following sketch:

A student of Jena became acquainted, in 1821, in Switzerland, with Karl Follenius and two other men, who confided to him the statement that "there was to be formed an association, among men already living in civic stations, for the purpose of overthrowing the existing governments; and that it was desirable that a similar association should be formed among young men." They proceeded to request the student to found such an association. He entered into the plan, and labored at Zürich, Basle, Freiburg, Tübingen, Erlangen, and Jena, in behalf of the society; at all which places, as well as at Halle, Leipzig, Göttingen, Würzburg, and Heidelberg, there were members as early as the summer of 1821. During 1821, 1822, and 1823, several other sections of it were established, consisting mostly, however, of only a few persons; and in all of them, so far as has been reported, great confusion and perplexity of ideas prevailed, no one knowing exactly what he wanted.

Many were, probably, induced to join the "Young Men's Union" by the compliment to their vanity implied in the immediate connection with the secret league of men, from which was expected a tremendous revolution tending to the improvement and renovation of Germany, and, perhaps, even of all Europe.

But they were startlingly undeceived by discovering, with certainty, that no such association of men existed. Part of them thereupon declared, that under these circumstances, the "Young Men's Union" was without any basis; and that it must, therefore, be dissolved. A majority, however, decided to continue their exertions more strenuously than ever, since the renovation of Germany must rest with them alone.

Thus, the phantasmal existence of the Union continued; it could neither live nor die. "It is clear," says the "*Information*," "that we

* This work was printed by C. Anton, with the express permission of the Royal Prussian Ministries of religion, instruction, and medicine. Halle, 1826.

can not discuss an actual organization of the 'Young Men's Union;' and that it would be in vain to attempt to follow up single ramifications of it to their origins, which were often accidental. We must rather treat of repeated attempts to accomplish an organization."

As the efforts in behalf of the "Young Men's Union" in Halle grew more and more efficient, they had an influence, most painful to me, upon my relations with the students. Whereas, they had previously been entirely open with me, and had conversed with me frankly respecting their lives, I could not but very soon observe that they were infected with wretched and foolish secrets and schemes. They could not communicate these to me, for they knew too well what were my opinions on them. I afterward found that, out of the most friendly feelings toward me, they had been entirely silent on these points, in order that no suspicion of participation might attach to me in case of any investigations. But this very silence sufficiently indicated to me that the young men, previously so firm in their honesty, were in great danger of being betrayed into secret, dishonest, and unlawful schemes. I felt myself necessitated to warn them once more, in a paternal manner, as clearly and distinctly as possible; and accordingly addressed to them all, in the year 1822, the following admonitory letter:

" *On the Re-establishment of the Burschenschaft.*

"I do not believe that the formal reorganization of the Burschenschaft by the students, in spite of their word of honor, and contrary to law, is to be apprehended; for, as the university overseer testifies, they speak the truth. Upon the dissolution of the Jena Burschenschaft, they wrote to the Grand Duke of Weimar, 'It was the will of your Royal Highness that the Burschenschaft be dissolved. That will has been carried into effect. We hereby declare, solemnly and publicly, that we have paid strict obedience to the command, and have, ourselves, dissolved our association, as was ordered,' &c., &c.

"In my judgment, these words express the true spirit of the Burschenschaft—open, true, and honorable. Every association which constitutes itself secretly, against the law and their word of honor, stands in direct opposition to this true spirit of the late Burschenschaft; and ought not, in my opinion, to be considered as an association of the class of that one, notwithstanding it may adopt its watchwords, colors, and all other externals.

"Such were my expressions to the academical senate in relation to the festival of January 12, 1821. May I never be obliged to give up the good opinion which I entertained when writing it.

"I still can not fear that any formal reorganization of the Burschenschaft, contrary to the word of honor given, and in contempt of the law, will take place. Who would advocate it?

"Suppose it should be said, 'You know the excellent purposes of the Burschenschaft; but it is impossible to attain them without the formal re-establishment of that body. Without a formal organization and establishment it will be impossible for us to hold together the students, and to lead them toward a common purpose.'

"To this I would reply: I ought not, strictly, to answer you at all, for you are seeking to cause a breaking of the law, and of the word of honor. Do you propose to defend this violation of law by claiming that the government has, on its part, destroyed the just condition ot affairs by its own injustice, and that, therefore, you feel yourself not bound by the law? How dare you say that law and right have not been violated by the young men themselves; and that, therefore, law and justice toward them are taken away? Have you forgotten Sand, and so many circumstances connected with him?

"But, even if injustice has been committed, dare you, for that reason, declare yourself free from all civil obligations? Was Socrates, then, in your opinion, a fool, because he drank the poison unjustly tendered him, rather than to flee? Follow no principle which you can not wish all the world to follow. Try every Christian commandment by this rule, and you will feel that the world would be happy if all should obey it. But if all were to cast loose from the State on this principle of yours—for when the government is unjust to one it endangers all—there would at once result a most fearful dissolution of all social bonds, a most terrific and bloody revolution. All the visionary and unbridled powers and passions of our nature would awake; hatred, envy, revenge, pride, ambition; the devil would stir up wicked hopes, and vain confidence in mere strength; and holy love would disappear in the waste abyss. Do you consider yourself powerful enough in intellect to quiet, guide, and rule these excited and rude powers and masses? Will you, a teacher and establisher of revolution, establish and maintain order? Beware of throwing out partial and frivolous words, which, as stimulants in real life, may become sad seeds of incalculable misery. Woe to you if you fool weak minds, and lead them astray with such words! And with this breach of law, the breach of word goes hand in hand. 'One word, one word—one man, one man,' our ancestors said. But, do you propose to begin the establishment of the German Burschenschaft by the violation of this truly German motto, and then to sing to your 'Union,' 'The world itself must pass away, and so the ancient proverb must?' Would you, Jesuitically, shelter yourself by that abominable principle that 'The end sanctifies the means?' In this direction points the cunning requirement, that we shall give up our healthy, simple moral instincts, and, instead of them, set up principles which an honest heart can not comprehend. And let us consider more closely that purpose of the Christian German Burschenschaft which is to sanctify these means. Was it not this, that the members were to live a common, free, open, true, pure, and affectionate life? And is the first step toward the accomplishment of that end, to be a breaking of the word of honor, and of the law? Have you, like the most unprincipled diplomatists, the greater morals and the lesser morals: the latter—Christian morality—for every-day life, and the former, the greater—devilish morality—for extraordinary occasions, which require lying and deceit? Are breach of one's word and of the law to be the consecrating ceremony at the entrance into the Burschenschaft? And must all the members live secretly, afraid every moment of being brought to an account, and contriving pettifogging shifts and tricks to get off with in case of need? What becomes of the simple innocence of an open and pure youthful life, with a good conscience, in whose place appears this concealed, secret, and light-shunning life? Are the young to train themselves, by such a course of life, into free Christian citizens? It is impossible.

"And however shrewdly all of your arrangements may have been made, however cunningly you calculate, be sure that good German honesty is best, and will always be best. Honesty stands longest. Arndt's verses are true of the German youth:

"'Trust thou not to a fair outside,
Lies and cheats thou canst not guide.
Arts and tricks will fail with thee,
Thy cunning, shallowest phantasy.'

"And in like manner will fail this trickish and secretly constituted Burschenschaft. It will soon be discovered, and broken up by expulsions.

"For these reasons I consider that, at present, the formal reorganization of the Christian German Burschenschaft would be a violation of law, and of the word of honor; unchristian, un-German, unwise.

"But is our youth so superannuated that it can not exist without a fixed form, without adherence to a letter? No law prevents you from living and laboring as friends in life and death, for the noblest of human purposes—for a free Christian intercourse. Must friendship be replaced by mere verbal fastenings, and a living intellectual tie by a lawyer's paper one? Must that mental power by which the better or more intelligent man influences his brother in God's name, be assured to him by a constitution?

"But if there are only a few individuals who are constituted capable of a profound and close association in life through love, it is better that these few should hold themselves purely and truly together, in independent friendship, than that efforts should be made to hold together, by prohibited ties, a great number of repugnant persons, and that the purpose should, at last, utterly fail. Woe to us, when our youth, even, shall be given over and consecrated to lovelessness; woe to youths who imagine that they can attain freedom by using their brethren wickedly and tyrannically, as blind tools! Oh, that our youth would purify themselves from every evil means, from every impure purpose; with a good conscience confess, before all the world, the good purpose at which they aim, and openly and freely demand from their instructors and officers, recognition and assistance in their truly holy endeavor! Who would dare oppose young men avowing their object to be a pure, active, loving life? Who can harm you if you do good? Oh, that Luther's free, and vehement, and powerful spirit could be a pattern for the German youth; that spirit which despised all low, stealthy, secret tricks and practices, and through divine and open confidence in itself, was unconquerable and irresistible!"

I was soon convinced that my appeal could not resist the force of the influence at work on the students. All confidence in the authorities was entirely at an end; for the students had experienced from them opposition, not assistance; and the opinion prevailed, that in order to realize the ideal of the Burschenschaft, it would be necessary no longer to co-operate with the authorities, but to oppose them; and that, on radical political principles, whatever stood in the way of that ideal must be removed. It was fancied that the "Young Men's Union" would lift the world to the condition of the angels.

We have seen that the Union was actually a nonentity. It was a fit subject for Aristophanes. But the times were too bitterly in earnest for this; and irritable and wicked consciences could neither understand nor endure any sport. The Union came to a tragical end. I had foretold, in my admonition, that if the prohibited Burschenschaft should be reorganized, it would soon be discovered, and broken up by expulsions. But the "Young Men's Union," in thinking to surpass the morality and lawfulness of the original Burschenschaft, foolishly passed beyond the sphere of its activity among young men, and attempted to interfere with the relations of actual life, of which it knew nothing, and which it was far from being competent to regulate or to change. Thus it happened that its members had to do, not with the paternal academical disciplinary court and the academical penalties, but with a criminal court and its severe sentence; that they were measured with the measure of the government, the existing state of which they had permitted themselves to attack. On the 25th of March, 1826, the High Court of Breslau passed sentence upon twenty-eight members of the Union, all of whom, except a few, were condemned to from two to fifteen years' imprisonment.*

This was the tragic end of the "Young Men's Union."

In 1822 my stay at Halle became unendurably painful to me. I still saw the same students whom I loved so well, but yet they were changed. I afterward found the names of twelve of them in the list of those condemned as just mentioned.

There was also a second reason, which had long annoyed me. I had been begging for three years that a collection of minerals might be purchased for the university, as the existing one did not at all fulfill the purposes of instruction. My request not being complied with, it was impossible for me to properly perform my duty as professor of mineralogy.

During this period of great uneasiness, my friend Rector Dittmar, while on a visit to me from Nuremberg, at Easter, 1822, invited me to take partial charge of his institution at that city. In October following I went to Nuremberg, examined the school, and consented. On returning to Halle, I applied to the two ministries under which I was an official—as mining councilor and as professor—for a dismission. I desire to commemorate the friendly manner in which the two ministers, Schuckmann and Altenstein, returned me my request, and advised me to recall my decision. But I had taken my resolution too firmly, and repeated my application. I received, May 30, 1823, through the ministry, the royal cabinet order which dismissed me. "In consequence," said the accompanying letter from the ministries, "the undersigned ministries do free you from your official duties, both in the university at Halle, and in the High Council of Mining, with thanks for your exertions there, and with the best wishes for your future prosperity."

I left Halle with very sad feelings. It was as if I were bearing to the grave all the wishes and hopes that I had nourished for ten years, ever since the year 1813, and for whose accomplishment I had fought and labored.

---

* Ten of them were imprisoned for fifteen years. Most of the twenty-eight were Prussians, but many other members were punished elsewhere. Most of them were, however, pardoned before the end of their term.

CONCLUSION.

The narration of our past experiences completely carries us back to time past, and so identifies us again with them, that we involuntarily write with affectionate interest of things which were so interesting to us. And although many things appear different to us in the course of time, yet we are unwilling to be too careful, and to weaken our delineation by subsequent criticisms. We may even, as Solomon admonishes, become incorrect by striving to be too much so. And it is equally improper to measure the past by the measure of the present —which was not then known nor applied—without reference to time and circumstances.

A reference to the eminent and long-continued usefulness of Schleiermacher will well illustrate this point. How many have thanked him for having first awakened them, at a time when they were sunken in a stupefying slumber under the poisonous influence of the vapors which arose from the dead sea of nationalism! And this, too, notwithstanding that subsequently a still deeper need separated them from him, to seek instruction and faith in eternal life from other preachers. Like them, I am grateful for the influence which Schleiermacher exerted upon me, although I afterward became unable to agree with his theological views.

It is not in the least my intention to defend all that I have related of myself, especially during my student life. I did not think it necessary to warn my reader, as he can become sufficiently acquainted with me, and with my views of Christianity, from this book.

My narrative ends with the year 1823, after which time I was for four years not at any university, and, accordingly, the concerns of those were out of my sight. When I was appointed at Erlangen in 1827, I found every thing very different from the north German universities, and every thing seemed to me to have changed.

The statements which follow are mostly derived from my experience during the twenty-seven years of my professorship at Erlangen. They relate chiefly to academical subjects, which have been much discussed within the last ten years, and upon which views and opinions have been very various.

I have stated my own beliefs as unequivocally, clearly, and definitely as I could, with the design of making both agreement and disagreement more easy; and not at all from any dogmatic assumption.

II. APPENDIX.

APPENDIX.

DOCUMENTS ILLUSTRATIVE OF THE HISTORY OF THE GERMAN UNIVERSITIES.

I. Bull of Pius II. for establishing the University of Ingolstadt.†

Pius, bishop, servant of the servants of God, in perpetual remembrance :—Among the happinesses which in this unstable life are offered us by the gift of God, it is not to be counted among the least that by assiduous study the pearl of knowledge may be found ; which points out the way to live well and happily, and makes the learned far different from the unlearned, and like God. And besides that, it introduces such to the clear comprehension of the secrets of the universe ; it assists the unlearned, and raises on high those born in the lowest places ; and for these reasons the Apostolic See,—a provident manager in things both spiritual and temporal—a careful distributor of its honorable abundance—and the continual and faithful helper of every commendable work,—in order that men may be the more easily carried to the attainment of so lofty a point of earthly condition, and to refund again with increase to others what they have gained, since distribution diminishes the quantity of other things, but knowledge increases by being communicated in proportion as it is diffused among more persons—exhorts them to prepare places for it ; assists and cherishes it ; and is itself accustomed, especially at the request of Catholic princes, willingly to make grants for its convenience and usefulness.

A petition lately exhibited to us on the part of our beloved son, the noble Louis, Count Palatine on the Rhine, Duke of Bavaria, imports that he, having long and providently considered that by the labors of those who pursue learned studies the Divine Majesty is worthily worshiped ; the truth of the orthodox faith illustrated ; virtues and good morals are acquired, and every species of human prosperity augmented, fervently desires, for the good of the common weal, that in his city of Ingolstadt, in the Diocese of Eystett—which is very fit for the purpose, and in which the air is temperate, and an abundance of the necessaries of life is found, and which has no other university within a circuit of almost a hundred and fifty Italian miles around it, or thereabouts—there may be founded a university in all the lawful faculties (*studium generale in qualibet licita Facultate*), where the faith may be promoted, the simple instructed, equity in judgment preserved, reason cultivated, the minds of men enlightened, and their intellects illustrated.

We, having attentively considered the premises, and also the eminent sincerity of the faithful devotion which the said duke has been proved to feel to us and to the Roman Church, experience a fervent desire that the said city may be embellished with the gifts of science, so that it may produce men eminent for mature judgment, crowned with ornaments of virtues, and erudite in the doctrines of the various faculties, and that there may be there a plentiful fountain of learning, from

* Schöttgen, 112.

† Mederer, iv. 16.

whose abundance all may drink who desire to be imbued with good literature;—and favorably inclining to the supplications of the aforesaid duke on that part, for the glory of the divine name, and the propagation of the faith, by apostolical authority do determine and ordain that in the said city there shall henceforward be a university, and that it shall there exist for all future time, in theology, canon and civil law, medicine, arts, and every other lawful faculty. And that readers (*legentes*) and students in it may for the future enjoy and use all privileges, liberties, exemptions, honors, and immunities whatsoever, and in the same manner as masters, doctors, and students in the University of Vienna do or can enjoy or use them. And that those who in process of time shall have merited the reward of superiority in the faculty which they study, and shall have sought a license to teach, that they may instruct others, or the honor of the master's degree, or the doctorate, may be admitted to the same by the doctor or doctors, or master or masters of such faculty, after strict examination, with the usual formalities. And those who have been examined and approved in the said university of the said town, and have obtained a license to teach, or an honor, may thereafter have full and free liberty of reading and teaching, both in the said city and in other universities where they may desire to read or teach, without other examination or approbation, notwithstanding the statutes, customs, and privileges of the University of Vienna, or of other universities, assured to them by oath, apostolical confirmation, or any other confirmation whatever, precisely as if special and express mention had been made of them, and of the entire tenor of them, in these presents, and of all other contrary matters whatsoever.

But we ordain that scholars in this university about being erected, taking an honor of any grade, shall be held obligated, and obliged, to take a proper oath of fidelity, before the Rector for the time being of the said university, according to the form given in these presents. And the form of the said oath is as follows: "I, a scholar of the University of Ingolstadt, in the diocese of Eystett, will, from this hour forward, be faithful and obedient to Saint Peter and to the holy Roman Church, and to my lord, the lord Pius the Second, papal pontiff, and to his successors canonically succeeding. I will not enter into any plan, agreement, undertaking, or act, to cause them to lose life or limb, or into any machinations or conspiracies for the derogation or prejudice of the person of any one of them, or of the authority, honor, or privileges of his Church, or of the Apostolic See, or of the Apostolic statutes, ordinances, reservations, dispositions, or mandates; neither, as often as I shall know of the agitation of any such thing, will I fail to impede it to the best of my ability, or to do whatever I conveniently can to signify the matter to our said lord, or to some other person, through whom it may come to his notice. But the counsels which shall be intrusted to me by them, their messengers, or letters, I will reveal to no one, to their damage. I will be their assistant against every man, for the retaining and defending the Roman primacy, and the royalties of St. Peter. I will be diligent to increase and promote, as much as in me lies, their authority, privileges, and rights, and to observe with care their statutes, ordinances, reservations, and dispositions. I will assist the legates of the Apostolic See honorably, and in their necessities; and will follow up, and fight against, to the utmost of my strength, heretics and schismatics, and such as shall rebel against any one of the aforesaid successors to our lord. So help me God, and these holy Evangelists of God."

Let no man whatever, therefore, infringe upon this our statute and ordinance, or with rash daring violate it; and if any shall presume to attempt it, let him know that he will incur the wrath of the omnipotent God, and of St. Peter and St. Paul, the Apostles. Given at Siena, in the year of the divine incarnation one thousand four hundred and fifty-nine, on the seventh to the ides of April. In the year of our pontificate, the first.

II. List of Lectures in the Faculty of Arts.

Prague, 1366.†

	Honorarium. Groschen.	Months.
Metaphysics,*	8	6
Physics,*		9
On the heavens,*	5	4
Generation,*	3	2
Sense and sensation,*		
Memory and recollection,*		
Sleep and waking,*		
Length and shortness of life,*		
Vegetables,*		
Ethics and Physics,*		9
Politics and Physics,*		6
Rhetoric and Physics,*		9
Œconomics,*		
Boethius de consolatione,	4	3
The old logic,	3	4
Prior (ethics ?)*	4	4

	Honorarium. Groschen.	Months.
Posterior (ethics ?)*	3	3
Topics,*	4	4
Treatise of Peter Hispanus,	2	3
Material Sphere,	1	1½
Algorism,		¾
Theory of the planets,	2	1½
Six books of Euclid,	8	6
Almagest,	1fl	12
Almanach,	10	6
Priscian (major),	2	2
De' Græcismo,	6	6
Poetria nova,	2	3
Labyrinth,	1	1½
Boetius on the discipline of schools,		
Doctrinale, 2d part,		

Erfurt, 1449.‡

	Months.
Physics,	8
On the soul,	3
On heavens and earth,	3
On meteors,	3
Lesser natural philosophy,*	2
Ethics,	8
Politics,	6
Œconomics,	1
Metaphysics,	6
Euclid,	6
Theory of the planets,	1½
Music,	1
Art of metrical composition,	1
Perspective,	3
Material sphere,	1½
Old logic,	3½
Prior (ethics ?)	3½
Posterior (ethics ?)	3½
Topics	4

	Months.
Elenchi,*	2
Peter Hispanus,	3
Suppositions, amplifications, restrictions, and appellations,	2
Consequences,	1
Biligam ?	1
Obligatory and insoluble propositions,	1
Priscian (minor),	3
Donatus,	1
Alexander, part 1st (Doctrinale),	1
Same, part 2,	1
Same, part 3,	1
Boetius on the consolations of philosophy,	1
Loyca Heysbri,	4
Poetria,	2
Computus,	1
Algorism,	1
Labyrinth,	2

Ingolstadt, 1472.§

	Honorarium. Groschen.
Lesser logic, and exercises,	
Old logic, and exercises,	24
Elenchi,	3
Obligatory propositions,	1
Physics, and exercises,	
Material sphere,	3
Euclid, 1st book,	1
Algorism, integers,	1
Some book on rhetoric,	1
Alexander, 1st part (Doctrinale),	3
Same, 2d part,	3
Prior (ethics ?) exercises,	10

(The preceding examined on for baccalaureate; the following for the master's degree.)

	Honorarium. Groschen.
Ethics,	
Metaphysics,	9
On meteors,	11
On generation and corruption,	3
On heavens and earth,	6
Lesser natural philosophy,	3
Theory of the planets,	3
Common arithmetic,	2
Topics,	6
On the soul,	11
Posterior (ethics ?)	3

Vienna, 1389.‖

	Honorarium. Groschen.
Physics,	3
Metaphysics,	9
Heavens and earth,	5
On generation and corruption,	3
On meteors,	5
On the soul,	5
Lesser natural philosophy,	3
Ethics,	12
Politics,	10
Œconomics,	2

	Honorarium. Groschen.
Boetius on the consolations of philosophy,	5
Euclid, 5 books,	6
Theory of the planets,	4
Perspective,	5
Bragwardinus on proportionate lengths,	3
On breadth of forms,	2
Albertus Magnus' summary of nat. phil.,	4
Old logic,	5
Peter Hispanus,	3
Prior (ethics ?)	3

† From "*Monumenta Universitatis Pragensis*," i. 1, 76. I give these lists as in the original sources, with their characteristic errors.

‡ Motschmann, i.

§ Mederer, iv. 93.

‖ Zeisl, 138. This list is headed, "We now assign the books ordinarily to be read, with the fees of the same, which no master may presume to augment." These fees will sufficiently indicate those for the other ordinary lectures.

Upon the above lists of lectures in arts, it may be observed:

1. The books which passed for Aristotle's are marked with a star (*), in the Prague list; as is also the Elenchi, in the Erfurt list, for the same reason. The latter, together with the Prior and Posterior (ethics ?), and Topics, belong to the new logic. The "old logic" (*Vetus ars*, *Logica vetus*) is not that of Aristotle.

Lesser natural philosophy.—"Part 6th of the Aristotelian Physiology, which disputes upon the general characteristics of living beings, such as memory and recollection, sense and sensation, sleep and dreams, . . . waking, respiration, old age, life, death; which three are called lesser natural philosophy (*parva naturalia*)." See *Monum. Univ. Prag.*, i. 2, 551, 564, 567.

2. *Honorarium, or fee* (*Pastus*).—At Prague, those who were unable to pay 12 gulden a year, might attend the lectures free. The professor was not to take more than the fixed fee for each lecture, nor, however, might he take less (by way of attracting scholars). If the smallness of his audience compelled him to discontinue his lectures, he was obliged to return to those from whom he had received it, the fee, less a part proportioned to the lectures read. Receivers or collectors corresponded to the present quæstors, and their office was "to collect the dues of the faculty; and accordingly *collecta* is the honorarium." (*Zeisl*, 138, 147.)

III. Bursaries. Burschen.*

"*Bursa:* 1. Purse, *bourse;* from the Greek of *βύρσα*, a hide, because they were made of leather. Jo. de Garlandia gives, as synonyms, '*marsupium*, *bursa*, *forulus*, *locusque*, *crumena*.'

"2. Chest, *ταμεῖον*, casket; but, more properly, a box for a specified purpose. In these *bursæ* or chests were deposited sums set apart for the support of scholars, or given by pious men for that purpose.† *Bursarius:* One who receives an allowance from a *bursa;* also, applied to such scholars in the universities as are allowed, on account of poverty, certain amounts from the chest set apart for that purpose, to enable them to complete their studies." (*Dufresne.*)

Chrysander wrote a treatise, "Why Students at the Universities are called Burschen. Rinteln, 1751." I extract the following from it:

"The chest from which poor students were supported at the Sorbonne was called *Bursa*, and such students, *Bursii* or *Bursarii*, *Boursier*. 'A *Boursier* was a poor scholar or student, supported by the *Bursa* of his college. The others, who supported themselves at the university of Paris by their own means, were called Studiosi, students.'" Hence the term was introduced to Germany.

In Italy, however, the students were called *Bursati*, because they were girded with a *bursa* or purse. Hence the stanza:

"Dum mea bursa sonat,
Hospes mihi fercula donat.
Dum mea bursa vacat,
Hospes mihi ostia monstrat."

That is: "While my purse tinkles, the host gives me delicacies; but when it is empty he shows me the door." A similar French stanza is:

"Quand ma bourse fait, bim, bim, bim,
Tout le monde est mon cousin;
Mais quand elle fait da, da, da,
Tout le monde dit, Tu t'en va."‡

The French *Boursiers* seem to correspond to the poor students of Germany, and the Italian *Bursati* to the rich ones.

---

* See an article entitled "Signification of 'Bursch' and 'Burschenschaft,'" in the *Academical Monthly*, May and June, 1858, p. 252.

† Merchants' purses were also called *Bursa.*

‡ This stanza is quoted by the pseudonymous Schlingschlangschlorum. See note, under chapter on "Personal Relations between Professors and Students."

IV. Comments of Landsmannschaften.

Extract from Comment of Landsmannschaft at ——f (Altdorf?), as in force in 1815.*

GENERAL PROVISIONS.

§ 1. The Societies bind themselves to put the present Comment into operation from the moment of its ratification, and to enforce the penalties fixed therein.

§ 2. If occasions shall arise for which the present Burschen-Comment does not provide, or if additional statutes are to be enacted, or if there is any occasion for a general council, two deputies are to be appointed from each Society, who shall exchange with each other the sentiments of the Societies; of which two, one, at least, must be an Old Bursch. The majority of voices, or in case of a tie, the lot, shall determine the result.

§ 3. The Societies bind themselves not to permit this code to come into the hands of a renouncer; but to cite its provisions, when necessary, only as if by oral tradition, and without giving any other source for them than general custom.

Title I.—Relations of the Societies to each other and to Renouncers.

A.—*Societies to each other.*

§ 4. Existing Societies ratifying this *Comment*, mutually guarantee to each other their existence as at present.

§ 5. No Society not now existing can be organized without the consent of those existing; nor can any existing Society be extinguished without the consent of all the existing Societies, or without sufficient and proved reasons. Nor can any new Society organize itself under the name of an existing Society.

§ 6. All the Societies have equal rights.

§ 7. In case of collisions between them, as, for instance, in differences for precedence, the major vote of the deputies, or the lot, in case of a tie, shall determine.

B.—*Between the Societies and Renouncers.*

§ 8. Every student, not a member of a Society, is a Renouncer.

§ 9. In case of doubt, the student shall be considered a Renouncer.

§ 10. Renouncers can enter only the Society of their countrymen; but if there is no such, they may enter any other existing one which is undetermined. *Novel:* but he shall not be recognized as such member by the other societies until so recognized by a major vote of the Convention of Seniors.

§ 11. On public festival occasions, the Societies shall be governed by the directory.

§ 12. Members of a Society have, everywhere, precedence over Renouncers.

Title II.—Distinctions among Students.

a.—*According to Birthplace.*

§ 13. A Pavement-beater (*Pflastertreter*), or Quark, is one whose parents live in the university town.

§ 14. A Cummin-Turk (*Kümmelturk*) is one whose parents reside within four miles of the university town.

b.—*According to length of stay at the University.*

§ 15. From the moment of matriculation, every matriculated student is a student qualified to fight.

§ 16. A Fox is one who

a. Has not yet been half a year at the university since his matriculation; or,

b. Comes from a university which the Burschen of the present university have degraded to the rank of Fox.

§ 17. A Brander or Brand-Fox is a Fox after his first half-year.

* Haupt, p. 185. The *Novels* or additions to this code are dated June 15, 1815. Haupt, p. 203.

§ 18. But any Fox may be made a Brander, or any Brander a Young Bursch, by his Society.

§ 19. A Pavement-beater, Cummin-Turk, or Fox, may not, without renowning, either consider himself insulted by those names, nor use them in insult.

§ 20. Excessive impositions upon the Foxes is by no means to the honor of a Bursch. If these border upon abuse, the Fox may demand satisfaction of the Bursch, or take the advantage of him.* And any Society may, besides, make the matter one concerning itself, if the insulted Fox is a member.

§ 21. In other matters, every Bursch has the prerogative over the Foxes and Branders, that the latter may not challenge him on behalf of an insulted person, nor make appointments, nor be seconds in a duel, nor give testimony in a case of dueling, nor preside, nor have precedence in dancing, nor give the pitch, nor ride with them in public processions, nor drink *Schmollis* to them, &c.

§ 22. A Young Bursch is one who is passing the first half of his second year; during the latter half he is Bursch. During the first half of the third year he is an Old Bursch, and afterward a Mossy Man (*bemooster Herr*).

§ 23. According to this reckoning of time spent at the university, if he have not been in dishonor (*im verschisse*) during the same, a student can become a Mossy Man during his fifth half-year at the university, if he has been previously promoted from the degree of Fox to that of Brander, or from that of Brander to that of Bursch.

c.—*According to the possession or lack of Bursch-honor.*

aa. *The Honorable.*

§ 24. Every student is to be reckoned honorable until he is expressly declared dishonorable (*in verschiss komm*) by the Society.

§ 25. In case of doubt, the party is to be held honorable.

§ 26. Every honorable student gives or receives the ordinary Bursch-satisfaction, according to his injury.

§ 27. If two honorable students give their word of honor to the truth of the same fact; or one for and the other against it, he who first gave it, as the injured party, is entitled to satisfaction from the other.

§ 28. If one Renouncer applies to another, or to a member of a Society, the term "dishonorable," &c., the injured party is entitled to fight him three times, with the choice of weapons, whatever the result of the duels. (!)

§ 29. A party insulted by a *pereat* may

1. Take a real advantage† of the other, and
2. Must fight a duel with him.

bb. *The Dishonorable.*

§ 30. For each dishonor (*verschisse*) is requisite:

a. A major vote of the deputies.
b. A sufficient reason.

Novel. And the Society concerned shall not vote.

A.—What constitutes dishonor of a student.

§ 31. Dishonor is either that from which the person dishonored can never escape, or from which he may be relieved after a certain time.

§ 32. Of what kind the dishonor shall be, always depends upon the decision of the deputies.

§ 33. Causes of dishonor are:

a. If a student breaks his word of honor.
b. If a member of one Society applies to a member of another Society, of whom

---

* "Advantage;" see this Appendix, p. 58.

† See this Appendix, p. 58.

he knows only the distinguishing tokens, the term "dishonorable," the former becomes thereby dishonorable.

c. Returning, to the highest verbal insult of "foolish fellow" (*Dummer Junge*), a further verbal or actual insult, or only threatening to inflict a similar verbal insult, after having been told that the party insulting is ready to fight.

d. Refusing the satisfaction which is demanded, or not knowing and seeking how to exact satisfaction for the term "foolish fellow."

e. Becoming a traitor in matters relating to the Burschen: as, for instance, by giving testimony against a student. (!!!)

f. Stealing, or being guilty of a great (!) piece of cheating at play.

g. Declaring one's self entirely free from the obligations of this Comment. (!)

h. Living in, or going to the house of a dishonored Philister.

i. Holding confidential intercourse with any dishonored person, except when strict necessity requires it. Persons violating clauses h and i, are first to be notified, by members of their own Society, to separate from the offenders; and, if disobedient, they become dishonorable with them.

k. Uttering a *pereat* against a whole Society.

l. Taking hold of an adversary's sword with the hand.

m. Bringing unequal weapons to a duel, as a broadsword against a rapier; or using weapons contrary to their purpose, as to thrust with a broadsword.

n. Intentionally thrusting or cutting after the seconds have called Halt!

o. Challenging without any reason.

p. Expulsion, with infamy, from a Society.

q. Letting one's self be chased away with a straight sword or a Jena rapier. *Novel.* But this shall be reckoned a shame (*Schande*) only.

B.—Dishonor of Philister.

§ 34. As under § 30, without the *Novels.*

C.—Consequences of Dishonor.

a.—*With Students.*

§ 35. The dishonorable has no claim to the honor or satisfaction of a Bursch. Any advantage may be taken of him.

§ 36. The dishonorable can not take part in any *commerce*, or any public ceremony.

§ 37. In duels between the dishonorable and Philister, the former shall receive no countenance, unless in case of insult, by the latter, to honorable Burschen.

b.—*With Philister.*

§ 38. The consequences of dishonor, with the Philister, depend on the kind of the dishonor; that is,

1. Whether the Philister is dishonorable on every account, or

2. Only on one; as landlord, for instance, or as artisan; in which case the consequences follow, of course (by § 33, h).

D.—Removal of Dishonor.

a.—*In the case of Students.*

§ 39. A dishonorable person may be relieved from his dishonor, according to its kind; and if he demand it, a member is selected from each Society, with whom he must fight. The choice of weapons belongs to such members, and not more than three duels must be fought with any one of them.

§ 40. Dishonor may be removed by unanimous vote of the deputies of the Societies.

§ 41. The person freed from dishonor re-enters upon all his rights as a Bursch.

b.—*In the case of Philister.*

§ 42. The dishonor of a Philister is removed at the expiration of the time for during which it was imposed.

TITLE III.—PROVISIONS ON INJURIES TO BURSCH-HONOR.

§ 43. An honorable student, receiving a verbal insult from another, or being pushed by him, may

a. Push him back again, or

b. Take the advantage of him, by calling him foolish fellow.

c. "Foolish fellow" is the highest verbal insult, and can be answered by no further insult; it can be followed only by a challenge. If one apply to another any other insulting expression, as "scoundrel," and other terms, the insulted person may knock him down or challenge him, and, after the duel, may address to him the same verbal insult. The term dishonorable, however, may not, under penalty of the punishments above specified, be used, except to a dishonorable person, upon whom both verbal and real insults may be inflicted.

§ 44. Insults from officers or honorable students from other universities come under the same rule.

§ 45. In case of a duel with a student of another university, they shall meet half way between the two universities. The person insulted shall fight the first three bouts with the weapon of his own university, and the last three with that of his opponent's.

§ 46. In the university prison, the Comment is suspended.

Extract from the Comment of the Landsmannschaft of the University of Leipzig, as in force in 1817.

TITLE II.—OF THE INSULT, OR ADVANTAGE.

§ 1. Whether honor be hurt, or not, is left to the feelings of each individual; but the convention has recognized certain expressions and actions, viz., those which are mortifying, or which undervalue one's honor and good reputation, as insults which every student is, as such, bound to answer by a challenge.

§ 2. Among verbal insults and verbal advantages are the terms "singular, arrogant, absurd, silly, simple, impertinent, rude, foolish;" and, as an epitome of the extremest verbal insult and advantage, "foolish fellow."

§ 3. For all these expressions an unconditional challenge must pass, unless they are withdrawn. Real insults can not be withdrawn. Insults given in intoxication are not to be noticed, unless they are afterward repeated, when sober.

§ 4. If any one thinks himself insulted by expressions or gestures, he may either proceed by means of the *coramage*, or take a verbal advantage; but must not send a challenge for that reason.

§ 5. If any one thinks himself not entitled either to challenge or to resort to the *coramage*, he may take the advantage: that is, may answer with a more insulting expression, and thus wipe out the lesser one.

§ 6. Real advantages are, a box on the ear, a blow with a stick, or any other assault with whip or stick. The offer of any such shall not be considered an advantage.

§ 7. The advantage can not be taken unless within three days of the receiving of an insult; but, if the aggressor can not be found, at his house, or elsewhere, within that time, the term begins anew, and so onward.

§ 8. There must be at least one witness when an advantage is taken. But if he who takes it shall give his word of honor to the fact, it shall be sufficient, if he belong to a Society.

V. Constitutions of Burschenschaften.

A.—Constitution of the General German Burschenschaft.

*Adopted on the 18th day of the month of Victory (October), 1818.**

GENERAL PRINCIPLES.

§ 1. The General German Burschenschaft is the free union of all the German youth engaged in learned studies at the universities; based upon the relations of the German youth to the coming union of the German people.

§ 2. The General German Burschenschaft, as a free Society, lays down, as the central point of its operations, the following received general principles:

a. Unity, freedom, and equality of all Burschen among each other, and equality of all rights and duties.

b. Christian German education of every mental and bodily faculty to the service of the fatherland.

§ 3. The living together of all the German Burschen in the spirit of these principles, expresses the highest idea of the General German Burschenschaft—the unity of all the German Burschen in spirit and in life.

§ 4. The General German Burschenschaft assumes existence, in order that the longer it lives, the more it may present a picture of the freedom and unity of its prosperous nation; that it may maintain a national Burschen-life in the development of every bodily and mental faculty; and in a free, equal, and orderly common life, will prepare its members for national life, so that each one of them may be raised to such a grade of self-knowledge, as in his own pure individuality to display the brightness of the glory of the German national life.

Constitution.

§ 5. As the General German Burschenschaft does not exist at any one place, it is livided into separate Burschenschaften, at the different universities.

§ 6. These Burschenschaften are, in respect to each other, to act as entirely similar parts—as parts of the entire whole.

§ 7. The constitutions of these separate Burschenschaften must coincide, as far as the above fixed principles, without any prejudice to any other peculiarities of each separate one.

§ 8. The General German Burschenschaft acts—

a. By an assembly of delegates from the separate ones, meeting annually, at the period of the eighteenth of the month of victory (October); to which each shall send, if possible, three delegates, with full powers, who shall bring with them the constitution, the customs, and the history of their Burschenschaft.

b. By the choice of a Burschenschaft for transacting business between one assembly of delegates and another, in order to conduct the common concerns. As a general rule, this appointment must not be passed from one Burschenschaft to another in any fixed succession.

Relations of the General German Burschenschaft to its members; the separate Burschenschaften.

§ 9. As in every well-organized Society the common will of the whole is above that of a single member, so in the General German Burschenschaft, the expressed will of the whole is above that of each single one.

§ 10. Any separate Burschenschaft which does not recognize, as its own, the common decision of the General German Burschenschaft, cuts itself off from the General German Burschenschaft by that very act.

---

* Haupt, p. 257.

Duties of the Assembly of Delegates.

§ 11. The assembly of delegates has supreme authority:

a. In controversies between the separate Burschenschaften;

b. In controversies of single Burschen with their Burschenschaft.

§ 12. It has power to scrutinize the constitutions of separate Burschenschaften, as well as to decide whether any thing in them agrees, or not, with the recognized fundamental principles. In the latter case it is to propose to the separate Burschenschaft the alteration of the inconsistent portion.

§ 13. The assembly of delegates shall usually begin its sessions with an examination of the constitution of the General German Burschenschaft, in order to convince themselves whether its form still expresses its spirit; in order that the progress of its spirit may never, in any way, be circumscribed by the letter.

§ 14. All propositions not having immediate reference to the above general recognized principles, or to the constitution of the General German Burschenschaft, whether they relate to the constitution or the customs of the separate Burschenschaften, shall be, after previous examination and approval by the assembly of delegates, by them laid before the separate Burschenschaften for acceptance, with request for agreement, as to something promotive of the beautiful idea of complete freedom; but still, whose non-acceptance can not injure the connection of the whole. All such propositions shall be either accepted or rejected by the separate Burschenschaften, and the result laid before the next general assembly.

§ 15. In all votes of the general assembly a majority of votes shall be decisive.

Duties of the Burschenschaft for Managing Business.

§ 16. The Burschenschaft in charge of the business has the precedence in the general assembly: that is, opens its sessions, leads the deliberations, and keeps the records.

§ 17. During the year its duties are the following:

a. It collects and arranges whatever is communicated to it to be laid before the general assembly.

b. It communicates all notifications, as quickly as possible, to the General Burschenschaft; for which purpose such notices are sent to it only, from the others.

c. It designates the place and time for the assembly of delegates.

d. It has charge of, and keeps in order the papers of the General German Burschenschaft.

e. It keeps the treasury of the General German Burschenschaft, and collects the contributions of the separate Burschenschaften; for which purpose each one is, half-yearly, to report all changes of its members.

§ 18. The Burschenschaft in charge of business shall report its proceedings to the assembly of delegates.

Relations of the separate Burschenschaften to each other.

§ 19. The separate Burschenschaften are to consider themselves equal parts of a great whole.

§ 20. All controversies between them must be settled, not by duel, but by the reasonable decision of the general assembly; unless they can be settled by themselves, or through the medium of a third Burschenschaft.

§ 21. Each Burschenschaft shall recognize all penalties inflicted by the others as just, and as binding on themselves, unless the General German Burschenschaft shall have declared them improper.

§ 22. It is, of course, understood that any member of one Burschenschaft, merely by declaring his wish, and by adhering to the customs of the university, can join another.

§ 23. Mutual hospitality is to be practiced.

RELATIONS OF THE GENERAL GERMAN BURSCHENSCHAFT TO SOCIETIES OUTSIDE OF IT.

§ 24. If a Society of German Burschen is established at any university where there is already a Burschenschaft, part of the general one, such Burschen are, by virtue of that fact, in disgrace; which, however, ends with the dissolution of such Societies, or secession from them.

§ 25. Where, however, Landsmannschaften or other Societies, having existed for a long time, are in operation, besides the Burschenschaft, the separate Burschenschaften shall conduct toward them as their character may require; and shall seek, as far as possible, to gain them over, in the way of persuasion, by exemplifying the truth to them, in part by their own whole life, and, where it seems likely to be effectual, by discussion. But if the Burschenschaft is attacked by them, and hindered in the free development of its principles, it must resort to the most efficient measures which the occasion may offer, and shall expect the utmost possible assistance from the General German Burschenschaft.

§ 26. With universities where there is no Burschenschaft, but only Landsmannschaften, the General German Burschenschaft has no further relation. But in order that these shall not become rendezvous for all sorts of disreputable persons, it will advise them of such Burschen as are known to it to be of bad character.

§ 27. If, however, there are, at such universities, individual Burschen, who desire to found a Burschenschaft, the General German Burschenschaft will supply all possible assistance to them, and pledges, in particular, the aid of the nearest university where there is already a Burschenschaft.

§ 28. Foreigners at any German university are permitted to proceed with their education in as free and national a manner as they desire; but, as it is not reasonable to expect that they, as foreigners, and as intending to remain such, should enter the German Burschenschaft, and labor in it for the good of the whole, and of individuals, they are permitted to form associations with each other. But an association of foreigners can never have a decisive vote in the general concerns of the Burschen; and they must, in all things, comply with the prevailing code of customs.

RELATIONS OF THE GENERAL GERMAN BURSCHENSCHAFT TO INDIVIDUALS NOT MEMBERS.

§ 29. With such Burschen as are connected with no Society, the General German Burschenschaft stands in the most friendly relations. It guarantees to them the fullest freedom which they can enjoy as men. But it properly requires from them to conduct themselves according to the code of customs prevailing at the university where they happen to be. To this end all honorable Burschen have a right to require that the customs of the university shall be read to them. Their affairs of honor with the members of the Burschenschaft shall be conducted according to the customs of the latter; but they may select for themselves honorable seconds and witnesses, but such as are acquainted with the code.

§ 30. If there are at the university associations other than the Burschenschaft, having different codes of customs, all Burschen connected with no Society, may, in affairs of honor with each other, proceed under whichever code they please; but, where they select that of the Burschenschaft, or where there is only a Burschenschaft, the latter may satisfy itself that the code will be properly adhered to.

§ 31. Against those refusing to conduct their affairs of honor on the principles of the Burschen, proceedings shall be taken according to their practice.

§ 32. The General Burschenschaft will use its means of protecting Burschen not in that Society against all treatment of an unjust kind, and unworthy of a Bursch, from those not Burschen.

§ 33. In consultations touching the good of the whole university, all honorable Burschen must naturally have part, whether members of the Burschenschaft or not.

General Festivals.

§ 34. The 18th of the month of victory is the permanent festival of the General German Burschenschaft. Every three years, when possible, this day shall be celebrated by all the German Burschen together, as a festival in commemoration of the first brotherly meeting at the Wartburg.

§ 35. The 18th of June is a festival for remembrance of all the German brothers at the other German universities.

B.—General portion of the Constitution of the Jena Burschenschaft.*

§ 1. The Jena Burschenschaft, as a part of the General German Burschenschaft, is an association of all the Jena Burschen who recognize as their own the general principles laid down in the General Constitution, and have given in their adherence to them by joining the Burschenschaft.

§ 2. The design of the Jena Burschenschaft must be that of the General German Burschenschaft, and it will promote that design within its sphere of activity; and will, for itself, also strive after the purposes therein proposed.

§ 3. In like manner will it, also for itself, carry out, in actual life, the idea of the unity and freedom of the German people; and will promote and maintain, in Jena, a national and upright Burschen-life, in unity, freedom, and equality, in the development of mental and bodily powers, and in a cheerful social intercourse; and will, by its organization, prepare its members for the service of the fatherland.

§ 4. The Burschenschaft adopts the code of customs as the only one which is right and suitable to the organization of the universities, and endeavors to maintain it, and by means of it, an honorable relation among the Burschen.

§ 5. Therefore it has supreme power in all affairs relating to the Burschen of our university.

§ 6. Only upon decisions relating to the interests of the whole university does it permit voting by those not members of the Burschenschaft; who are, otherwise, to be treated as those having themselves resigned their right to vote, since nothing prevents them from joining the Burschenschaft.

§ 7. For this reason every Bursch is bound, in every matter in which he consults with Burschen, to have reference to the privileges of the Burschenschaft.

§ 8. The Burschenschaft, as a separate organization, can exist only in unity and order, and in a free and public social intercourse, such as is proper for Burschen.

§ 9. In order to secure its own existence, the Burschenschaft establishes a constitution, in which it sets forth its relations in proper order; so that each member may comprehend the sentiment and spirit of the Burschenschaft, and may be able to instruct himself in what relation he stands, and what he must do and avoid, in order to become a worthy member of the Society.

§ 10. The Burschenschaft appoints, as its head, a managing board, to whom it intrusts the management of affairs, as it is impossible for the whole body to transact them.

§ 11. In order to secure itself against any attempts upon the rights of the whole body, it appoints, together with the managing board, a committee, as a supervising authority.

§ 12. But the decision is reserved to the Society in all cases which nearly concern its own whole existence; as the making of laws, and as a tribunal of ultimate appeal. And it shall also decide upon such decisions and ordinances of the managing board as are brought before it by the non-concurrence of the committee, or by the appeal of individuals.

§ 13. In order to secure the obedience of its members to its laws, it establishes a code of penalties.

* Haupt, p. 264.

§ 14. As the maintenance of the Burschenschaft renders necessary many expenditures of money, it pledges each of its members to a contribution to the common funds. It establishes a treasury.

§ 15. In order to maintain in the Burschen-life the ancient knightly exercise of fencing, and that each member of the Burschenschaft may be skillful enough for a combat in defense of his honor, the Burschenschaft establishes a fencing-room. It, however, also favors other bodily exercises, since it recognizes bodily development as especially necessary to a German education. For this reason the Turning-place (*Turnplatz*) is under its protection.

§ 16. In order to promote friendship and pleasure in the social intercourse of the members of the Burschenschaft, it rents a Burschen-house, and supplies it with every thing proper for that purpose.

§ 17. Upon all occasions of celebrations by Burschen on days which are festivals for every German, the Burschenschaft will appear as a public participant at the ceremony. It establishes and arranges banquets for pleasure, and also more serious celebrations.

§ 18. A general view of the chief heads of the Constitution of the Jena Burschenschaft is as follows:

A. Organization as to the business concerning the Society:
  1. Managing board.
  2. Committee.
  3. Decisions of the whole Burschenschaft.
  a. Sections of the Society.
  b. Assemblies of the Burschen.
  4. Course of business.

B. Entrance into and departure out of the Burschenschaft.

C. Relations of the members as individuals—Rights, Duties.

D. Penal code.

E. Treasury.

F. Fencing-rooms.

G. Burschenhaus.

H. Burschenschaft festivals.

SPECIAL PART OF THE CONSTITUTION.

Managing Board.

§ 19. The managing board consists of nine managers, and three candidates for the managership.

§ 20. The managing board is chosen every half-year, for six months, by the Burschenschaft.

Official Duties of the Managing Board.

§ 21. The managing board is the representative of the Burschenschaft, and all matters are under its charge which relate to the whole Society. It exercises, in their name, judicial, executive, supervisory, and managerial authority.

§ 22. Above all, it is to watch over the credit and honor of the Burschenschaft, and to promote it by every means in its power.

§ 23. It exercises judicial power, in that it decides all cases which come before it under the laws; or where none of them deals with the case in hand, after the analogy of existing laws, and in accordance with justice and conscience.

§ 24. It exercises executive power, by carrying into execution the decisions of the Burschenschaft.

§ 25. The board watches over the observance of the laws and conformity to the code. It decides upon quarrels, and all affairs of honor between Burschen, which are brought before it. And accordingly, each manager has authority to stop any duel which appears to him to be contrary to the code, and to cause it to be investigated.

§ 26. It is the right and duty of the managers to give friendly admonitions to the other members of the Burschenschaft in reference to their relations as Burschen.

§ 27. The board manages all external business of the Burschenschaft, and conducts its correspondence.

§ 28. It fixes the time and place of the assembly of the Burschen.

§ 29. It has charge of all general festivities, of the Burschen-house, the fencing, and especially the gymnastic exercises, and the financial affairs of the Burschenschaft.

§ 30. It is the especial duty of the managers to fight such duels as are upon points involving the whole Burschenschaft.

Official Duties of the Individual Managers.

§ 31. In order to the proper execution of its duties, the managing board apportions offices among the nine members as follows: one shall be speaker, one secretary, one treasurer, one manager of the fencing-room, one of the Burschen-house, one steward, one umpire of the gymnastic council, and one historiographer.

§ 32. All these offices are conferred by the board for the whole half-year, except that of speaker, who is to be appointed every month; and must not be reappointed at the end of his term.

§ 33. The character of these offices makes it necessary that the secretary and treasurer should hold no other office; but all the others may be speaker at the same time.

The Speaker.

§ 34. The speaker is to call meetings of the board whenever necessary. He is bound to do the same upon the requisition of any member of the Burschenschaft.

§ 35. He is the proper person to be applied to in all matters relating to the Burschenschaft.

§ 36. At sessions of the board he is to preserve quiet and good order, and may, for that purpose, take away the privilege of voting. In all the business of that body he has the precedence, and the first vote.

§ 37. The speaker is to call meetings of the assembly of the Burschenschaft. He opens and closes them, maintains quiet and order in them, and is to take the lead in the business.

§ 38. If he is prevented from performing his duties, his last predecessor is to supply his place; and, in case of his failure, a person chosen *pro tempore.*

The Secretary.

§ 39. The secretary is to record, at sessions of the managing board, and of the assembly of the Burschenschaft, a proper account of the proceedings.

§ 40. He has charge of the archives of the Burschenschaft, and is to keep all their papers in order.

§ 41. He is to enter all new laws in the constitution, and to note, also, the repeal or alteration of old ones.

§ 42. He is to inform applicants for joining the Burschenschaft of the established mode of proceeding.

§ 43. He has charge of forwarding all letters, and authenticates all documents issued by the managing board.

§ 44. In the absence of the secretary, the historiographer is to supply his place.

The Treasurer.

§ 45. The treasurer has the management of all the finances of the Burschenschaft, and the care of all its housekeeping arrangements.

§ 46. The treasury of the Burschenschaft is in his charge.

§ 47. He is to render a quarterly account of his official proceedings to the committee, together with the necessary vouchers.

§ 48. In his absence, the steward is to take his place.

The Manager of the Fencing-room.

§ 49. He is to supervise the fencing exercises of the members, and to keep order in the fencing-room.

§ 50. He is, half-yearly, to lay before the managing board, an order of fencing exercises, and must keep a list of fighters.

§ 51. He is to have charge of, and keep in good order, all weapons, standards, defensive apparatus, and all other such property of the Burschenschaft.

§ 52. He is to select all witnesses for the Burschenschaft at duels.

The Manager of the Burschen-house.

§ 53. He has the oversight of the Burschen-house; and, accordingly, all complaints, by and against the landlord there, are to be brought to him.

§ 54. He is to make the necessary arrangements in the assembly-hall for the assemblies of the Burschenschaft.

§ 55. He is to adjust the minor details of the Commerces, and all other festivals, after consulting, previously, with the managing board respecting them.

§ 56. At the beginning of every half-year he must lay before the board a plan ot arrangements for Commerces.

The Steward.

§ 57. He is to see that the duties of hospitality, on the part of the Burschenschaft, toward Burschen from abroad are fulfilled, and has charge of their entertainment. For this purpose he is to possess a list of the dwellings of all the members of the Burschenschaft.

§ 58. He has the care of any Burschen who are ill.

The Umpire of the Gymnastic Council.

§ 59. He is to attend at such meetings of the council as may take place.

The Historiographer.

§ 60. He is to keep the journal of the Burschenschaft, and to have the history of it written up for presentation at the general assembly.

§ 61. At every election of speaker, he is to announce it to the managing board.

The Candidates.

§ 62. The candidates for the managership must attend the sessions of the board, and have an advisory vote therein. But if acting members are absent, they are to take their places, and to cast deciding votes.

§ 63. They are, also, to assist the managers in the performance of their duties, by all proper means.

Meeting of Managers and Course of Business.

§ 64 a. The sessions of the board are of two kinds, viz.:

1. Those in which accusations are made against individuals, and the trials thence arising are had.

2. Those in which discussions and decisions are had upon the various matters entered upon the business-book of that session, as far as they need no further investigation; and generally, upon all other matters affecting the Burschenschaft.

§ 64 b. The penalties inflicted are to be executed, partly in private meetings of the managing board, and partly in public ones.

§ 65. Assemblies of the first kind are to be held at the speaker's room, or at some other suitable place, to be fixed by him.

§ 66. These assemblies are to consist of the speaker, secretary, and two other managers, who shall attend in regular order.

§ 67. Besides the managers, no one is to be present, except such as are to bring accusations, or to be tried; and the latter only till their business is settled.

§ 68. Except these assemblies of the managers, all sessions of the managers are public: that is, all members of the Burschenschaft may attend them, being silent.

§ 69. The managers are to hold a public meeting, usually, every week, at a fixed time; when practicable, at the Burschen-house, at which they shall endeavor to transact any business coming up. In urgent cases, extraordinary sessions may take place, which are to be notified by handbills, and to which the speaker shall summon the managers.

§ 70. Any one not attending a meeting, unless he have a sufficient excuse, of which the board is to be the judge, and which must be previously communicated to the speaker, either orally or by writing, must pay a fine of one reichsthaler to the treasury, and loses his vote at that meeting.

§ 71. If a member, without a sufficient excuse, comes a quarter of an hour after the appointed time, he is to pay eight groschen; if half an hour, sixteen groschen.

§ 72. After the expiration of a quarter of an hour the speaker is to proceed to business.

§ 73. During the meeting the speaker must have the laws lying before him, in order, in doubtful cases, to be able to refer to them.

§ 74. The speaker has the precedence, and conducts the business. In voting, he votes first, and then calls upon the other managers, in succession. He, only, is authorized to stop the voting, and to recall attention to the question under discussion.

§ 75. In public meetings, the following order of business is usually to be observed: First, the managers take up the business-book of the committee; then the trial book; and then only, other oral or written business may be attended to.

§ 76. After the managers have ended their deliberations, the speaker is to inquire of the audience whether any of them has any thing to offer. Until that time they must all preserve silence; and for the decision of each matter, some one must furnish new facts, not before considered, permission to state which must be given by the speaker.

§ 77. At the end of the meeting, the secretary must read over the proceedings.

§ 78. The decision of the managing board, in all matters, is made by a majority vote.

§ 79. A public sitting can only be held with nine members present. If nine managers are not present, those who are may, in very urgent cases, fill up their number.

§ 80. At the first session of the new board, in every half-year, when the offices are apportioned, the duties of the board must be read over from the constitution.

§ 81. In the decision of cases, witnesses, documents, and the word of honor shall be testimony. The witnesses must be two Burschen in good standing, and must be able to authenticate their testimony by their word of honor. In cases, however, where other testimony is wanting, Philisters who are known to the board to have such correct sentiments on the subject of honor as to be competent to give their word of honor upon any matter, may be admitted to testify.

§ 82. No manager may give a decision upon any affair which is his own, or in which he is a witness. The same rule is to be observed in decisions by the committee or by the Burschenschaft.

§ 83. No manager may, in the performance of his duty, use insulting expressions; and this is the rule for all authorities.

The Committee.

§ 84. The committee shall consist of twenty-one acting members, and seven candidates for membership, who are to be chosen half-yearly, by the Burschenschaft, for a half-year.

§ 85. The doings of the committee have a twofold relation.

§ 86. As a whole, it is, as a supervising authority, to observe that the managing board acts in conformity to the law, and not beyond its authority.

§ 87. Immediately upon observing any irregularity of this kind, it is its right, and its duty, to advise the board of the same, and if the latter does not act accordingly, to bring the matter before the Burschenschaft.

§ 88. The committee is also to review all decisions in cases not clearly and definitely determined by the law, and to approve or reject the decision of the board upon the same.

§ 89. In order that the committee may be able to exercise its supervisory and approving power, the business-book of the managing board must be laid before it every week, with all the papers relating to it. It must also examine all letters of the managing board, before they are dispatched. It is, also, after the board, to decide whether the same shall be laid before the Burschenschaft for approval or not.

§ 90. The individual members of the committee are at the head of the sections of the Burschenschaft.

Apportionment of the Offices.

§ 91. The members of the committee shall choose, from their own number, by a major vote, a speaker and a secretary, the latter for a half-year, and the former, who is not re-eligible at the end of his term, for one month.

§ 92. The speaker is to maintain quiet and order in the meetings of the committee, and to conduct their deliberations.

§ 93. The secretary is to have charge, in their meetings, of the business book.

§ 94. In the absence of the speaker, his last predecessor, or a substitute chosen for the occasion, shall supply his place.

§ 95. The committee shall usually appoint to the headship of twenty sections of the Burschenschaft, the remaining nineteen members of the committee and the first candidate. The sections are to be chosen for these by lot.

§ 96. The candidates have advisory votes in the meetings of the committee. If members are absent, they take their places, and have deciding votes.

Meetings of the Committee, and their Business.

§ 97. The meetings of the committee are public. The audience must here, also, be silent, until the speaker, at the conclusion of the business, shall give permission to some one.

§ 98. The committee shall meet weekly, at some fixed time (if possible at the Burschen-house), to dispose of current business. In urgent cases, special meetings may be called, which shall be notified by public handbills, and to which the speaker shall summon the members.

§ 99. Every committee-man absent from a meeting, without a sufficient excuse, which shall be previously given to the speaker, either in words or in writing, and of which the committee shall judge, shall pay a fine of one reichsthaler to the treasury. Any one a quarter of an hour late shall pay eight groschen; and if half an hour, sixteen groschen.

§ 100. After a quarter of an hour, the speaker shall commence the business, and shall conduct it.

§ 101. During the meeting, the speaker must have the constitution before him.

§ 102. In voting, the speaker shall give the first vote, and shall then call upon the secretary and the rest of the members in order. He, only, has the right to interrupt the voting, and call attention to the question under discussion.

§ 103. At the end of the business, the speaker is to read over the proceedings.

§ 104. Decisions shall be by a major vote.

§ 105. In matters relating to the individual sections, the secretary shall give to the manager of the section copies of the proceedings of the board and the committee, and of all other documents relative to them.

§ 106. At meetings of the committee, the secretary is to collect the results of votes in the sections, and to enter them in a book kept for the purpose, in order to hand them over to the managing board.

The whole Burschenschaft as a Voting Body.

§ 107. The whole Burschenschaft decides upon cases to which the authority intrusted to the managing board does not extend. It possesses, also, exclusively, the law-making and ultimate judicial power; and appoints its own officers, by electing them.

§ 108 a. New laws, and alterations and repeals of old ones, are examined and discussed by it, and decided upon by voting. Such decision is, however, only valid when two thirds of the number of votes are in its favor, such two thirds to be a majority of the whole number of voters. For instance, if there are 300 members entitled to vote, if all these vote, 200 are necessary to adopt the law; but, if a less number vote, then two thirds of their votes are requisite to adopt the law; but a majority of all the voters, that is, in this case not less than 151, is necessary.

§ 108 b. In other cases, where no law is to be determined upon, the Burschenschaft decides by a majority of those actually voting; but two thirds of all the voters must vote in all cases except those in which a majority of all capable of voting is concerned.

§ 109. In every case where the managing board and the committee differ, the decision is left to the Burschenschaft.

§ 110. Any member may appeal to the Burschenschaft against any decision of the managing board which he thinks unjust, even if approved by the committee. But he must previously lay the reasons of his opinion before the board and committee, in writing; and can not bring the matter before the Burschenschaft until such reasons are rejected. All complaints for violation of duty by the managing board or committee, either by one of them against the other, or by individual members, are also to be brought before the Burschenschaft.

§ 111. The managing board must lay all important letters before the Burschenschaft before sending them. If one voice is given against them, upon inquiry, the Burschenschaft must decide on sending them by a vote.

§ 112. All other cases, not including the introduction of a new law nor the repeal of an old one, whose decision does not belong to the managing board, or which the latter, though authorized to act on them, considers of sufficient importance to be decided by the Burschenschaft, must also be brought before that body and decided by it.

§ 113. All special taxes must be consented to by the Burschenschaft.

§ 114. The Burschenschaft must also authorize the institution of special festivities.

§ 115. Election of managing board and committee, as well as of all important officers appointed temporarily, must be made by the Burschenschaft. Those not present lose their votes; and for such elections no fixed number of voters can be set. The accounts of such special officers are also to be submitted to the Burschenschaft.

§ 116. The Burschenschaft may act either through assemblies of its separate sections, or through general assemblies.

Sections of the Burschenschaft.

§ 117. The whole Burschenschaft is to be divided into twenty-one sections, which are to consult and vote upon propositions to be laid before the whole body for decision. It should here be remarked, that in such decision, it is not the votes of the sections, but those of the individual members which are counted.

§ 118. The managing board constitutes one of these sections, and the other twenty are to be formed from the other members of the Burschenschaft, as follows:

§ 119. At the beginning of each half-year, four managers, to be designated by the board, shall divide the members into four groups, according to their standing; of Candidates, Old Burschen, Young Burschen, Foxes. Each of these four groups they are to divide, by lot, into twenty sections; so that an equal number of each standing shall be in each.

§ 120. If new members are admitted into the Burschenschaft during the year, they shall be, in like manner, apportioned to the sections by the secretary of the committee.

§ 121. Each of these twenty sections shall, by lot, select a committee-man as manager, who shall preside over its meetings, and maintain order and quiet therein.

§ 122. Each section shall select, from among its own number, a secretary, who shall have charge of the business-book at meetings, shall record votes, read over the proceedings at the close of each meeting, and subscribe them, after the speaker.

§ 123. In the absence of the speaker, the secretary shall take his place, the papers to be delivered to him by the former.

§ 124. The speaker must have the constitution before him during the sessions, in order to refer to them in doubtful cases, and especially in order to assist individuals in the knowledge of it.

§ 125. The meetings of the sections shall be held as often as is necessary. The manager shall call together the members of it by public handbills.

§ 126. Any one absent without having presented to the manager a sufficient excuse, to be judged of by him, shall pay a fine of eight groschen; and any one a quarter of an hour or more late, shall pay four groschen.

§ 127. No meeting shall be valid where there are not present two thirds of the members of the section.

§ 128. At the first meeting of the section, the portion of the constitution relative to it must be read.

Meetings of the whole Burschenschaft.

§ 129. The meetings of the Burschenschaft are for the following purposes:

1. To inform it, through its representatives, of whatever occurrences are of importance to it.
2. To submit motions to it, respecting laws or other matters.
3. To bring complaints for violations of duty by the managing board or committee.
4. To make appointments and offer complaints.
5. To hold consultations.
6. To vote upon proper matters.
7. To elect officers.
8. To choose new members.

§ 130. The secretaries of the managing board and committee must read, in these meetings, the proceedings of those bodies, and the papers connected with them.

§ 131. The first meeting in the half-year must be held within a fortnight after the conclusion of the lectures. The choice of officers must be made at this and a subsequent meeting. At the first regular meeting after this, the sections relating to meetings and to taxes must be read.

§ 132. A meeting must be held, usually, every fourteen days, and special ones in urgent cases.

§ 133. The call to these meetings is to be by a public notice on the bulletin-board. Every member must, therefore, examine the bulletin-board daily, for notices respecting the Burschenschaft. These notices must, however, be put up before 9 A.M.

§ 134. Any one not attending at the time indicated by the call must pay a fine of eight groschen. Excuses must be laid before the speaker of the section, who is to judge of their sufficiency.

§ 135. In meetings, the members sit by sections, which are to be numbered by the manager, who will mark delinquents. The managing board will sit in sight of the assembly, and the committee one side of it.

§ 136. Every one will sit in the meeting with uncovered head. Smoking, and bringing in of dogs are strictly forbidden; as are, also, all conversation, and expressions of approbation or displeasure.

§ 137. For the sake of good order, it is necessary that all should remain at the meeting until the close of it. Only urgent excuses, to be given to the speaker, can form an exception.

§ 138. At the end of a quarter of an hour, after the speaker has called to order, the meeting shall be opened with a song.

§ 139. Quiet and order must be observed in the meetings. The speaker, and the managers with him, are to maintain the same.

§ 140. The speaker is to direct the order of business. At the beginning of the meeting, he is to announce the purpose of it.

§ 141. Every one is entitled to express his sentiments in the meeting, being only holden to do so in a manner respectful to the assembly.

§ 142. Any one desiring to speak must stand before the meeting, and turn toward it; and when he has spoken, return to his place.

§ 143. No one may interrupt another, and the speaker must reprove any one doing so.

§ 144. It is the right and duty of the speaker to end the discussion of a subject when he considers enough has been said upon it. But he can not forbid any one complained of from setting forth his grounds of justification, even if he considers it inexpedient, and that the subject has been sufficiently discussed.

§ 145. The speaker shall close the meeting after inquiring twice whether any one desires to speak.

§ 146. The time of the meeting shall not be unreasonably prolonged. Two, or at most, three hours shall be the rule. Urgent cases may justify exceptions.

§ 147. All persons being bound to observe a proper respect for the meeting, all insults between individuals are forbidden. Any person insulted shall bring the offense to the notice of the speaker, who shall inquire of the offender whether he intended an insult; and, if such was the case, he shall cause him to retract it, and shall administer to him a public reprimand. The same rule shall be observed in case of personalities in the meetings of the managing board or of the committee, or between the manager, as such, and the audience. And the same rules hold good in the sections.

Course of Business.

§ 148. The proceedings in all matters relating to the Burschenschaft shall be as rapid as possible, as only in that manner can active life be maintained in the Society. The following rules, as to details, shall be observed:

§ 149. All matters in which the committee must concur with the managing board shall be laid before the former in the business-book of the latter. If the committee concurs, the decision takes effect, unless an appeal is lodged to the Burschenschaft within three days after its announcement.

§ 150. If the committee does not concur, the matter is referred back to the board in the business-book of the committee. The board can then either accept the amendment of the committee, when the decision takes effect, or can adhere to its decision as first made, in which case the matter will be submitted to the next assembly of the whole Burschenschaft.

§ 151. In decisions to be made by the whole Burschenschaft, the following shall be the mode of proceeding:

§ 152 a. First, in motions for new laws or the repeal of old ones. These may be made either by individuals or by the managing board. In the former case, the motion must be laid before the managing board in writing. The board shall pass it, together with its own opinion, over to the committee, which shall also express an opinion upon it. At the next meeting of the Burschenschaft the speaker shall give notice of the decision. The secretary of the committee shall also, in this meeting, cause the section managers to enter, in their section-record, the motion, with the opinions of the board and the committee.

§ 152 b. No motion respecting a law can be laid before the whole Society, which is not put into a clear and legal form for voting on.

§ 153. The managers of the sections shall now lay the motion before their sections for consultation. These consultations, being a preparation for the general consultation, must be completed between the meeting of the Burschenschaft at which the subject was introduced and the next one. The motion will then be brought before the latter.

§ 154. The motion shall be voted upon in the sections. This voting must be finished before the next meeting of the committee, the time of which is to be announced by the speaker of the committee, in the proper general meeting. At such meeting of the committee, the secretary, to whom all the section managers must hand in their business-books, shall enter the result of the vote in a book kept for that purpose, which he shall pass over to the managing board. The secretary of the managing board shall then enter the new law, or the repeal or alteration of the old, in the constitution, and to lay it before the next general meeting, from which time it goes into effect.

§ 155. All matters coming before the Burschenschaft on appeal, whether by disagreement of the committee and managing board, or on the part of individuals, shall, in like manner, be announced in the general meeting and voted on in the sections. In these cases the voting may be without discussion; but otherwise the same proceedings are had as in the case of new laws. The result of the vote is announced, at the next general meeting, by the managing board. What is decided by the Burschenschaft takes effect from its announcement by the managing board.

§ 156. The same proceedings are to be had in all matters which, although not respecting laws, still come before the Burschenschaft for decision through the managing board.

§ 157. If one voice is given, at the call of the speaker, against the sending of letters laid before the Burschenschaft, the question shall be discussed, and decided by vote.

§ 158. A decision, by vote, in the general meeting, may be had upon all subjects not admitting of delay.

§ 159. Elections shall be conducted as follows:

§ 160. In the first meeting of the half-year, the speaker of the past half-year, or another of the managers, shall announce that a new election is to be held, and shall remind the members of the duty of choosing according to their best knowledge and convictions. Ballots, printed for the purpose, shall then be distributed to the voters, upon which they shall write, with a clear description, the names of their candidates, without subscribing their own names: that is, twelve for the managing board and twenty-eight for the committee.

§ 161. On a day immediately following, the Burschenschaft shall convene again. The letters of the alphabet shall then be distributed to fifty members, one letter to two. The speaker, to whom shall be joined a committee-man, for assistance, shall read the votes. The fifty members shall, upon their word of honor, observe strictly, how often the names beginning with their letters occur. The votes shall then be counted, and the result announced. The three out of those chosen for the managing board who shall have the fewest votes shall be the candidates; and in like manner the seven of those chosen for the committee. Votes to choose those members of the managing board who are actually chosen to the committee, shall be counted for them for the latter place.

To avoid irregularities, any one may have the ballots preserved for reference to the time of the announcement, at the next meeting of the Burschenschaft, and may inform of any such irregularities.

§ 162. In case of an equal number of votes for several candidates, the lot shall decide among them; and the same in all other elections.

§ 163. The same mode of election shall be followed in filling vacancies in the board and the committee, and at special elections.

§ 164. In all cases where delay may be injurious to the Burschenschaft, the managing board, alone, shall make the decision; but is answerable to the Burschenschaft for it.

§ 165. During vacations, there shall be formed, from any managers and committee-men remaining, a body, to consist of at least five members, and which, if managers and committee-men can not be found, shall complete its number from any members of the Burschenschaft remaining in Jena. In important cases, this body may call meetings of such members of the Burschenschaft as remain in Jena. But any decision by such meeting is provisory only, and becomes binding only by vote of the Burschenschaft.

§ 166. In all matters for the decision of which those not members of the Burschenschaft are to be called on to act together with it, the business shall be introduced by the Burschenschaft before those not members take part in it. The meetings of Burschen are to be conducted under the same forms as those of the Burschenschaft.

§ 167. When any decision has been lawfully made, it is the duty of the managing board to enforce the fullest and most punctual obedience to it.

Entrance into and Departure from the Burschenschaft.

Acceptance and Entrance.

§ 168. Every student at this place may present himself for admission into the Burschenschaft.

§ 169. The candidate must possess the following qualifications:

a. He must be a German: that is, he must speak German, and acknowledge himself a German by nation.

b. He must be a Christian.

c. He must be honorable: that is, there must be no disgrace attaching to him, either as a citizen or as a Bursch.

d. He must belong to no association whose laws or purpose conflict with those of the Burschenschaft.

e. He must have been a Bursch for at least a quarter of a year.

§ 170. Burschen wishing to enter the Burschenschaft are to apply to the secretary of the managing board, who shall record their surname and given name, place of birth, university where and time during which they studied.

§ 171. The secretary shall read the names of such candidates at the meeting of the Burschenschaft, and shall post them up at the Burschen-house. These steps are to enable any persons having objections to such candidates as are deficient in any of the above requisites, to state them to the managing board.

§ 172 a. If no such objection is made within fourteen days, the constitution shall be read to the candidates, by the secretary; and if, upon inquiry, they continue in their desire to enter the Burschenschaft (silence to be taken as an affirmative), they shall be admitted at the next meeting of the Burschenschaft.

§ 172 b. If any objection is alleged to the admission of a new member, and any disgraceful matter alleged, the Burschenschaft shall decide, by vote, upon his admission.

§ 173. The proceedings at admission shall be as follows:

After an address by the speaker, to the candidates, who shall be seated before the assembly, the secretary shall read to them, slowly and distinctly, the form of admission; and if they shall answer "Yes" to the questions therein, they shall give their word of honor to the speaker to observe the conditions of the same.

§ 174. The form of admission is as follows:

"You stand before this honorable assembly to take the joyful vow which shall admit you into our midst. I, as secretary, ask you, N. N., in the name of the Jena Burschenschaft, solemnly and publicly:

"Do you recognize the sentiment and spirit which belong to the provisions of our constitution? Do you recognize the sentiment and spirit which animate our fundamental principles, and give them power and form? Do you acknowledge yourself a German by nationality; and do you acknowledge that, without a German life—without a profound sympathy in the weal and woe of our fatherland—our Burschenschaft can not exist for its purposes? Do you declare that, in the fundamental principles of the Jena Burschenschaft you find your own principles; that you will, within and without that society, with your body and life, defend the principles and life of the Burschenschaft; and that as with the Burschenschaft, so with the German people, you will stand or fall? Then give your word of honor to the speaker."

§ 175. By giving their word of honor, the candidates become members of the Burschenschaft, and are, from that time forward, to be treated as such; and are at once to be apportioned, by the secretary of the committee, to the sections.

Dismission from the Burschenschaft.

§ 176. A member of the Burschenschaft ceases to be such:

a. By being dismissed by the Burschenschaft.

b. By himself seeking a dismission.

c. By ceasing to be a student.

§ 177. A member desirous to leave the Burschenschaft must make written application, with his reasons, to the managing board.

§ 178. The request having been granted by the managing board and the committee, and having been signified to him, he ceases to be a member.

§ 179. Any one a member of the Burschenschaft at leaving the university, remains an honorary member of it, unless himself renouncing membership, or afterward excluded for dishonorable conduct.

§ 180 a. Honorary members have all the privileges of actual members, so far as they can be enjoyed by one not a student: namely, the right of taking part in the meetings of the Burschenschaft, and of casting deliberative votes; of participating in all the festivities of the Burschenschaft, &c.; also, the right of hospitality, and other aid from the Burschenschaft, so far as they can give it. He must, however, also undertake all the responsibilities which the enjoyment of those rights implies.

§ 180 b. All those leaving Jena as members of the Burschenschaft shall be solemnly dismissed at the last meeting of the Burschenschaft. The details of the occasion shall be arranged by the managing board.

Relations of Individual Members to the Burschenschaft and to each other.

Rights and Duties.

Relation to the Burschenschaft.

§ 181. It is the duty of every member to watch over the honor and reputation of the Burschenschaft as over his own honor; and everywhere, as much as in him lies, to promote its unity and prosperity.

§ 182. Full and punctual obedience to all the laws is a fundamental principle of the Burschenschaft; for that body can only exist as a whole, and accomplish its purposes, by strict order.

§ 183. Every member unconditionally recognizes the decisions of the Burschenschaft as binding laws, whether they were opposed by debate and vote or not.

§ 184. Every one must quietly submit to whatever punishment may be inflicted upon him according to law.

§ 185. Every member must, so far as time and circumstances permit him, assist in every thing directed by the Burschenschaft as a whole.

§ 186. Every member is bound to assume every office to which he is elected, and all its rights and duties. If there are reasons not permitting him to perform the duties of the office, he must lay the evidence thereof before the managing board for examination; but during the examination he must perform the duties of the place, since his election renders this necessary.

§ 187. Every member must obey the officers of the Burschenschaft so long as they do not exceed their authority.

§ 188. Especially strict obedience is due to the decisions of the managing board and of the committee, unless an appeal is to be legally brought to the Burschenschaft.

§ 189. If any officer has exceeded his authority, and thereby done injustice to any one, information must be given to the managing board.

§ 190. Every member is bound to inform the managing board of any gross violation of the constitution or code of customs; and no performance of this duty can subject him to the charge of tale-telling.

§ 191. All members are bound not to mention publicly, that is, in the presence of Philister, any matters whose publicity might be dangerous to the Burschenschaft; for, though that body is by no means a secret society, it can not proceed entirely without some operations not public.

§ 192. Every member has, in all circumstances, the fullest right to the most powerful and active assistance from the Burschenschaft which it can afford.

Relations of the Members to each other.

§ 193. The relations of the members to each other are altogether equal; and no appearance of gradation of rank can, at any time, be allowed.

§ 194. All difference of birth is put entirely out of the account; and every member is holden to consider the rest as his brothers, seeking a common object with him.

§ 195. In order to mark the closeness of their bond of unity and brotherhood, all the members shall use, to each other, the pronoun "thou."

§ 196. For this reason every member is bound, in duels, to obtain a second and a witness from the Burschenschaft.

§ 197. The only difference to be recognized among members of the Burschenschaft is that which greater or less experience naturally occasions. Accordingly, the members do not possess deciding votes in the Burschenschaft until the second half-year of their life as students.

§ 198. No member can be chosen manager until the third half-year of his student-life, nor committee-man until the second.

§ 199. But these distinctions shall not occasion any younger member to be reckoned inferior to an older; for it is only individual excellence, not years' standing, which can be alleged in favor of members.

VIOLATION OF LAWS.—PUNISHMENTS.

§ 200. The Burschenschaft shall punish in its capacity as:

1. Upholder of the code of customs; inasmuch as it visits with a penalty every

infraction of the code, and declares the loss of honor or "disgrace" (*verruf*), pronounced by the code, to be incurred by students guilty of dishonorable practices.

§ 201. 2. An association; in which capacity it must protect itself against violations of its laws by members, and must, for that purpose exercise its judicial authority over them.

§ 202. Punishments for violations of the laws of the Burschenschaft are either fines or loss of honor.

§ 203. Fines are inflicted for unpunctuality at meetings and at the fencing-room. Details are given in their appropriate places.

§ 204 a. All fines must be paid before the first of the following month. Any one then unable to pay must fix a term of payment, upon his word of honor, which must not be more than four weeks.

§ 204 b. Every manager of a section, or of the fencing-room, is bound to collect all fines due, and is holden for them if he neglects to do so; and he must hand them over, monthly, to the treasurer.

§ 205. Punishments by loss of honor are as follows:

1. Admonition, by the speaker, for neglect of duty.

2. Reproof and censure in proportion to the fault.

a. Before the managing board, privately.

b. Before the same, publicly.

c. Before the meeting of the Burschenschaft.

§ 206. The speaker shall administer all reproofs, after they are approved by the managing board; and in the terms which he uses to characterize the fault he must use no insulting expressions; for a judicial officer can not be supposed to intend insult.

§ 207. 3. Expulsion from the Burschenschaft may take place when the conduct of a member has rendered him unworthy to remain such: that is,

a. When a member has incurred the penalty of disgrace;

b. Or when he has committed a transgression for which disgrace is not the proper punishment.

§ 208. 4. Disgrace is incurred by any member asserting any thing disrespectful to the Burschenschaft; either by insulting the whole Society, or the managing board and committee, or by opposing himself to the decisions of the Burschenschaft.

§ 209. All these punishments are either

1. Prescribed by law for fixed cases of misconduct; in which case the managing board inflicts them as prescribed; and in cases where it does not recognize an exculpation as sufficient, an appeal, as hereinbefore provided, may be brought to the Burschenschaft.

§ 210. Or,

2. No fixed cases are prescribed for their infliction. In such case the managing board, with the approval of the committee, inflicts admonition or reproof; against which an appeal lies to the Burschenschaft.

§ 211. The whole Burschenschaft must decide, by major vote, upon the expulsion of any member, at the instance of the managing board, in cases where the laws do not expressly prescribe that penalty.

Finances.—Treasury.

§ 212. The managing board has control of the finances.

§ 213. The sources of income of the treasury are three:

a. Half-yearly taxes.

b. Special assessments.

c. Fines accruing.

§ 214. The following are the regulations for levying taxes:

§ 215. Every member must pay one and a half per cent. of his income, whose amount he must state, on his word of honor, at his entrance into the Burschenschaft; but those having an annual income of less than a hundred thalers are free from all regular taxes. But all free tables and stipends must be included in the stated amount of yearly income.

§ 216. For the sake of good order, the fixed taxes must be paid half-yearly, in advance; and the last day of May for the summer term, and the last of December for the winter term, are fixed as the terms at or before which every member must pay. But as it may happen that members may be unable to pay at that time, the treasurer may fix a further term, not to exceed six weeks after the above, at which such members must give their word of honor to pay.

§ 217. Any one not paying at the fixed time, and not appointing any term of extension, shall be expelled from the Burschenschaft.

§ 218. At payment, every member shall receive a voucher from the treasurer.

§ 219. In order that no blameworthy carelessness may subject any member to the penalty of disgrace for a breach of his word of honor, this law relating to taxes shall be read in the first regular Burschen meeting of each half-year, and the speaker shall, at such time, remind the assembly of the obligations of the word of honor.

§ 220. Special taxes, when necessary, shall be laid by the managing board, and assented to by the Burschenschaft. These taxes must be paid by every member, even by those having less than a hundred thalers income. Such taxes, when small shall fall equally upon all members; but, if of importance, shall be apportioned according to income. The latest term allowed for their payment shall be fixed, on the word of honor, at fourteen days after consent by the Burschenschaft; but for taxes falling heavily on individuals, they may be permitted a further respite.

Fencing and other Exercises.

Fencing-room.

§ 221. The Burschenschaft shall have a fencing-room for its own use.

§ 222. Every member of the Burschenschaft is bound to attend at the room four times a week, on fixed days, and at fixed hours. Exceptions can only be made in favor of those in their last half-year, or those whose circumstances make it impossible, of which proof must be laid before the managing board.

§ 223. Every member has the right to require fencing practice; and every one who can fence is bound to do so.

§ 224. Every member must keep his fencing apparatus in good order, that there may be no intermission in the practicing.

§ 225. Any one injuring the fencing apparatus of another, is bound to have it, at once, put in good order again, and the possessor is not thereby to lie under the accusation even of the shadow of selfishness.

§ 226. All instruction from any third party is forbidden; and only the master shall instruct the scholars.

§ 227. At the designated hours, managers shall have charge of the fencing-room, shall keep it in order, make out lists of delinquents, and collect fines.

§ 228. Further details shall be left to the managing board, who shall determine them half-yearly, in the fencing regulations.

Gymnastics.

§ 229. The gymnasium is under the protection of the Burschenschaft. All further details and arrangements shall be made by those exercising, with reference to the exercises.

§ 230. A manager shall always sit in the council for gymnastics.

§ 231. The regulations for exercising shall be laid, by the gymnastic council, before the managing board and committee for approval. If this is withheld, they must be changed, unless the gymnastic council choose to proceed entirely without connection with the Burschenschaft. The maintenance of the regulations approved by that body, is guaranteed by it.

§ 232. In winter, the swinging exercises shall be practiced in the fencing-rooms, at hours when they will not interfere with the fencing.

Burschen-house.

§ 233. As a common Burschen-house is a principal means of closer union, harmony, and social intercourse, it is incumbent upon every member to frequent it as much as possible.

§ 234. It is the duty of the managing board to provide such a one, and to fit it up properly for the accommodation of the students.

§ 235. All festivities relative to the Burschenschaft shall be held in the Burschen-house, if there is room sufficient.

§ 236. All public meetings of the managing board, committee, and Burschenschaft shall be, if possible, held at the Burschen-house.

§ 237. Above all things, a retiring-room must be provided at the Burschen-house, and kept in good order.

§ 238. That the Burschen-house may, at all times, be in good reputation, every member pledges himself, upon his word of honor, to the regular payment of the landlord.

Public Festivities.

§ 239. Public festivities by students are either:

a. By the Burschenschaft, and therefore general; or,

b. By individuals; in which case the details of arrangements, as far as not repugnant to the Burschenschaft, are entirely left to the undertakers.

§ 240. The Burschenschaft shall arrange commerces, festive processions, funerals, &c.

§ 241. Regular commerces shall be, a Fox commerce, at the beginning of each half-year; a commerce at the change in the protectorate, and a farewell commerce at the end of the half-year. The manager of the Burschen-house may, in connection with the board, arrange as many smaller commerces as he chooses.

§ 242. Further details relative to the commerces shall be contained in the commerce regulations, which the manager shall give out half-yearly.

§ 243. Great and general festivals shall be celebrated as follows:

On the 18th of June, in memory of the founding of our Burschenschaft and of the battle of Belle Alliance; also as a memorial festival of all the fraternity of Burschenschaften; and the 18th of October, by this Burschenschaft, unless celebrated by the general meeting of all the Burschenschafts, in memory of the battle of Leipzig, and of the first union of all the German Burschen in the General German Burschenschaft.

§ 244. The Burschenschaft must order other special festivities.

§ 245. The details of such festivals shall be left to the managing board, with consent of the committee, as shall the designation of the officers of them. Managers and committeemen have a prior right to be appointed such officers.

§ 246. Every member is bound to take part in all the festivities of the Burschenschaft, as far as possible, and to observe the regulations made for order on such occasions.

VI. Answers of the German Universities to the Jena Burschenschaft.

Berlin, August 25, 1817.

Greeting:—

Dear Brothers:—We will willingly contribute, according to our ability, to the festival of October 18. Many of our number have already departed; but we shall send some deputies to the Wartburg, and shall inform all the students here, in order that any one who desires it may be present. A song will be sent as soon as possible. And so adieu.

ERLANGEN, August 23, 1817.

GREETING :—

Dear Friends :—On the 19th of August we received your most welcome invitation to the Wartburg. In regard to this festival of October 18th, we are profoundly delighted that the wish which we entertained, even before it occurred to you, is already fulfilled. We think it altogether good and judicious to have chosen the 18th of October instead of the 31st, for the time when the German Burschen from most of the German Universities are to learn to know and love each other; and the order of exercises, also, seems to us judiciously arranged, as not only providing for our own enjoyment, as Burschen, but as not neglecting the worship of God, whose blessing is the first requisite to all that is good. Your friendly invitation is right welcome to us, and several of us will have the greatest pleasure in accepting it; we only hope most earnestly that a similar one has been sent to all the Burschen of our country, in order that perhaps a larger number from among us may clearly demonstrate and comprehend the great and glorious movements now in progress on German land, and among German Burschen; of which we can certainly afford no sufficient representation.

If any one shall be found among us able to furnish a song for the festival, we will send it to you as early as possible.

In pleasure at the coming gathering.

GIESSEN, September 3, 1817.

Friends and Brothers :—Your friendly invitation to the celebration of the jubilee of the Reformation was welcome to us; and we count much upon this united festival to promote the uniting together of the various German Universities.

According to the plan proposed, all of our number who will take part in the festival, will be in Eisenach on the 17th of October.

We all find the arrangements for the festival appropriate and good; and certainly no one can fail to be impressed with its liberal and magnanimous spirit. But you will, without doubt, agree with us, that at this celebration in remembrance of so noble a deed of a free spirit, any powerfully spoken word for our fatherland and union in it, must do good. To this end we are of opinion that no one who feels himself impelled thereto, should be prevented, either by previous arrangements or any other means, from delivering his views in a public address. There will be sufficient time, after the close of the festivities to which you have invited us, which can not be better occupied.

Whether any song will be received from us, we can not inform you in advance, as it depends on certain individuals, who will care for the seasonable sending of it to you.

GÖTTINGEN, August 22, 1817.

In relation to the friendly invitation to a general festival of Burschen, on the 18th of October, at the Wartburg, we are very much pleased with it; and believe it will be universally recognized as very expedient for the Burschen of the various German Universities, an opportunity being given, to become acquainted with each other. For this purpose we shall send a number of representatives, and as many other Burschen will be present as shall be able. To that end we shall seek to make this, our resolution, known, as far as possible, to the remaining Burschen.

HEIDELBERG, September 6, 1817.

GREETING, AND A GERMAN GRASP OF THE HAND :—

Dear Friends and Brothers :—We have been so much occupied with various matters as to be unable to return an earlier answer to your welcome letter. Do not, therefore, be vexed at this somewhat late answer, as it was rendered necessary by external circumstances; and receive the assurance of our truest love and solicitude for your welfare. May heaven bless our united endeavors to form one people, filled with paternal and brotherly virtues, and whose love and harmony may make up for mutual weaknesses and faults. We reciprocate your German goodness of heart with like feelings, and hope that by means of those who shall follow our example, this divine union will be destroyed by no dissension.

The invitation to Eisenach, for October 18th, has exceedingly pleased us. This appropriate and lofty festival, the birthday of faith and of freedom, will be the day of the foundation of love for us. It is unfortunate that so many of our much-beloved brethren have departed in various directions; some home, and some to other universities. This will deprive us of many ornaments, and you of the pleasure of knowing them. But, of those who remain, a part will come without fail; who are delighted, in advance, with this glorious festival, and with the personal brotherhood of those of congenial minds.

In case any songs should be composed by us, we will forward them to you.

LEIPZIG, August 30, 1817.

FRIENDLY GREETING:—

Dear Brothers:—You here receive the required answer to your friendly letter of the 11th of this month, in which you advise us of your intention to celebrate, in a festive manner, the jubilee of the Reformation, in connection with the festival of the battle of Leipzig, on the 18th of October, at the Wartburg, near Eisenach, and invite us, in a friendly manner, to this celebration. The worthy celebration of a time in many respects so memorable and inspiring to every German, and the proposed festive assembly therefor, of so many German Burschen, has our entire approbation, and we thankfully accept your invitation. Only, we are grieved that we can not answer it as numerously as we should have wished, because the 18th of October comes in our vacation, when nearly all of our students have left Leipzig, most of them having gone home, perhaps to the furthest province of Saxony. We have, therefore, in a general assembly of 22d August, determined, "to send a deputation of from four to six Burschen to Eisenach on the 18th of October of this year, in the name of the Leipzig Burschen, to take part in the gathering of the Burschen of all the German Universities, who are to assemble there to celebrate the jubilee of the Reformation and the anniversary of the battle of Leipzig."

Our deputies, and the other Leipzig students who are to take part in the celebration will, agreeably to your wish, be in Eisenach on the 17th of October. We will also provide that a song appropriate to the day shall be composed and sent in good season.

Hoping that we have thus satisfied your wishes, we bid you farewell.

MARBURG, September 2, 1817.

TO ALL OUR BROTHERS AND FRIENDS AT JENA, A FRIENDLY GREETING:—

Even before we received your invitation, several of our Burschen had determined to celebrate the 18th of October, the day of so many new institutions, at the memorable Wartburg. For this reason we have, with the more pleasure, accepted your invitation, and have determined, in any case, to send some deputies (whom, however, the favorable opinion of such a Burschen festival will cause to be attended by several companions), to this gathering of the German Burschen. We hope that the spirit of German patriotism and freedom will prevail, and, treading down all party spirit, will insure us a prosperous issue.

We wish you all good fortune.

ROSTOCK, September 2, 1817.

SCHMOLLIS, GENTLEMEN:—

We have received your friendly letter of August 11th, and hasten to send you our answer.

VI. "Dr. Bahrdt with the Iron Forehead; or, the German Union against Zimmermann."

(From the Universal German Library, vol. 112, part 1, p. 213, &c.)

"Of the work itself we shall say nothing. All Germany is agreed that it was a shameful blemish upon German literature, and surpassed every thing that could be imagined for contemptibleness and malignant defamation. The most completely shameful and entirely unpardonable invention of all, was placing the name of Herr Von Knigge upon the title-page of this lampoon as its author. Any one capable of permitting himself this base contrivance must have destroyed all his own appreciation of honesty. Not only to print the most outrageous calumnies, the most vulgar insults, but to publish the name of an innocent man as author! This was going very far!"

"The work "*Bahrdt with the Iron Forehead*," excited, everywhere, the greatest displeasure. So much susceptibility to honor and honesty was left in Germany, that such a vulgar attack upon respectable people, must, of necessity, be everywhere abhorred. This composition was, moreover, of such an atrocious nature that curiosity was excited as to where it could have originated. Still, the author would, perhaps, not have become known, and this vile production would have sunk still sooner into the profound oblivion where all such contemptible and vulgar writings soon sink, had not a remarkable judicial investigation (by the Hanoverian Chancery of Justice), been set on foot to discover the author.*

"This commission, little by little, found out that the lampoon was printed at Graiz, in Voigtland. This, of course, led to tracing the person from whom the publisher received the manuscript. At this point Von Kotzebue, to conceal himself, had recourse to a means of protection which no man could have permitted himself to use, unless he had already issued so shameful a lampoon upon so many reputable persons. That is, he undertook to help himself out with a threefold false testimony. Counselor Schultz, of Mietau, having been in Weimar at the same time with Von Kotzebue, at the request of the latter, engaged the engraving of the vignette, which was, in itself, good enough, with the copperplate engraver Lips, and caused his secretary to transcribe the MS. He gives his word that he received it, and returned it, together with the copy, unread; a statement which the circumstances render probable. A traveler accidentally saw a copy of the engraving in the possession of Herr Lips, and this gentleman, who was wholly innocent in the matter, and who knew nothing of the purpose of the vignette, mentioned, incidentally, by whom it had been put into his hands. This came to the knowledge of Kotzebue, who feared a judicial summons to Mietau, which he afterward did, in fact, receive. He therefore wrote in great trouble, to Herr Councilor Schultz, requesting him, if he should be called upon to testify, not to tell the truth, but to state that he had received his commission from Herr Gauger, a bookseller in Dorpat. He added the assurance that he would furnish him an ante-dated letter from this Herr Gauger, in which the affair should be put into his hands accordingly, and this letter he was to lay before the court as testimony. This, therefore, constituted a double false witness. But not content with this, he prevailed upon a man in Reval (by means best known to himself), by the name of Schlegel, to state that he was the author of "*Bahrdt with the Iron Forehead*," and to authenticate this falsehood to be the truth by declaring it before an imperial notary public. This false explanation is printed in No. 14 of the work, and has appended the act of the imperial notary before whom Schlegel declared this falsehood true."

* This was caused by the Hanoverian Klockenbring, who had been vilely attacked in the work. This writer, "who had been a deserving servant to the Hanoverian government, and a useful author, was so much affected by the attack as to fall into a dangerous mental condition. 'Woe to the author,' says the writer in the *Universal German Library*, 'who has upon his conscience such consequences from his writings.'"

"But the affair did not take the turn which Von Kotzebue intended. In spite of the notarial instrument no one was deceived, for a moment, into thinking Schlegel the author of the pasquinade. It was, indeed, stated in the Jena *Gazette of Literature* (Schlegel had studied at Jena), that he was not capable of producing the work. Councilor Schultz had also already indignantly refused the request that he would bear false witness. To prove his intention, he sent the original letter, in which Von Kotzebue had asked him to be guilty of this crime, to a friend, and related, in a letter to him, the true course of the affair from the beginning. He requested this friend to permit any person to whom these letters could be interesting, to read them.

"But Kotzebue found that all these base expedients would not avail him, and he finally decided, on the 24th of December, 1791, to declare, publicly, in the newspapers, that he was the author of the scandalous production."

VII. Substance of the Tubingen "Statutes for the Formation of a Students' Committee."*

"These statutes recognize order, quiet, and good morals, as properly required of the students, especially by means of voluntary co-operation on their own part, and in particular on the part of such of their number as have the confidence of all. The substantial part of them is as follows:

"The committee consists of fifteen members, chosen freely from the whole body of students. Its duties are, to communicate the wishes of the students to the academical authorities, and to consult with them as to the practicability and mode of accomplishing them. In case of any injury to any student, as such, they are to apply to the authorities for assistance. If the disciplinary authorities have occasion to give warnings to the students, it reports them to the committee, that it also may give a warning. In case of severer punishments, also, the fact is to be communicated to the committee, that they may state any grounds of mitigation. A later ordinance, of December 21, provides that, on occasions of investigations, where punishment is to be inflicted, the committee of students is to be advised, not of the first information received, but of the result of the investigation; that it may allege any matters in mitigation.

"The committee is also entitled to lay before the university authorities any proposals from the acceptance of which it may anticipate improved results from the university course. It is under the protection of the university authorities in the performance of its duties, and any injuries to a member of it are to be punished with double severity.

"Every member of the committee binds himself to set a good example of obedience of the laws, and to labor to promote the improvement of his associates in morals and honor. The committee is bound to assist in repairing breaches of the public peace; and in the absence of the authorities, to uphold, to the best of its ability, the means used to restore order. It is to use its power to compose enmities between students, and, as far as possible, to oppose every attempt of one student to insult another, or unlawfully to vindicate himself. Every member is also bound to warn his fellow-students against any association of a secret character, or avoiding publicity, and to use his influence to prevent any of them from joining with any such association. If any evident disturbers of peace among the students make their appearance, or persons whose actions render them unworthy the name of students, the committee is bound, after trying the virtue of admonitions, to inform the academical authorities of them."

---

* Klupfel, p. 318.

VIII. Extract from an Address by Wolfgang Heyder, Professor at Jena, delivered in the year 1607.

Such a vicious student prays not at all to God, and in accordance with such recklessness, when reproved by any one, even mildly, says, "The hogs, although they neither fear God nor call upon him, yet grow fat on their food in the sty."

He goes unwillingly past a church, not to mention his entering it. He is as rare a bird in the church as a black swan in the African forests. Of preachers he says, "They are passionate, morose, eccentric fellows, whose great enjoyment consists in attacking, reproving, and abusing others; damning them in the pulpit, and sending them to hell. They are always harping on the same string; singing the same old song that everybody has heard a thousand times and more."

He neither has at hand the Holy Scriptures, in which the Son of God has commanded us to search, nor does he think it necessary to read in them, unless when he has been in some quarrel, and been so pounded that he can scarcely breathe, and begins to despair of his life. Then he borrows a Bible from his neighbor, and tries a few verses, just as they occur to his stupid head, but with discomfort, for he gapes with idleness, and scratches his head with the difficulty of reading. But as soon as the barber tells his client to be of good hope, the sick man throws away that old book, and at once resumes his former course.

The base desires which find nourishment in such a life, completely destroy all susceptibility to honor, all love of virtue, and all pleasure in study; and, indeed, extirpate their very seeds. He thinks not of wisdom, nor of ability, nor of honorable studies, nor of the welfare of church or state; but he is absorbed with contemptible tricks, sloth, idleness, drinking, harlotry, fighting, wounds, murder.

If you happen to enter his room, I ask you what will you find for furniture; what will you find? In the first place, no books—for what has such a hot, or frantic soldierly fellow to do with cold and spiritless studying?—or perhaps a few carelessly thrown away under seats or in corners, defiled with dust, eaten by moths, almost destroyed by mice.

If you look up and down, you will see hanging on the wall a few swords and daggers, of which most would not bring three *heller* when the time comes to pay the Rector's bills. And there are are a few guns, which he has from time to time not been ashamed to steal from the suburbs, between some shingled house and the barn full of grain. You will see armor, or steel gloves, with which our giant appears, not unarmed, at the fighting-ground; and doublets, wadded and well-filled in with cotton, tow, hair, or whalebone, so that if a quarrel happens they will stand a sword-thrust.

You will see a few bowls and many glasses awaiting new guests. You will see cards, draught-board, dice, and other means of destroying money and youth.

He attends the public course either not at all, or very late; and hears no lectures, unless he gets caught in the audience, like a hound in a bath.

The lazy marmot either sleeps until noon, or sits at a vulgar drinking debauch, preparing himself for the skirmishing of the night, so that men may see how boldly and actively he will act.

When both streets and chambers are still, and both men have gone to rest and the birds have left off singing in the boughs, and the beasts are sleeping in their dens, then he starts up, with great bangs on posts and doors, and breaks forth from where he had been abiding, armed and surrounded by his followers. Then you have to hear such a frantic horror and tragedy; such a roaring, groaning, hallooing, shrieking, raging, knocking, and throwing of stones, and many more such actions, as, if one of the one-eyed giants had done them, would have brought all Sicily together, and have banished the rioter to eternal misery.

Where one lives whom he thinks his enemy, God preserve us! how many devil's and fool's actions does he perform before his door! how does he kick the door with his feet! how does he throw stones at the window!

He must needs assault the most blameless people, against whom not Momus himself could allege any thing, with such lies, slanders, abuses, and shameful stories, that, although they are all false and pure inventions, something will always be believed, and suspicious minds will be kept uneasy.

When he meets either other students going home, or peaceful citizens, he falls upon them like a murderer or open highwayman, with bare and drawn sword, and while the swearer utters an unimaginable number of oaths, he cuts and thrusts at them, strikes them, wounds them, knocks them down, stamps on them, strangles them, snorts, rages, and behaves exactly like a devil sent out of hell in human shape; and sometimes he injures his adversary, and sometimes carries off his booty with wrath and fury. Or, if the time and place will not endure this, and others will not suffer him to shed swiftly men's blood, and wreak his anger upon them, the ambitious bully requires him with whom he desires to fight to appear at a future day, and requires it with frightful cursings and maledictions. The hour is fixed, and the conditions stipulated, exactly as if he were about to take the field, and lay out an encampment for an army.

And if the summoned party is not prompt in attendance, he must pass for the greatest rascal of all the rascals that ever lived or will live; and probably these announcements are made: "If you are an honorable fellow, meet me early to-morrow morning; if you are of honorable birth, fight me; if you are better than a gallows-thief, set to with me."

When the battle is ended, the university officer comes up and summons our centaurian brawler and man-eater before the Rector. When he appears before him, our cut-and-thruster firstly begins stoutly to deny every thing he did, and for which he is accused and summoned, with a hardy impudence truly wonderful. But when he is convicted, he seeks other devices to escape; and swears that may the devil fetch him if he had not drank so much that he had quite lost his senses, and could neither hear nor see; and that he has forgotten all the things he did or said, and can only very indistinctly remember any thing at all about them.

But all the while that he will not know any thing of the matter, he has every circumstance of it in his mind, and can plead whatever may best serve to excuse his share in the transaction, as skillfully as if Simonides had given him a most masterly training in the art of memory. When the decision is declared, and our young leader must either pack off out of the place, like a tormenting devil whose very shadow harms good people, or must crawl into prison, then you will see what an impassioned advocate he is about his honor. His heroicals surpass all the Stoics and the philosophers, the Aristideses, Rutiliuses, and Catos, and he harangues about his honor with the most brazen impudence.

He requests that his punishment may be remitted; he has just come out for the first time, after being sick; his family will be branded with a disgrace which can never be wiped out. In his country those who have been imprisoned are reckoned infamous; he must have some communication with his friends before undergoing his penalty; and, moreover, there is so much cold and stench in the prison that he cannot be placed there without losing his health, which no money will buy him back.

But when he absolutely must go in, who can tell how horribly he rages about it, and how pitifully our soaker laments! He says he was always a pious fellow, but a little trifle uneasy after drinking. The Rector's official term will come to an end soon, and when he gets out he shall have some new windows, and an everlasting hatred.

They contract mighty debts for board and lodging, which they are never able to pay. But when pay-day comes, and they are called on for the debt, and have to write home, they deceive their parents or guardians about it.

They write, first of all, for their board-money, but with large additions. After it they put down, but with great reluctance and economy, of course, what they have squandered on feast-days, birth-days, and entertainments. After these come the falsest things: "Our landlord married a wife at New Year's, and we had to give her, beyond all measure, a Hungarian ducat for a gift for good fortune; seven *groschen* to each child (there are five), and an *orts-thaler* to each of the servant-girls. And in like manner it was necessary to spend money on each fair-day, of which there are two a year here. And I studied myself into a fever by sitting up late nights, and had to lie abed with it six whole weeks. This cost me eight *thalers* to the apothecary, four to the doctor, three to the barber, and the sixth of one to the boy who brought the medicine and gave it to me.

"I have attended various extra lectures, with great benefit, and paid the instructor who read them, and who values his knowledge highly, six *gulden*, which he refused at first, and wanted one more. I have bought the best and handsomest books, for I could get along as well without them as I could fly without wings. And I owe the bookseller twelve ducats, which I must pay as soon as possible. I have some clothes, to be sure, but my boy has just run away, and stole both my cloaks, my hat, and my purse, with what money I had left, so that I must have some more clothes, which are not to be had for nothing." With such impositions as these they fool their parents and guardians, and also make the insulting charge of avarice against men to whom they have never paid so much as a pear-stem.

Wherever our young gentleman goes, he gives out that he is anxious to marry. He represents himself as an only son, and having very wealthy parents. If his suit prospers, he is going to take his bride to the Fortunate Islands.

He borrows money of his acquaintance, and gets goods on credit at the shops, and with these he befools and entices the poor girl, who most gladly believes what she wishes, and sometimes grants favors which she ought not. But very soon after that, when his desire is satisfied, he pretends an occasion to be angry, and transfers his love to some one else.

His clothes, though not of costly material, are of a foolish and ridiculous pattern. He is first to take up a new fashion, and first to throw it away again, when it is a little out of date.

With hair like a crow's head, and his dog's face scarred up, he is far worse than Virgil's vagabond, Achæmenides.

There is no noble aspiration in him, nor any good habit. He wallows in the filth of his wickedness. His course of villanies hardens him until he loses all sense of shame, and he pursues his evil ways with no reminder from his conscience.

He holds all laws and restraints of authority not worth a snap, and is forsworn and reckless to God—scarcely believing that He exists and governs the world by His wisdom.

After thus passing his university course in neglect of study, debauchery, and folly, he is summoned home, though unwilling; unless, as commonly happens, he is for his heroic virtues cut off like a pestilential member, and rejected from the number of students. He leaves, almost always, yellow, lean, sunken-eyed, lame, toothless, marked all over with scars and bruises. Such are the rewards of his honorable and angelic life.

When he gets to his native place, he is in no great hurry to see the faces of his parents and friends. He turns from a lion to a hare; and in his anguish hides in dark corners, seeks intercessors in his mother, sisters, brothers-in-law, and relatives, and by means of their prayers and entreaties, obtains leave, with great difficulty, to crawl, with what of himself he has not gorged and guzzled away at the university, into his father's house, and to snore and lie hid there. It is months before he has courage to appear on the public streets; the reason, because he will be spit upon and jeered at by every soul he meets. After this he will find himself obliged to follow a different course of life.

IX. Synonyms of Beanus.

Schöttgen says: The Pennals, or young students, have many other names, which I must give in order, in several classes. Some they receive on account of their youth, and as new students, as for example:

1. *Quasimodogeniti*—which excellent expression, used by the Holy Ghost itself, men have shamefully abused.
2. *Neovisti*—perhaps from *neophytus*, a tyro, but with a coarse terminal change.
3. *Crowbills*—as if, like young crows, or other birds, they were yet yellow about the bill.
4. *Housecocks.*
5. *Heifer-calves.*
6. *Sucklings*—as having only just left home, where they had been nursing infants.
7. *Bacchants*—a name, as is well known, applied to all not regularly deposed.
8. *Innocentes*—as not having got far out into the world. By an abuse of theological terms, it was also said that they were *in statu innocentiæ.*
9. *Half-papen*—a name given them at Rostock, meaning half-students. All students were anciently termed *papen*, but at present this term has become one of abuse, which the vulgar are accustomed to apply to students.
10. *Beani*—applied to those not deposed.
11. *Shovers*—because they pretend to be students too soon, and try not to serve out all their Pennal year.
12. *Tapeworms*—for it was pretended that they were full of all manner of uncleanness inside, and so they were given, or, rather, forced to take all sorts of things.
13. *Imperfecti*—because they are not declared free from their obligations; as opposed to the *Absoluti.*
14. *House-pennals; house-goblins; family-foxes* (*stammfeix**)—these names are given to such as are afraid of Pennalism, and stay long at home before going to the university.

X. Meyfart's Aretinus.†

Meyfart (p. 126) relates how the student Aretinus, after leaving the gymnasium, went to the university.

"He hastens to Athens, arrives there, and almost before he has set his foot within the gate, there meets him that man-stealer, that gallows-bird, and destined to be broken on the wheel Kunz Sawrüssel,‡ a monstrous abortion, who ought to be driven from the earth and from the neighborhood of reasoning creatures.

"This beast, I say, recognized Aretinus, as he had formerly attended the preparatory schools with him; and quickly he overclouds his wolfish visage with gloomy wrinkles, pricks up his ass's ears like Egyptian grave-stones, stretches his heavy chops as many ells wide as an elephant, begins to stare out of his eyes like a lion and to make tiger-claws of his hands, mutters a few words between his dog's teeth, curses angrily. He does not insult nor approach the young man, however, but runs after some of his like, and finds, by great misfortune, a filthy vagabond and lewd talker, the vilest of all two or four footed beasts, the most cursed and stinking boar of the mud. He finds him in a public drinking-house, having crammed his foul paunch, and not only wet himself with beer but bathed himself in it; and

---

* In the letter quoted at p. 46, of Duke Albrecht of Saxony to the University of Jena, in 1624, *Feux* is used as a synonym of Pennal. Is *Feux* our present Fox? Compare an article entitled "How comes *Reineke Fuchs* into the universities?" in the Academical Monthly, for August and September, 1853, especially p. 407.

† On Pennalism and Deposition, see "The Academical Life of the Seventeenth Century," by Dr. A. Tholuck, pp. 200 and 279.

‡ *Sawrüssel*, i. e., Hog-snout.

stirred himself up, not to foolishness, but to raging and raving madness. This fellow Sawrüssel informs that a young gentleman has arrived, and those of the place must consider what is to be done. Sawrüssel has scarcely addressed himself to this traitorous abyss (who ought to be decorated with a rope), when behold, all the caves of hell open, and the devils incarnate pour forth from their throats nothing but fearful blasphemies against God, terrific revilings of His name, shameful curses upon the holy sacraments, so that I doubt whether even Rabshakeh the Assyrian had attained to more than a shadow of their recklessness.

"They hold a consultation, and the resolution is adopted that the young gentleman (those who enact it being very old gentlemen, not having the yellow off their bills yet, or their spittle wiped off) must be bravely stirred up, abused, and subjected to tribulation. What further happens? The time comes when these beasts lie down to rest, and the watchman has proclaimed the tenth hour of the night. But now these fellows get up—Sawrüssel, Vollfrass, Schling-Kühe, Gassen-Eule, Geil-Spatz,*—and put their swords at their sides, in order to be able to enforce their designs, and get themselves to Aretinus' lodging. There they neigh like horses, roar like lions, bleat like calves, bellow like cows, grunt like hogs, baa like sheep, hop about like magpies, woodpeckers, and apes; a worse crew than the desert goblins of the wastes of Babylonia, of which the prophet speaks; more freakish than the Zihim and Ohim, stranger than ostriches, more poisonous than dragons.

"Meanwhile these mud-birds asperse the name of Aretinus, break in his windows, and spit out thousands of shameful lies about his honored parents.

"After this they enter Aretinus' room, uninvited and unwelcomed, sit down, snort and bluster like executioners who come into the torture-chamber and see the prisoners, ask for nothing, order every thing, and make Aretinus have beer and wine brought in, and whatever else they fancy.

"They send off also for a martyr-master and torturer, who comes to the feast, and our pious Aretinus has to let himself be struck, insulted (scolded is too mild a term), pounded, punched, thrown about, and abused.

"He is made to crawl under the seats, make a fool of himself, snuff the candle, carry round the liquor, pour out, rinse the glasses, and do more than a slave's services. Neither is he safe at the lecture-room, church, choir, or even at the altar, when he would receive the beloved pledge of Jesus. For this devil's brood, to keep him faithful to his new obligations, stand close at his side, wink, beckon, laugh, and point with the finger at the good Aretinus, until the sacred services are over."

XI. Emperor Leopold's Charter to the University of Halle, Dated October 19, 1693.†

We, Leopold, by the grace of God elected Emperor of the Romans, always Augustus, and of Germany, Hungary, Bohemia, Dalmatia, Croatia, Sclavonia, &c., King, Archduke of Austria, Duke of Burgundy, Brabant, Styria, Carinthia, Carniola, &c., Margrave of Moravia, Duke of Luxemburg, and of Upper and Lower Silesia, Wirtemberg and Tecka, Prince of Sweden, Count of Hapsburg, Tyrol, La Ferette, Kyburg, and Gortz, Landgrave of Alsace, Marquis of the Holy Roman Empire, of Burgau, and of Upper and Lower Lusatia, Lord of the Marches of Sclavonia, Portus Naonis, Salines, &c., do grant and make known to all persons, by the tenor of these presents. Since we were elevated, by the favor and permission of the all-powerful God, to the high office of the imperial majesty, we have considered that the obligations of our office do in an especial manner require us carefully to follow the example of our ancestors, the Roman emperors and kings (who, among the other cares of their supreme power, have thought it especially worthy of their dignity to establish, found, and strengthen the various academies, gymnasia, and universities in the

* Hog-snout, glutton, cow-eater, street-owl, lust-sparrow.

† Koch, i. 453.

Holy Roman Empire); that the study of the liberal arts and sciences, which are appropriate and necessary for the government and preservation of the commonwealth, may be cherished and incited by proper honors and rewards, and may by our means be happily promoted. Whereas, therefore, the Most Serene Frederic, Margrave of Brandenburg, Duke of Magdeburg, Stettin, Pomerania, and of the Cassubii, Burggrave of Nuremburg, Prince of Halberstadt, Minda, and Carmina, Count in Hohenzollern, Arch-Chancellor of the Holy Roman Empire, Prince Elector, and our own most beloved relative, has humbly made known to us, that having long considered in what manner he could confer upon his faithful subjects some singular benefit whose fruits should not be of one age only, nor should redound to the benefit of cotemporaries alone, but might endure, and accrue to posterity, he had judged nothing so likely to conduce to the solid happiness of both governors and governed, as to have opinions so directed that youth, especially those approaching maturity, after having prosperously completed their preparatory studies in the lower schools, shall be carried through a higher course of study, imbued with the best learning of every kind, and formed, as it were beneath the eyes and in the sight of their parents, in such a training as, with the blessing of God, may make them useful to the republic. And whereas, among the means of attaining this felicity, the first place is due to those higher schools, which are, as it were, indispensable institutions for the receiving of youth from the introductory ones to more learned studies, shaping them by a superior course of discipline, and at last taking them, as if from a full treasury, thoroughly fitted for undertaking the employments of the republic. And whereas the aforesaid Most Serene Prince Elector hath desired of us, since he, almost alone, of all the princes of Lower Saxony, is not possessed of such a most useful seminary, we should in our kindness deign to grant him, as far as in us lieth, authority to establish such a high gymnasium or academy, in his city of Halle, in the territory of the dukedom of Magdeburg, and subject to the Holy Roman Empire, which in point of privileges and immunities, shall be upon an equal footing with the other privileged universities of Germany, Italy, and France (saving nevertheless our authority, and saving also the supreme jurisdiction of the said Prince Elector, our petitioner, and of his successors), in which academy to be erected, the professors of each several faculty may have power, after a previous rigorous examination, to grant the titles of Doctor, Licentiate, Master, and Bachelor, to those worthy of and entitled to them; who, having been thus promoted, may use, enjoy, possess, and have the pleasure of (*gaudere*), each and every the favors and privileges had by those of the same degrees in other universities; and moreover, in which academy to be erected, the doctors and scholars, with the consent of the said Prince Elector and his successors, may enact their own statutes, make ordinances, and create and appoint a Pro-Rector and Pro-Chancellor (the dignity of Rector and Chancellor remaining with the Prince Elector as founder, and with his successors), and other university officers; and moreover, that the person holding the rectorate of the same university shall possess the dignity of count palatine, and that the conferring of arms and insignia upon the several faculties to be established in the university may be as a favor permitted to him, the Prince Elector, our petitioner. We, from the singular and benignant affection which we entertain toward the Most Serene Prince Elector of Brandenburg, have thought proper to grant (and do by these presents graciously grant), in reply to his petition, in manner following, for his pleasure, and do graciously concede to him, authority to erect in the aforesaid city, subject to us and to the Holy Roman Empire, a higher gymasium or academy and university of all such laws, arts, and sciences, as are accustomed to be publicly set forth and taught in any gymnasium, university, or academy throughout all our dominions and those of the Holy Roman Empire, in such manner as we give and grant the aforesaid power and privilege in these presents, with deliberation, from mature consultation thereon had, and of our certain knowledge; that is to say, so that the said gymnasium, or academy, and university may be founded and erected by the said Most Serene Prince Elector at Halle (without any prejudice, however, to neighboring universities); and when it shall have been erected, with all the professors, doctors, and students contained in it, and shall contain a body of youth cultivating the study of letters in it, and such other persons as pertain to it, it shall possess equal rights and dignities, and all immunities, privileges, liberties, honors, and franchises as are used, enjoyed, possessed, and delighted in by the other universities of Germany and their members. And we desire, and by the same our imperial authority do decree, that professors and fit persons may be appointed by the said Prince or by his delegates, to profess (*profiteri*) in the said university, and to hold public lectures, disputations, and recitations (*repetitiones*), to propose arguments for public discussion, to interpret, comment, and explain, and to do all scholastic acts, in the mode, manner, and order which is accustomed in other universities. And if the course of study shall have been successfully pursued, and shall be carried on further, and if a proper honor or grade of dignity shall be decided upon in acknowledgment of talent or good conduct, and such as may merit at any time the worthy reward of their labor, shall seek the same; we enact and ordain that a tribunal of professors and doctors shall be formed, and that any who shall be judged worthy to receive the prize for their contest (the most fit and excellent being selected), shall first submit to the observances to be conducted by such doctors and professors, according to the usual custom of other universities, and to a rigorous and diligent preparatory examination (the honesty of which we charge upon the consciences of the professors), and that those submitting themselves for examination, and causing themselves to be presented to the university authorities by respectable and honorable persons, according to custom and to the statutes, may then be admitted to the examination itself, and, the blessing of the Holy Spirit having been invoked, may be examined; and if found and judged fit and sufficient, may be created bachelors, or masters, or licentiates, or doctors, according to the science and learning of each; and may receive the dignity thereof, and be invested with the same by the imposition of the hat, the giving of the ring and the kiss, and may receive and have conferred upon them the usual ornaments and insignia of the said dignities; and that bachelors, masters, licentiates, or doctors created and to be created in the said university ought to and may, in all places and territories of the Holy Roman Empire, and in all other countries and places, freely do all acts of professors, reading, teaching, interpreting, and commenting, which other professors, bachelors, masters, licentiates, and doctors created in other privileged universities may and ought to do by right or custom.

Moreover, we receive the same university, to be erected as above by the aforesaid Most Serene Prince Elector in his duchy of Magdeburg, into the peculiar protection, safeguard, and patronage of ourselves and our successors, Roman emperors and kings; and we ordain and decree by these presents, that scholars who shall receive any dignity or degree in the said university may rejoice in and possess, and can and ought to use, enjoy, rejoice in, and possess, all and singular the grants, honors, dignities, pre-eminences, immunities, privileges, franchises, concessions, favors, indulgences, and all other things whatever, which the universities of Heidelberg, Tübingen, Cologne, Ingolstadt, Friburg, Rostock, Julia Helmstadt, Strasburg, and other privileged universities, and doctors, licentiates, masters, bachelors, and scholars in any one of the aforesaid faculties who are created to or honored with any dignity or degree, rejoice in, use, enjoy, and possess, in any manner whatever, by custom or by law. Any privileges, indulgences, prerogatives, grants, statutes, ordinances, exemptions, or other things whatever to the contrary notwithstanding; all and singular of which, of our certain knowledge, deliberate purpose, and proper motion we repeal, and ordain to be repealed by this our charter; provided, nevertheless, that neither professors nor students shall therein teach or write, or permit to be taught, written, maintained in public lectures or disputations, or secretly or openly spread abroad, either by writing or books, any thing scandalous or contrary to good morals, or adverse to the Constitutions of the Holy Roman Empire.

And we moreover do graciously concede and bestow upon the doctors and scholars, for the time being, of the university to be erected, after the manner of other universities, but with the previous consent had of the aforesaid Frederic, Prince Elector of Brandenburg, and his successors, the faculty and power of enacting statutes, making ordinances, and of creating and appointing a Pro-Rector and Pro-Chancellor (we having chosen that it should rest in the free will and good pleasure of the Prince Elector as founder, and of his successors, to reserve to themselves the dignity of Rector and Chancellor, or if, and as often as they shall choose, to grant to the university the free right, usual in other universities, of electing a Rector and Chancellor), and such other officers as their pleasure or necessity may require. And that the aforesaid Most Serene Prince Elector of Brandenburg and his successors may further experience our gracious sentiments toward this erection and foundation, we have, of the motion, knowledge, and authority aforesaid, conferred, given, and bestowed, and do by the tenor of these presents graciously confer, give and bestow, upon the Pro-Rector to be appointed or elected in the manner already prescribed, or who shall, in succession, at whatever time be filling the office of Rector in the same university, the dignity of Count of the Sacred Lateran Palace, and of our Cæsarean Court and of the Imperial Consistory, and do graciously aggregate him to and inscribe him with the number and company of the other counts palatine.

Decreeing and ordering by this imperial edict, that from this time forward successively, as long as and while he shall fill the office of said Pro-Rector, he may and shall use, enjoy, and rejoice in the privileges, grants, rights, immunities, honors, exemptions, customs, and liberties below written, in manner as the other Counts of the Holy Lateran Palace have hitherto used and possessed the same, or do in any way use and possess them, by custom or by right. And first, that he may, throughout the whole Roman Empire, and in all countries and places, create and make notaries public, or scribes and ordinary judges, and to give and grant such office of notary, or scribe and ordinary judge, to all persons worthy, skillful, and fit for the place, and to invest any of them, by pen and pencase, as the custom is; provided, however, that from such notaries public or scribes and ordinary judges created by him and from each of them, in the place and in the name of ourselves and of the Holy Empire, and as a pledge of fidelity to the Roman Empire, he shall take their corporal and proper oath, in this manner: That they will be faithful to us and to the Holy Roman Empire, and to all our successors, Roman emperors and kings, legitimately succeeding, and will not enter into any design contemplating danger to us, but will faithfully defend and promote our good and our safety, and to the extent of their power prevent and avert our damage. That, moreover, they will fairly, correctly, faithfully, and without any pretense, contrivance, falsehood, or fraud, write, read, draft, and dictate all instruments, public and private, last wills, codicils, testaments, all acts of judges, and all and singular such other things as it may be required from them, and any one of them, by obligation of the said offices, to draft or write, not regarding hatred, money, rewards, or other feelings or favors. And that they will faithfully, according to the custom of their locality, read, draft, and write all writings which they may be required to draw for public purposes, upon clean parchment, not upon erased documents or paper. That they will promote, to the best of their ability, the causes of their guests (*hospitalium*), and of those in distress; and bridges and public roads: that they will faithfully retain in secrecy the testimony and words of witnesses until they shall have been regularly published; and shall well, fairly, and honestly do all and singular such things as shall in any way whatever pertain to the said offices, either by custom or law. And that such notaries public or scribes and ordinary judges to be created by him may, throughout the whole Roman Empire, and in all other places whatever, draw, write, and publish contracts, acts of judges, instruments and last wills; supply attestations (*decreta*), and authorizations in all contracts requiring any such thing, and do, publish, and exercise all other things which pertain and are known to belong to the office of public notary or scribe and ordinary judge. Decreeing that all instruments and writings made by such scribes, notaries public, or ordinary judges shall have full faith in court and elsewhere; all constitutions, statutes, and other things making to the contrary, notwithstanding. In like manner, by our said imperial authority, we grant to the aforesaid Pro-Rector, or person who shall be filling the office of Rector, that he may have power and authority to make, create, and invest as poets laureate, persons fit therefor and excelling in the poetical faculty, by the imposition of the laurel and the giving of a ring; which poets laureate so created and invested by the same, may have power and authority in all cities, communities, universities, colleges, and schools, of all places and countries of the Holy Roman Empire, and everywhere, freely and without any impediment or contradiction, to read, instruct (*repetere*), write, dispute, interpret, and comment in the science of the said poetical art, and to do and exercise all other poetical acts which other poets and persons adorned with the poetical laurel have been accustomed to do and exercise, and to use, enjoy, possess, and rejoice in all and singular the ornaments, insignia, privileges, prerogatives, exemptions, liberties, concessions, honors, pre-eminences, favors, and indulgences, which other poets laureate, appointed in whatever places and academies, rejoice in, enjoy, and use, either by custom or law. And, moreover, we grant and bestow upon the aforesaid Pro-Rector full power to legitimate natural children, bastards, children of prostitutes and concubines, and incestuous children in marriage or without it; and all others, although infants, and whether present or absent, begotten or to be begotten from illicit or damnable intercourse, whether masculine or feminine, by whatever name called, whether other legitimate children exist or not, and without their consent having been sought for (*iis etiam aliter non requisitis*), and whether their parents be living or dead (the children of illustrious princes, counts, and barons being nevertheless excepted), to restore to them and any one of them, all and singular, legitimate rights, entirely to take away all stain from their birth, by restoring and habilitating them in all and singular their rights of succession and inheritance of paternal and maternal possessions, even from intestate relatives by both father and mother, and in all legitimate honors, dignities, and private agreements, either by contract or by last will, or in any other manner whatever, whether in court or without, precisely as if they had been begotten in legitimate matrimony, all objections from illegitimate birth being completely quieted. And that such legitimation of them so made by him as above, shall be had and held to be done with entire right and lawfulness, not otherwise than if it had taken place with all the legal forms, the defect of which we will and intend to be specially supplied by imperial authority (so nevertheless, that such legitimations shall not prejudice legitimate and natural heirs and children); so that those so legitimated, after having been legitimated, shall be, and shall be held to be, and may be named, and can and ought to be named, in all places, as if legitimate and legitimately born of the house, family, and descent of their parents, and have power and authority to bear and carry the arms and insignia of such parents; and, moreover, that they be made noble, if their parents were noble, certain laws notwithstanding, which provide that natural children, bastards, children of prostitutes and concubines, and incestuous children, whether in marriage or without it, and all others begotten or to be begotten of illegal or damnable intercourse, cannot and ought not to be legitimated while natural legitimate children are living, or without the wish and consent of the natural and legitimate children, or paternal relatives, or of the lords of the fief; and especially the Novels, "*How natural children may be enfranchised,*" *passim*;* and *Liber Feudorum*, "*If there be a controversy between the lord and paternal relations about a fief*;"† and Code, title *Jubemus*, 6, "*Of the emancipation of children*;"‡ and other similar provisions, which laws, and each of them, we ordain to be expressly and intentionally repealed; and notwithstanding the provisions of contracts aforesaid, and of the last wills of deceased persons, and other laws, and their enactments and customs, although they are such as require to be recited or of which special mention ought here to be made; which, in abrogation of, and intending to abrogate them, in this present case at least, we do of our certain knowledge and the plenitude of our imperial power, totally repeal and will to be repealed.

And, moreover, we give and grant to the aforesaid Pro-Rector, or person filling the office of the Rectorate, power and authority to appoint guardians and curators, and to remove the same, for legitimate subsisting causes; to restore infamous persons, whether by law or fact, to good fame, and to purify them from every sign of infamy, whether inflicted or to be inflicted, so that thereafter they shall be held fit and proper persons for all and every transaction, and may be promoted to dignities; also to adopt children, young or adult, and to make, constitute, and ordain them such; also to emancipate children, legitimate and to be legitimated, and adoptive; and to consent to the adoption and emancipation of all and singular, both of infants and adults; and to declare those supplicating it to be of full age, and to give their authorization and decree to that effect; also to manumit servants, and in like manner to give their authorization and decree for any manumission, either with or without the use of the official rod; and to alienations by minors, and transactions by those not enfranchised (*alimentorum*); and to restore to their rights minors, churches, and communities injured, the other party having first been summoned for that purpose, and to grant to them or either of them full restitution, the legal order of proceeding being always preserved.

Lastly, we grant and bestow upon the aforementioned Most Serene Prince Elector of Brandenburg free authority and power of conferring peculiar arms and insignia upon each of the faculties to be established in said university, which they shall have power and authority to use whenever necessary, or at their pleasure, in public writings, edicts, ordinances, and other acts, in place of a seal; saving, nevertheless, as to all the foregoing, our Cæsarean authority, the supreme jurisdiction and all the authority of the founder himself and his successors, and the rights of all other persons whatever.

Let no man, therefore, of whatever state, rank, order, dignity, or pre-eminence, infringe upon the grants and powers of our concession, erection, confirmation, indulgence, protection, countship palatine, and other our privileges above inserted, or with rash daring make opposition to them, or violate them in any manner. And if any one shall presume to attempt to do so, be it known to him that he will incur, without power or remission, both the heaviest indignation of ourselves and of the Holy Empire, and a fine of fifty marks of pure gold for each offense; of which we decree that one-half shall go to the imperial fisc—that is, to our treasury—and the remainder to the aforesaid Most Serene Prince Elector of Brandenburg and to his successors. In testimony whereof these letters are subscribed with our hand and attested by the attachment of our Cæsarean seal. Given at our City of Vienna, on the nineteenth day of October, in the year one thousand six hundred and ninety-three, and of our reign over the Roman Empire the thirty-sixth, over Hungary the thirty-ninth, over Bohemia the thirty-eighth. LEOPOLD.

---

* Novels, 89, *passim*; see *Corpus Juris Civilis*, ed. by Kriegel and others, 3 vols. royal 8vo., Leipsic, 1856, vol. iii. p. 397, *et seq.*

† Lib. Feud., 11, 26, § 11; ib., vol. iii. p. 860.

‡ Cod., viii. 49, 5; ib., vol. ii. p. 559.

APPENDIX XIV. THE UNIVERSITIES IN GERMANY, IN THE SUMMER OF 1853.

UNIVERSITIES.	NUMBER OF TEACHERS.						NUMBER OF STUDENTS.													
							THEOLOGIANS.													
	Ordinary Professors.	Extraordinary Professors.	Honorary and Assistant Professors.	Private Teachers	Teachers of Languages and Exercises.	Total.	Catholic.		Protestants.		Law, Finance, Forests.		Medicine, Surgery, Pharmaceutics.		Philosophy and Philology.		Whole number of Foreign.	Total Matriculated.	Not matric., attend lectures.	Total matriculated and not matriculated.
							Native.	Foreign	Native.	Foreign	Native.	Foreign	Native.	Foreign	Native.	Foreign				
Basle,	21	3	3	12		39			8	30	6	2	5	13	2	1	46	67		67
Berlin,	52	41	Acad. 7	60	8	168			149	39	526	106	254	62	253	110	317	1491	675	2166
Bern,	13	17	2	8		40			34	1	51		57	1	12	1	3	157		157
Bonn,	47	13		24	8	91	202	4	47	12	248	35	86	8	153	67	126	862	34	896
Breslau,	39	15		24	14	92	246	3	37	1	271	3	88	6	146	5	18	806	31	837
Erlangen,	26	10	2	4	5	47			132	72	131	5	63	5	15	8	90	431		431
Freiburg in the Breisgau,	26	1		7	4	38	151	37			51	4	52	13	15	4	58	327	29	356
Giessen,	31	16	2	7	1	57			45	1	161	18	108	41	26	2	62	402		402
Göttingen,	46	21		28	14	109			80	34	98	123	125	78	67	64	299	669		669
Gratz,	16	3	Suppl. 4	6	3	32	94				173	1			72	3	4	250	93	343
Greifswald,	25	8	7	10	5	55			25		55	2	80	1	35	6	9	204	4	208
Halle,	35	10		19	7	71			283	51	147	14	58	7	50	6	78	616	45	661
Heidelberg,	34	12	1	33	11	91			49	24	77	423	48	57	9	32	536	719	33	752
Jena,	24	22	8	6	10	70			57	46	74	23	60	25	49	86	180	420	12	432
Innsbruck,	15	1		2	4	22					179		51	6	17	1	7	221	33	254
Kiel,	17	11		9	6	43			25		50	3	38	4	12		7	132		132
Königsberg,	30	8		16	6	60			52		168		70	4	49	4	8	347		347
Leipzig,	44	32	2	27	4	109			105	50	262	79	150	94	36	18	241	794		794
Marburg,	29	12		14	7	62			79	7	45		65	12	32	7	26	227	20	247
Munich,	50	14	11	15	4	94	199	38			791	58	277	87	405	45	228	1893		1893
Münster,	10	4		3	1	18	164	23							124	17	40	328		328
Olmütz,	10	1		1	1	13	130				70							200		200
Prague,	37	24		23	4	88	135	4			465	1	294	12	111	3	28	1025	144	1169
Rostock,	21	3		7		31			15	5	49	5	19	5	9	1	16	168		108
Tübingen,	37	13	Ass't. 3	20	6	79	116	45	123	28	178	35	98	22	88	10	140	743		743
Vienna,	56	15		35	10	116		1	30		741	3	875	42	103	5	78	1964	439	2403
Würzburg,	30	7	1	3	5	46	91				186	5	103	199	118	3	207	705		705
Zurich,	19	16		16		51			20		35	4	76	18	28	8	30	189	16	205

III. TREATISES ON ACADEMICAL SUBJECTS.

IV. ESSAYS ON ACADEMICAL SUBJECTS.

I. Lectures. Dialogic Instruction.

The talented Theremin wrote on the universities in 1836. He discussed, principally, their defects and faults; and believed that many, if not most of them, would be remedied by one universal cure; namely, the disuse of the received mode of instruction, and the introduction of the dialogic form instead of the monological one of the usual lectures.

This theory indicates a pseudo-genius, who would know every thing better than others, but knows nothing well.

The defects of many lectures are plainly to be seen, and have often been attacked. Professors have been pointed out who have read the same manuscript for a series of years, or rather chanted, in a wearisome monotone, from them; and students who stolidly wrote down the matter thus delivered; and it has been asked, "What is the use of these notes since the invention of printing? If the professor's manuscript is worth so much, let him print it."

To read the same manuscript year after year would seem entirely inadmissible; and, in fact, is, as a rule. But there are exceptions which must not be overlooked; especially that where a master of style has worked up his manuscript with artistic care, to a degree of excellence as high as he can reach, and feels that any alteration must be not for the better, but for the worse. If such a speaker even adds no remarks to the written matter, the rule *vox viva docet* (it is the living voice that teaches), is still true of his mere reading. His tone, his accent, even his gestures, enliven his words, and each hearer feels that the speaker is addressing him. If the manuscript were printed, reading in silence, to one's self, could not entirely fill the place of the *viva vox*. This is a case which has happened, though very seldom; and it occupies a middle place between oral teaching and writing books.

But it is clear, at least, that the practice of repeatedly reading the same manuscript should not be unqualifiedly condemned, especially where the professor has labored continually, thoughtfully, and fruitfully in his department; and when, in consequence, his lectures, though always on the same basis of substance, are a stem which every spring puts out new leaves and blossoms.

The teacher who prepares his notes with quiet but thoughtful and careful industry, in the silence of his study, is altogether to be preferred to the pseudo-genius, who dares to enter the desk substantially altogether unprepared, because he intends to give himself up to the inspiration of his genius. Such pretendedly inspired *improvisatori* do not, it is true, want for words, but their words are destitute of all substance—of any actual truth.

Of different character was one young man who trusted, with the utmost confidence, to the field of knowledge which lay quite at his command. He had often ridiculed the professors' notes, and proposed to have nothing but an entirely free lecture. Upon his first appearance in the lecturer's desk, he spoke, for the first quarter of an hour, with confidence, rapidity, and freedom; for the second, his delivery was, in spite of himself, moderate, slow, and hesitating; and when the third quarter commenced, he was forced to go into bankruptcy. Saying, with great mortification, "Gentlemen, my materials have escaped me," he closed.

Even a most distinguished teacher, who is completely at home with his subject, will not enter the desk entirely unprepared—without having previously prepared his lecture with care. And it is, of course, much more necessary with teachers not so accomplished, young ones especially, even if they do not prepare their lecture as carefully as if for the press, at least to write out a more or less full skeleton arrangement. They are, otherwise, in danger of embarrassment or repetition.

Lectures differ with regard to taking notes of them, especially in this: that some instructors are accustomed to use short distinct sentences of a compendious nature, which they give as themes to be expanded; while others speak in a more flowing style, leaving the hearer to seize and write down whatever he can.

To discuss the latter practice first:—It is not an easy matter to take satisfactory notes of such a lecture. All who are not sufficiently skilled in short-hand to take down every word—an accomplishment necessarily rare—must use no small intellectual exertion in an extempore condensation of what is said, and the selection, on the spot, of the most important matter. Such note-taking certainly can not be charged with being merely mechanical work; it is rather to be feared that it requires too much from the audience. It is only necessary to compare different notes of one lecture, to see what great differences there are as to capacity for doing this work. Many such notes show such a lack of it, and so much misunderstanding, as might well drive the instructor to the practice of formal dictation.

If the instructor has carefully and advisedly placed the more important portions of his lecture in precise and clear statements, which concentrate in themselves many facts and much thought, he must, naturally, desire that his hearers shall understand this, and shall, accordingly, take down these propositions accurately, in order that they may afterward be possessed of an analytic compend which will serve to recall the course of the discussion to their minds, and to enable them to reproduce it. Hearers who do not take down such statements, show faulty indifference and lack of intelligence.*

To determine the qualities of a good lecture is difficult, because different subjects require to be taught in different ways, and particularly because instructors proceed, and must proceed, according to their individual endowments, in the most various modes. How different, for instance, were the lectures of Werner, Steffens, and F. A. Wolf, though each was a master in his own style. Werner's lectures on mineralogy and geognosy were confined within the limits of experience. He spoke calmly, intelligibly, and instructively; his pupil, Steffens, on the contrary, with winged enthusiasm. Empirical facts served the latter only for the building-stones of the architectonic structure of his inner natural history of the earth. He hurried his hearers along with him; and without having the exclusive purpose of communicating to them empirical facts, he awoke in them a desire for the acquirement of them. Wolf, again, taught in a manner still very different. A thoroughly learned, acute, and enthusiastic scholar in the ancients, elements, seemingly the most repugnant, were united in him,—learning, enthusiastic love, keen criticism; and these traits, together, made his lectures, in the highest degree, at once attractive and instructive. Thus might be described many teachers, who each taught in a masterly manner, but each in a style quite peculiar to himself.

The gifts of a teacher are often measured by his acceptability to the students. Such a rule is, however, not correct; for a competent judge must be able to pass both upon the substance of a lecture, and its style and delivery. But pupils who sit at the feet of a teacher can not, generally, have any well-founded opinion as to whether he is thorough in his department, and therefore entitled to full confidence. And accordingly, it is frequently and lamentably the case, that empty, ignorant declaimers give most satisfaction, while the quiet delivery of the most profound professors is found wearisome.† This complaint, in particular, is often made of the latter, that they do not stimulate their hearers. But is it the sole fault of the teacher that his discourse does not stimulate; and are not the hearers themselves often to blame, as lacking in

* A compendium might fill the place of this dictation; and would, indeed, gradually proceed from it. To read from a compendium prepared by another, must usually be, to an independent instructor, who has other purposes than to do a mere "forwarding business," no less irksome than to wear another man's coat, which does not fit.

† Eloquence must contain something agreeable, and something real; but what is agreeable must be real.—*Pascal.*

intellect and receptivity?* F. A. Wolf says, in academical discourses, that he requires of the professor to teach the truth, and this not in the manner of an actor, but in a style adapted to his subject and his audience. Then, addressing the students, he adds: "Of you it is required that you have your ears open to the lectures."†

I will here add a remark on the maxim "*Vox* VIVA *docet*." The proverb *Docendo discimus*, "Teaching teaches us," has reference to the reaction of his occupation upon the teacher. But this means not only that the knowledge of the industrious teacher increases by his occupation, but has a second and deeper meaning.

For, if an oral address makes a much more profound impression upon an audience than mere quiet reading, he, on the other hand, who merely writes books for a public entirely unknown to him, fails entirely of that inspiriting influence which comes to the speaker from a circle of dear and attentive hearers. How great this is, is indicated by a remark of F. A. Wolf, who says, "I have long been accustomed to the pleasant stimulus which comes from the development, eye to eye, of my thoughts before an attentive audience, and from the vivid reaction which is so easily felt from it by the teacher; and this awakens an inspiriting voice within me, every day and every hour, which is as quickly silenced by the seat before the empty wall and the insensible paper."

To return from this digression—I would refer particularly to lectures in some real studies, in which the teachers must require the students to have not only their ears, but their eyes open. How great a defect often exists in this particular, I have already observed in the chapter on instruction in natural science. Many are far more attracted by quite unreal words, by chatter about things, than by the things themselves. Suppose a picture, by Raphael, to hang on one wall, and some declaimer to stand opposite, who delivers, in poetical prose, a high-flown oration upon the picture—would not most of any audience turn their backs to the picture and give their whole attention to the declaimer? So entirely is it the practice to learn by words only, and to make no use of the eyes.

This brings me back to the beginning of my discussion: to the comparison of the methods of teaching by lectures and by dialogue.

---

* See Raumer's *Pädogogik*, part ii, p. 352.

† "*A vobis exigitur ut ad novas auditiones afferatis aures.*" What he means by *aures* appears from another of his addresses, delivered at the opening of his seminary, in 1787, viz.: "Had I entertained the personal views so usual with many, I should have prepared my discourses rather for the ear than for the understanding. But I know that my business is, not to procure a multitude of hearers, but to promote thorough knowledge." I refer, further, to the excellent observations by Wolf, given in Raumer's *Päd.*, part ii. p. 351, *et seq.*

It is sufficiently evident, when the number of the audience is great, that the latter is impossible; that Savigny could not have used it on the pandects, with his audience of three hundred, or Neander, on church history, with the hundreds of his; aside from the fact that it is a method not adapted to these studies.

But it is equally certain that the mode by lectures will not instruct in empirical mineralogy, botany, zoology, &c., where distinct bodily vision is requisite; or, at least, where the pupil must receive practical instruction at the same time, as in the case of applied chemistry. Many other real studies are in the same category, which have, even now, long been taught only in private seminaries and courses of lessons, as the catalogues show. Such are the studies which such private seminaries, for exegesis, homiletics, catechetics, dogmatic history, and philosophy, offer to teach. Students in these escape from the passivity which is necessary at a lecture. The teacher deals with them, not as one man, but directs himself to each one; and every one, whether orally or in writing, must give active co-operation, and apply and learn to use his faculties, under the direction of the teacher.

This clearly presents the contrast between instruction by lectures and by dialogue.

But suppose the case that where a study—as mineralogy—absolutely requires the dialogic method, the audience is so numerous as to make it quite impossible for the teacher to direct his attention to each individual, and to instruct him alone, what is to be done? I know no better plan than, where possible, to subdivide the number, and instruct each section separately. It is more profitable, where forty persons attend a course of six lessons, to instruct each half of them during three lessons, than to instruct them all together during six.*

But how frequently are mineralogy and other studies taught from the chair to hundreds! It is, at the same time, admitted that, without examining the stones themselves, the completest descriptions of them are altogether useless, and that those who have not seen the stones themselves, can not represent them in their minds. This defect it has been sought to remedy by sufficiently awkward means. One exhibits his specimens from the desk only, even to his most distant hearers; although even the nearest can get no satisfactory idea of them. Nor is any fixed idea of them obtained by another method, of passing the specimens before the painfully staring eyes of the students, in cases, on a table, like a shadow on the wall. By these means the pupils receive only words; and do not become acquainted with the things

*See Raumer's *Päd.*, on instruction in natural science, part iii. p. 158; and part ii. p. 442.

themselves. They remain in real ignorance, unless they afterward are able to examine thoroughly mineralogical collections.

In conclusion, one great advantage should be mentioned which the dialogic method has over that by lectures, namely: that it enables the teacher to obtain a personal acquaintance with the students, and thus to put himself on friendly terms with them. It is an uncomfortable thing to lecture, year after year, to an audience of strangers, even if Wolf is right in saying even the silent students before us have a reactive influence on their teacher.* One often wishes to say to the silent hearers, "Speak, that I may see you."

II. Examinations.

F. A. Wolf, in an academical address, opposed the Greek mode of teaching, by dialogue, and advocated the method by lectures. In order that the students might, to some extent, enjoy the advantages of the ancient method, there should be, he said, examinations and disputations; and he added, "Do not be afraid of these terms; such exercises will be of great service to you."

Where Wolf, sixty years ago, told the students not to be afraid, it would now almost be necessary to say it to the professors, if they were about to advocate Wolf's views on examinations, in order that they might not be discouraged by the numerous opponents of all examinations whatever.

We will adhere, in what relates to academical laws, to the principle that no law which is made with reference to the bad shall stand in the way of the good.

Many claim that this is the case with all examinations established by law; and that they should, therefore, all be discontinued.

But should this be so in all cases? Are there not occasions when examinations are quite indispensable? We reply, yes: there are such cases. Examinations of stipendiaries may be an example. The founders of charities for the support of such persons usually require strictly that their funds shall be given only to students, industrious, and of unblemished character. The professors are to decide whether they are of unblemished character, and industrious. But how can they judge of the diligence of their hearers, especially when the latter are numerous; and when, besides, as is frequently the case, they are so near-sighted that they cannot recognize the students, except those who sit nearest the desk?

* It must be remembered here, that Wolf, partly through his seminary, and partly otherwise, knew very many of his hearers, and, therefore, was more influenced by their presence than would have been the case with professors having no such acquaintance, or not a near one.

Mere corporeal presence does not decide the question. A certain professor observed that one of his pupils was invariably present; but also observed, very plainly, that he always occupied himself in reading one book, which its uniform indicated to have come from a circulating library.

A Prussian ministerial circular, of 13th January, 1835, requires that instructors, in giving certificates, should act with the strictest care and conscientiousness; and recommends them to be observant of their hearers, "in order that they may be enabled to say, with certainty, whether individuals have attended their lectures diligently or not." And, it adds, "it will be well for all those whom the number of their hearers, or their near-sightedness, prevents from sufficiently close observation of all, to intrust to some older and proper student from among them, the business of a beadle or assistant, for the maintenance of punctual attendance."* So it is not to be the professors, but their assistants, who are to give the certificates; and what sort of students would submit to that sort of management? Another circular, of 29th June, 1827, recommends to imitate one instructor who, "in order to judge better of the diligence of his hearers, sent round, at unexpected times during his lectures, a list, which those students present were to sign."† I have known this experiment to be tried; but those present were accustomed to enter their absent friends; so that once, the name of an absent one was inadvertently entered twice, by two of his friends. In another list were entered such names as Plato, Aristotle, &c.

Such modes of ascertaining the diligence of hearers seeming inadmissible and unsuitable, the question recurs, How shall the professors arrive at a reliable judgment upon that diligence; and particularly on the point supposed, namely, their merits in reference to stipendiary allowances?

The answer is,—Unless they would declare themselves quite improper persons to give certificates to stipendiaries, they must, themselves, examine them. Only such professors are excepted as use a dialogic mode of teaching; for they have no need of making a special examination of their hearers, since they examine them daily in teaching them, and thus gain a thorough acquaintance with them. The benefit, however, of subjecting these students to an examination, consists in this: that their grade can be certified to, not merely by the instructor whose lectures they have attended, but by all professors assisting at the examination.‡

* Koch, ii. p. 511. † Ib., ii. p. 201.

‡ Accordingly, the regulations of 3d May, 1835, for the Bonn Seminary, for all the natural

That idle students, with evil consciences, should object to the examinations for stipends, is natural, and does not trouble us. We attach more weight to the views of their better fellows. These, as they have often informed me, are quite satisfied with the plan. They readily see that, in competing with ignorant companions for these stipends, they have a material advantage in the examination, which enables them to prove themselves worthy of preference.

I wish it were not to be said, that "those who decide in the matter of these stipends make little inquiry about academical testimonials; the motives which decide their selection are quite different." Although this charge may be true of many, it certainly is not universally so. I, myself, have known one excellent man, who had an important influence in deciding the appropriation of many stipends by cities, and who was exceedingly conscientious therein. He complained bitterly, to me, that so little reliance could be placed on many of the academical testimonials, in forming his decision.*

This charge of disregard to such testimonials must be entirely withdrawn. Others must answer for their own actions in reference to the matter of such stipendiaries, and we professors for our own; and we must act according to the best of our knowledge and belief, without regard to consequences. We are especially bound to appropriate such support, as far as we can, to the better class of students. It must, naturally, pain us to see immoral and idle students wasting the stipends which our pious predecessors intended for useful purposes, while the most industrious ones are destitute of means of support, and can, with difficulty, get through their studies. But how distressing must it be, when we have to accuse ourselves of having been, by careless and unconscientiously given testimonials, the cause of such miserable injustice!

What has thus been said of the examination of stipendiaries, applies to all cases where conscientious academical testimonials are required;

---

sciences, say, that for a certificate for a member of the seminary, "no special examination is necessary, inasmuch as the attendance, itself, at the seminary, is a constant examination." (Koch, ii. p. 629.)

* A student applied to me for a certificate with reference to a stipend, without having been previously examined, pretending that he had obtained such from others without a previous examination. But on being made to stand an examination in mathematical geography, it appeared that he knew nothing at all about Copernicus. Suppose I had given him, on his assurance, a good testimonial, and he had handed it in, with his application, to the collator, and the latter should question him on the same subject, what must he think of me, on discovering his excessive ignorance? Undoubtedly that I gave testimonials most unconscientiously, and that I was not to be relied on. In giving every such testimonial, we should ask ourselves whether we could certify to the same after an expert had examined the applicant. We may err, it is true, in our examination of such students; but such error is human, excusable, and no blemish on our official honor.

and of the absolute necessity of those examinations there ought scarcely to be a doubt among honest men.

As to other examinations, where this necessity is not so evident, opinions differ.

Although, as has been said, the better class of students are in favor of the stipendiary examinations, they consider themselves somewhat annoyed by other ones. Yet they allow that they are, by means of them, obliged to a useful review of the lectures. Young medical students, who must, at their examination for practice, stand an examination in mineralogy, have confessed to me that it was only the expectation of this examination which kept them from giving up the lectures, even during the first weeks of the course. In the progress and at the close of it, however, they found that in mineralogy, as in all studies, the commencement may probably be difficult, and even wearisome, to beginners who have no knowledge of what they are to learn.* Their perseverance, however, they said, was rewarded, for they ultimately became interested in the study, finding great pleasure, especially in the mathematical beauty of the crystals. From that period they pursued their study without any reference to the coming examination.

Thus the examinations have a good influence, even on the better class of students, who might seem to have no need whatever of such a stimulus; it is admitted that the less industrious, and the idle, need such exterior incitements. With regard to these, it is only to be inquired whether the examinations actually cause industry, and whether it is an industry of the right kind.

Laws, it is true, can not make men industrious; but this is no reason why we should become anarchists. If idle persons are constrained to labor, it may, in time, become agreeable to them; but without constraint they will neglect it entirely.

Still, objections are made against all academical examinations, of every kind.

1. F. A. Wolf said, "They study ill who study for examinations; well, who study for themselves, and for life." When our objectors cite this remark, they should also consider that Wolf also said, that examinations will "be of valuable service" to the students. The former observation was evidently aimed at those low-minded students who, without any love of learning, busy themselves with it only so far as is absolutely necessary in order to pass a decent examination.

What well-intentioned student would, in that sense, "study for ex-

* Let any one remember the beginning of his studies in language; his learning by rote of *mensa* and *amo*.

aminations?" But he might, however, be influenced in respect to his studies, by a judiciously ordered future examination, thus far: that, by a proper selection and limitation of subjects for examination, they would direct him to an appropriate choice of studies. An expectation of a future examination would also be needful to lead him to a preparatory self-examination as to what he knows with certainty, and what not; in order that, by means of the self-knowledge thus acquired, he may endeavor to fill up deficiencies in his knowledge, and elucidate what is obscure.

Capable examiners will also, in most cases, easily distinguish between candidates who have labored with genuine love of learning, and have made their studies actually their own, have intellectually assimilated them, and such as have merely hung themselves about with all manner of materials; have laid in matter in the vestibule of their memory, to be displayed on occasion of the examination, and afterward thrown contemptuously away.

Nor can we partake in the apprehension that an illiberal character will be impressed on all the students by the examinations. A nature which is illiberal and vulgar will remain so, examined or not; and one which is liberal and noble can not be demoralized or vulgarized by all the examinations in the world.

2. A second charge against the examinations, related to the former, seems to touch the honor of the students. Examinations, it is said, are for schools,—for boys, who are unable to control themselves, and require the guidance and stimulus of teachers. Students are emancipated from such control; to examine them is to treat them like school-boys. Such a pretense pertains especially to students who are glad to shelter their idleness under the noble patronage of freedom and honor.

It seems to be forgotten that examinations are used before the period of student-life, and after it too: namely, the state examinations. Why should examinations be dishonorable to students, as putting them in the place of boys, and be no dishonor to candidates for public offices? It is also overlooked, that school examinations are shaped, both as to form and subjects, according to the character of the school, and academical ones according to that of the university; and also that the term examination includes two very different ideas. No university examiner will treat the students like gymnasiasts; yet he may justly require that their attainments shall not be at, or under, the level of those of the gymnasium; so that he may have to ask some questions such as would be prominent, however, only at a school examination.

It may, perhaps, be imagined, that since I thus defend the examinations, and seek to refute so many objections to them, I am blind against the many faults and evils connected with them. This is far from the case; I have, during my professorship of more than forty years, had abundant opportunity to become acquainted with those faults and evils. Let us turn our attention to them.

1. While many persons are lately opposing all examinations of any kind, others can not have enough of them; and would, by their means, oblige all students to the most industrious labor. At Mainz the students are examined every week. At this place, even, the same students were, heretofore, examined every half-year, in two examinations near together,—one for their general progress, and one for stipendiary allowances. It is evident how superfluous, and even harmful, such a practice must be.

2. It is an evil, especially in the larger universities, that the number of candidates is very great, so that the time which can be devoted to each must be made very brief. How can it be possible, ask many, to discover in ten minutes whether a candidate is well acquainted with a study or not? But this, though certainly an evil, is not so great a one as it might, at first sight, appear.

Suppose a candidate is to be examined in three departments, and that an average of eight minutes is employed on each, he will be examined twenty-four minutes in all. Any one who observes the examination attentively, and observes particularly the character of the candidate's answers, and how he deals with difficult questions, can form an opinion, very soon, on his capacity and mode of study. The examiner can, moreover, abridge the proceeding, by selecting questions which, without requiring too much from the candidate, shall yet be real *experimenta crucis*, and such that scarcely any further ones need be put to one who answers them clearly and correctly.*

But the evil arising from a large number of candidates may chiefly be remedied by this: that all who have been instructed in the dialogic method, in seminaries or otherwise, being as well understood as if already examined, need very little further examination, or none at all, as has already been observed in relation to stipendiary examinations.

3. It is charged that a large share of the examiners lack the requisite skill in examining. Some, it is said, are not satisfied with any answer which is not given precisely according to their own preconcep-

* In an examination on mathematical geography, the most ignorant candidate can easily learn by rote how many zones there are, and what are their limits; but an answer to the question, How must I travel, so that during a whole year, the sun shall pass my zenith every noon? could, with difficulty, be learned by rote, but would have to be prepared on the spot, from knowledge already acquired.

tions; and are unable to enter into any statement made from another point of view, and justly to judge of it. Others limit themselves to some fixed question, and adhere pitilessly to it, though they may see that the candidate is not at home on the subject; instead of seeking to find out, by other questions, whether he is not better acquainted with a second or third subject, &c. Others, again, fail in this: that they give the candidates no opportunity to answer the questions which they put to them, but answer them themselves; thus, of course, not being able to have any opinion about the candidate, and yet delivering one upon him; and so on.*

4. It is said that the result of the examinations is uncertain, because candidates are so different; some of them being entirely at their ease during the examination, and answering questions with entire presence of mind, while the timid and bashful often lose their presence of mind so entirely as not to be able to reply to the slightest question; while, notwithstanding, they are often much more capable than such ready answerers. Must not this cause erroneous and unjust estimates?

Evils resulting from incapacity of examiners and bashfulness of candidates will be remedied by written examinations. But if the examiners have even a moderate knowledge of their duties, they will be able to reassure the timid, and not to over-estimate readiness. In any event, a better estimate of the candidates can be made by an oral examination, as to whether they are in an error or on the right track, and to ascertain whether their minds are in active operation, or their modes of thought are unwieldy. But, if a written examination is the only one used, oral conversation with the candidates upon their work, when done, is still very necessary, for more than one reason.

It is very usual to give three marks at examinations: distinguished, good, and bad. These are not sufficient, and often leave the examiners in a perplexing situation. They will give the first only in the most remarkable cases of excellence, and the last only in the very worst cases. Thus, the intermediate mark is that most frequently given, and to candidates of very different attainments; some near to one of the extremes, and some to the other. The use of five marks would remove this unfair equalization.

* Meiners, in his work on the German Universities, makes charges against the examinations, honorable neither to students, professors, nor himself. A university where vulgarity prevails is beyond help.

III. Compulsory Lectures.—Freedom of Attendance.—Lyceums.—Relations of the Philosophical Faculty and its Lectures to the Practical Branches.

Compulsory lectures have been opposed from all quarters, and, in general, with great justice. But it must first be determined what this ominous term means.

There are academical studies which the student can sufficiently master by himself, from books; and others for which distinct teachers and means of instruction are indispensable. To the latter belong most of the practical natural sciences, and most departments of medical study. The very nature of these pursuits require such, without any legal enactments; though the lectures on them are still not compulsory ones. The medical student must attend lectures on anatomy and obstetrics; he can not pursue them by himself. But, still consider these not as compulsory lectures, but merely as in themselves necessary.

While, in former times, not only all the subjects were prescribed on which lectures must be attended, but also the persons who were to deliver them, and their order, at present the opposite extreme prevails; even so far that it is demanded that it shall not even be required of a student to live at the university, or to attend so much as one lecture. The questions naturally arise here, Why, then, do the students live at the university at all? and, if this demand be reasonable, Why should there be any universities?

The reason of establishing compulsory lectures, and the order of attending them, is clear. It was because the students, especially beginners, were unacquainted with the right method of studying. They were, therefore, assisted, and in the simplest way, by the definite peremptory prescription of a course of study.

This conception was very excusable, so far as it relates to the entire ignorance and indecision of so many students, especially new-comers, as to the selection of lectures to be attended. It was considered how frequently, at leaving the university, students said, "If we could pursue our studies over again, we would take an altogether different course." And it was believed that the fixing of a course, to be closely adhered to, would save them their hesitation at the beginning of their university life, and their repentance at the end of it.

In later times, the ancient strictly compulsory rule was relaxed, as if to make good Taubmann's definition of a student—"an animal which will not be forced, but persuaded." This was the case in Bavaria, and in Prussia. The faculties of the Prussian universities published courses of study, but with the express remark that they did not prescribe, but only advised them. In the course for medical students, at Berlin, of

August 3, 1827, it is said, "As every student must desire, not only to have before him a general view of the lectures which he is to attend while a student, but also to see them arranged in a suitable order, that he may be under no misapprehensions in selecting, the medical faculty publishes the following course for their students, at subscribing to a course, as paternal advice; and requests that every one, in case of any doubt relative to the course, will apply to his fellows, or to the dean, or some other member of the faculty; inasmuch as nothing can be more desirable to them than to afford all the assistance in their power, in order to the best use of the student's exertions."* Then follows the course of lectures for each of the eight half-years. For example:

"*First half-year.*—Encyclopedia of Medicine; Botany, with excursions; Osteology; Physics; Greek and Latin lectures, Mathematical and Philosophical lectures; as the student may require."

The course of study (in Latin) of the theological faculty at Bonn, of 3d June, 1829, says: "Wherefore, either comply with this, our advice, or, if you have one to propose better adapted to the peculiar character of your studies"† . . .

In the course of study, however, laid down by the theological faculty at Halle, for their students, in 1832, they say, without more ado, that the students are in great need of good advice. "The study of theology," they observe, "is always, as a long experience has taught us, begun by very many persons who have no clear idea of its extent, of the connection of its parts, or of the most proper method of becoming familiar with it. Indeed, only a few have an opportunity, before leaving school, to acquire this previous and so necessary knowledge. Hence so much uncertainty and error in choice of lectures, so many mistaken estimates of the comparative importance of different matters, so much lack of a regular plan of study, even where there is serious industry; and hence the loud complaints so frequently heard at the close of the academical course, of discovering, when it is too late, a mode in which those years might have been much better used."

But this plan does not arbitrarily determine that certain lectures must, or must not, be attended by students; it only fixes the order in which they should be heard; it advises; is, in fact, a compendious system of hodegetics.

Obligatory attendance is the less objectionable, as theological, legal, and medical students must pass a government examination at the end

* Koch, ii. p. 201.

† Koch, ii. p. 204. See same, p. 209, for philosophical course at Halle; p. 216, for theological course there; p. 235, for theological course of 1837, at Bonn; p. 239, for jurisprudence there; p. 245, for medicine there.

of their studies, and present, at this, certificates of the lectures they have attended. No person can present himself as self-taught; and even if such a preparation be admitted in some studies, the examiners would, and with propriety, examine him very strictly upon them, to ascertain what he had accomplished for himself.

The practical courses of the three faculties might properly be called compulsory courses, although they do not so appear to the students. Even the less industrious of them do not consider whether or no they will attend lectures on exegesis and dogmatics, the pandects, or anatomy. Every one is anxious to pass, with credit, the government examination on these studies, and thus to obtain a recognized standing, and an appointment.

What is true of the students of theology, law, and medicine, is also true as to philological and mathematical lectures, of those of philology and mathematics, in the philosophical faculty, who intend to become teachers. But what is the case with such lectures of the philosophical faculty as are not practical—do not refer directly to a future profession? As for medicine, the statutes of the medical faculty at Bonn say, § 20,* "With the regular medical course must be pursued, either before it or parallel with it, a philosophical preparatory course, to include the following studies of the philosophical faculty: classical philology, logic, psychology, mineralogy, botany, zoology, physics, and chemistry." On these the medical student is examined, and must have a certificate of the examination.† There is a similar examination of medical students (the so-called examination for admission) at Erlangen; the subjects of it being zoology, botany, mineralogy, physics, chemistry, and pharmacognosy. These studies seem to be regarded as belonging, not to the general, but to the professional education of a physician.

Gymnasium pupils are obliged, without making any selection, to learn whatever is taught at the gymnasium; and the students are under a like necessity with respect to professional studies. But what is the fact as to those lectures in the philosophical faculty, which have no direct relation to the theological and juridical professional studies, but only to general education? This question is difficult to answer, because different opinions prevail respecting it in different countries of Germany, all of which have again been modified, in many ways, in the course of time, sometimes very materially, as appears from the example of the university of Erlangen.

Here, formerly, every student was obliged, during his first year, to

* Koch, ii. pp. 246, 260.

† See Koch, ii. pp. 66, 72, the ministerial rescripts of January 7, 1826, and October 23, 1828.

attend lectures on general history, physics, logic, philosophy, mathematics, and natural history; at the end of which time the unhappy fellows were examined, all at once, in all these heterogeneous subjects; and only after passing their examination satisfactorily were they allowed to proceed to professional studies.* These six courses were called, in derision, Fox lectures;† they were attended, listened to, usually, with repugnance and carelessness; and much pleasure was felt when the concluding examination (Fox examination) was over.

It is evident how discouraging and burdensome this arrangement must have been for any professor who loved his science, and the successful teaching of it; and it was not less extremely unsuitable to the students, and unfavorable to all free and right-minded education. For these reasons measures were taken against the regulation; a proceeding the more necessary, because the philosophical faculty was sharply distinguished from the three other faculties by the fact that the students were under its tuition during their first year, but heard no lectures from it during their other years at the university.

But, still further, it was but a step to the idea of entirely separating the philosophical faculty from the university, and of establishing, instead of it, distinctively Protestant institutions elsewhere, called lyceums. A lyceum, for both Catholics and Protestants, was actually established, in 1839, at Speyer, which, for a long time, caused annoyance to the university of Erlangen. The danger came still nearer when, especially in 1843, there was a serious plan for setting up two Protestant lyceums in Ansbach and Baireüth. If this plan had succeeded there would have been an end to the university, and we should have had professional schools instead of it. Against this very important scheme, I published, in 1843, the following article:‡

LYCEUMS.

Gymnasiums have an important and definite difference from universities, in that they give general education only as a basis for professional education; while the arrangement by faculties characterizes the universities, and is to facilitate the passage into practical life. Even in the highest gymnasium classes, the future theologians, jurists, and physicians, without distinction, recite the same lessons; while, in the

* Beginners were always *permitted* to attend an introductory course during that first year, but *obliged* to attend the six courses in the philosophical faculty.

† With a reference to the "foxes," or freshmen.—[*Trans.*]

‡ "*Gazette for Protestantism and the Church*" ("*Zeitschrift für Protestantismus und Kirche*"), for 1843. I give the article, with very little alteration, because I yet adhere to the same views.

first year at the university, it was and is the practice to give lectures introductory to professional studies.

This distinct character of the gymnasium and university may become confused, namely: by adding to gymnasium studies arranged faculty-wise, by using the first one or two years of the university like those spent in the gymnasium, for studies of a general character; or, by the erection of hybrid institutions, to stand between the gymnasium and the university, for the purpose.

Of gymnasiums with academical departments, there are several examples. Thus, the Dantzic gymnasium has three faculties, which are distinguished in the upper two classes. The theological faculty taught dogmatics, polemics, and even exercises in preaching were introduced; the jurists lectured on the institutions, and on federal law; and the medical faculty on anatomy and physiology. It was not until lately that the authorities discontinued "the medley of university and preparatory school." In like manner, at the Stargard gymnasium, were, formerly, read lectures on exegesis, church history, the institutions, and anatomy. Here, also, the conviction followed, that such a confusion "must be harmful to the studies proper to the school." A result was, as might have been expected, that the "collegial students, considering themselves students, and not boys, acted accordingly; not regarding the school-hours, attending recitations only as they saw fit, and occupying themselves, during them, as they chose." In the year 1770, we are told, "this nuisance with an academical constitution," was discontinued.

The experiment which a minister made, toward the end of the last century, of introducing into the gymnasium, for future law-students, the Institutes of Heineccius instead of Tacitus and Virgil, excited universal displeasure.

The gymnasium recognizes no professional studies, and should recognize none, unless it designs prematurely and violently to impress upon unripe boys a useless professional education.

Now to discuss the second question: Whether it is advisable to interfere with the character of the universities, by devoting the first year, or two years even, to general studies, excluding those of the faculties; and by making this period only a continuation of school studies—a mere preparatory course for professional studies—so that the students shall entirely complete their general studies, in order afterward to devote themselves as exclusively to their professional studies?

There are many reasons against it. The graduate of a gymnasium has prepared himself, to the best of his ability, for the final examination there. Having passed this successfully, he is usually received at the university, to the same studies with which he had been occupied before. He had spent years in studying the classics at the gymnasium, and continues them at the university; he has taken pains to make himself acquainted with the facts of general history, and is made to do the same again, and to be examined on them again; he has studied pure mathematics, and has to study them again. Thus, he is commonly occupied with reviewing what he knows; a species of study in which he can have no interest.

It is, of course, not intended that general studies shall at once be entirely discontinued, but that the school method of teaching them should be replaced by an academical one. The latter can, usually, only be introduced where the student has been gradually ripened and prepared for it. If, for instance, the student of law has previously studied the history of law, or the theological student, church history, with how different a feeling, understanding, and interest will they then return to the study of general history, in which all the elements of human development present themselves, and appear as one great whole, in the most complicated and vivid interaction. In like manner, it might be asked, whether the young theological student, after his long occupation, at the gymnasium, with the classics, should not make a pause with them, while he studies biblical exegesis, and only afterward apply himself again to classical philology, with the view of studying the relations of the classical and sacred languages, and worlds.

It is certain that several of the studies of the philosophical faculty would be pursued much more profitably in the latter part of the university course than in the former; and in a method worthy of a university, independent and free, from pure love of the science, instead of merely for the sake of answering questions on a lesson. But this latter objectionable practice prevails so much the more, as the students, during the first, or so-called philosophical years, are obliged to pursue the most inconsistent studies, of which they must give account in the examination for advanced standing.* This mode of study is universal in the lower grades of school study; but, in the higher ones, the requirements are too numerous even for the best scholars; they can not, with interest and pleasure, study, all at once, logic, general history, mathematics, physics, natural history, and philology. And, if they are still compelled to hear lectures on them all, they feel a genuine re-

---

* That is, the examination at the end of the first university year, for a transfer to the professional studies.

pugnance for these so-called compulsory lectures; even the best of them despair of receiving any benefit from them, and most of them care only to make a passable appearance at the examination, and are profoundly glad when they are past the philosophical year.

Any one who has attended one of these examinations for advanced standing, and who knows what pains the examiners have to take to ask childish, easy questions, and how even these questions remain unanswered in various ways, will never deceive himself into believing that general education is furthered by such a mode of studying.* Many may, perhaps, at once blame the professors, as destitute both of zeal and of skill for the awakening of interest and love for their department of study. Even if this might be true of some one or other individual, it can still be demonstrated from experience, that even the most conscientious and competent professors are in the same unpleasant situation. And those acquainted with the facts can also testify, that even the best-disposed students perform these prescribed studies, mostly with indifferent spiritlessness, and are as glad as the rest when they have finished their first year at the university.

How entirely different would it be, if the student of theology, law, or medicine, besides his professional studies, should, in every term, attend one or more lectures from the professors of the philosophical faculty; with what pleasure would he listen, and how much would he be stimulated and strengthened in his professional studies! The very lectures which would produce this quickening effect are disgustful to our present students. The reasons have been explained. One of the greatest jurists of Germany has a very valuable observation on the subject. "Here," he says, "arises a question: Shall juridical studies be commenced as soon as in the first university term? By all means. The first ideas of the profession to which the student is to devote himself can not be too early secured. Historical, literary, mathematical, and philosophical studies are very far from being excluded by this plan. But one who insists on becoming familiar with all these before hearing lectures on the Institutions, acts as judiciously as if he should take, all at once, his dessert for a whole week, and should eat nothing else as long as that will last him. Evidently, he will receive less pleasure than from an alternation of food, besides that he will often disorder his stomach."†

---

* There are even men of penetrating intelligence, who earnestly desire to advance the cause of general education, and to oppose a mere drill preparatory to professional study, who do deceive themselves in this way, and consider that an opponent of the "philosophical year" is a traitor to the cause of general education. Quite the reverse!

† Hugo, in the "*Civil Law Magazine*" (*Civilistisches Magazin*), i. 57.

It is a most discouraging, and even terrible thing, for a professor in the philosophical faculty to have his lectures considered compulsory ones. The consequence is, that all connections of an elevating character between him and his hearers ceases; and there is the greatest danger that, from that time forward, all true feeling and respect for his department will die out of the hearts of the students, and that, in the same proportion, ignorance will prevail there.

Savigny,* whose clear views, lofty character, and long experience render his opinion, on subjects connected with universities, more valuable than that of most persons, observes upon those lectures which the students are obliged to attend. The original reason, he says, was the laudable one (in itself), of carrying the students, by attendance on lectures of various kinds, to a thorough, free, and complete stage of development. But, where this plan is carried out compulsorily, and in opposition to the peculiar tendencies of the pupils, nothing will result except an ignoble false pretense, for the sole purpose of securing a certificate which will satisfy the formal requisitions. So little can the communication of knowledge succeed when enforced by any external compulsion.†

To proceed now to institutions in which the characters of the gymnasium and the university are confounded in a hybrid organization—to the lyceums.

If the first university year is devoted to philosophical studies, the result of the arrangement is to divide the university into two parts; since the philosophical studies are distinct from the professional. But still, most of the new-comers attend introductory professional courses, and their lives are those of students.

But if the philosophical faculty is established in lyceums at a distance from the universities, the separation becomes an entire one, and the character of a German university is entirely lost, whether as to studies or discipline. Instead of the universities we have special schools.

Savigny says, of the German universities, "Their common character consists in this: that each of them includes the whole body of knowledge, instead of being limited to a single department, as is often the case in the special schools of other countries." The superiority of this

* "System and Value of the German Universities," by Savigny, in Ranke's "*Historical and Political Gazette*" (*Historisch-politisch Zeitschrift*), September, 1832, p. 569, &c.

† Sufficient warnings cannot be given against university arrangements intended to control the bad, but which are actually a hindrance, and even injury to the good. Thus, for instance, bad students are forced into a hypocritical appearance of industry, a dead pharisaical labor, and at the same time the honest, sincere industry, and profitable studies of the better ones are made useless.

character, he adds, has been so often and so thoroughly shown, that he forbears to discuss it.

Thus, the erection of lyceums breaks up the character of our universities. One even moderately acquainted with the organization and influence of the philosophical faculties, will have no doubt of this. A lyceum will be an independent philosophical faculty, existing by itself; but such a faculty can only prosper when it is conjoined with the other faculties, and gives them, and receives from them, mutual vigor. The theological, juridical, and medical faculties, separate from the philosophical, would sink into mere preparatory schools for gaining a living in future; while the isolated philosophical faculty, wanting its relation to the serious requirements of life, and of the future profession, is without substance or aim. On the other hand, the closer and more complete the union of the philosophical with the other faculties, so much more efficient and scientifically thorough will the spirit of the university be.

The hybrid character of a lyceum, which is neither a gymnasium nor a university, must have the worst effect on its pupils, and impress a similar hybrid character on them. They can not be school-boys, and would willingly be students; but are, in fact, neither the one nor the other. It is a question, also, how the teacher is to manage them. It is too late for school discipline, and yet they can not be granted the entire academical freedom. But, though not granted, they will take it, and will be the more disorderly, in all respects, because they are under no wholesome restraint from the older students.

In reference to the foundation of lyceums, there are some considerations of importance, if they are to be not mere phantasms, but are to be actually efficient. Very important amounts of money will be required for this purpose. Let it be considered how great is the annual amount required for the professors' salaries of a philosophical faculty; the capital represented by their physical and natural historical collections, their botanic garden, and, above all, by their part of the university library; which may be estimated at two thirds of the whole number of books;—add, also, the annual expense for maintaining and increasing these collections, &c., and the total of the sum thus required for such a foundation will be astounding. And in this we are considering not at all the endowments of great universities, but at what is required for the smaller ones; what is so absolutely indispensable for instruction, that, in their absence, the most valuable lectures will be empty words, destitute of basis or efficiency. But if it be designed to diminish the expense of organizing a lyceum, by, so to speak, improvising a body of teachers, by intrusting the different departments to persons who may be occupying other situations at the place of the new institution, this will show that the office of a professor in the philosophical faculty is altogether undervalued and under-estimated. One seriously interested in his vocation as teacher, especially in the present busy and progressive age, will find abundant labor for himself; his office will demand the whole man; and can not possibly be filled as a mere occupation. But one who has the self-confidence, beside his other employment, as preacher, gymnasium teacher, or otherwise, to undertake that of professor in a lyceum, will only show that he was not wholly devoted to his former occupation—that his whole heart was not on it. But, if this charge be undeserved, he will need to be much on his guard lest, by over-estimating his own powers and under-estimating his new duties, he do all his work by halves, and, according to the old proverb, "between two stools, fall to the ground;" and so neither suffice for the old office nor for the new one.

Thus, all considerations oppose the introduction of lyceums, and none favor it. They break up existing organizations to the foundation. F. A. Wolf says: "In my opinion, great and universal changes are not advisable at any university. The useful results of the ancient organizations we already know, and continually enjoy. In order to a better one, experiments must be made, to form an opinion; and such experiments might be costly in many ways."

To this warning of Wolf's, may be added this, from Savigny: "So many causes have always tended to the dismemberment of Germany, that it may very well seem necessary to direct our attention to whatever good things are common to the whole nation; both for the sake of rejoicing in their possession, which secure the continuance of our national prosperity, and to direct us toward the means of maintaining them. Among the most important and valuable of those common possessions are, at this time, to be reckoned our universities."

The common character of these common possessions of Germany, the universities, we have delineated, and have shown that that character, according to Savigny's own views, would be entirely destroyed by the introduction of lyceums.

Wherever this shall happen, the mutilated universities will no longer be among the good possessions common to the German people, and be institutions of study for all the German races. They will excommunicate themselves; and, degraded into special schools, can no longer be reckoned entitled to equal privileges with the other German universities.

With sacred earnestness, and full of the importance of the subject, the judicious Savigny writes: "The universities have come down to us, a noble inheritance from former times; and it is a point of honor with us to leave them in a condition improved, where possible, and at least not made worse, to coming generations. It rests with us whether they shall remain as they are, or whether they shall sink or rise. The judgment of posterity will require an account of them at our hands."

Relations between the Philosophical Faculty and the Professional Studies.

Measures were now taken at Erlangen against the philosophical compulsory lectures. In 1844, instead of the one so-called philosophical (or Fox) year, two years were set apart, during which the student, beside the philosophical compulsory lectures, might attend professional ones.* In 1849, a further very important step was taken, by removing all compulsory attendance, and providing, instead, that every student must, during his university course, attend eight philosophical courses, of at least four lectures each; these eight to be selected at his pleasure, and no examination to be held on them.

It is evident that this plan would much satisfy the wishes of the better students; for they could now attend with interest such lectures as were suited to their scientific tendencies and capacities. But it is also not to be wondered at that some evils also resulted from it. It can not be denied that idle students could misuse the freedom given them to indulge in mere idleness. But no one who remembers the most lamentable results of the previous examinations of such idle students upon the compulsory lectures attended by them, will desire, for the sake of such results, to circumscribe the honorable freedom of the industrious. From my own convictions, I accordingly reject the compulsory lectures, and from my heart rejoice in the freedom of the better sort of students in making their selection. Still, I must repeat my observation, that they often hesitate about their choice, especially in the beginning of their studies; and that, on the other hand, they frequently wish, at the end of them, that they had attended many lectures whose value, and had not attended many others whose uselessness, they learned too late.

Let us consider, once more, the lectures of the philosophical faculty. The beginner, who hitherto, at the gymnasium, has had no choice as to what he shall study, and what not, has now before him the catalogue of lectures, for a selection at his pleasure. Most of them select

* This new arrangement was announced to the students, July 20, 1844, in an excellent address, by my honored colleague, Prof. Doederlein.

under the advice of older students; and accordingly often fall into the hands of those who advise them, during the first year, to refrain altogether from study, and rest after the labor of the gymnasium. The better minded have to decide whether they will continue their studies at the gymnasium, or will suffer these to rest, for a time at least, while they pursue studies which were not taught at the school. So far as my experience goes, most of them select the former course, as if they were afraid of a journey into an unknown country.

In any case, most of them are in great need of good advice. But what instructor will show them the way? Will not the philologist recommend philological lectures especially, the historian historical ones, &c.? Not that this will be from vulgar and egotistical motives, but only from the natural and necessary preference of every one for his own department. Very few professors have so far mastered the different studies as to be capable of lecturing on a comprehensive system of hodegetics.*

It has been attempted to simplify and ease the selection, by having each of the three faculties, in the plan of study which they draw up for their students, recommend to them lectures upon such subjects in the philosophical faculty as are most closely related to their respective professional studies. The faculty of law, for instance, would recommend historical lectures; of medicine, natural historical; of theology, philological.

However simple this expedient may seem, it is still to be feared that these recommendations to the students of each faculty will cause them to turn their backs upon all studies not recommended, as being foreign to their purpose, which is far from the case. Natural science, for instance, will usually not be recommended to students of theology, law, or philology. In after life these students will commonly have no opportunity to become acquainted with these studies, nor could they do so at the gymnasium. It is only at the university that an opportunity offers to fill up these omissions in their education, and to acquire a knowledge of nature. Here are offered teachers and means of instruction. Ought theological students, &c., now, not to improve the opportunity, at least to gain a glimpse into a world which has hitherto been strange to them, and which will usually remain so, if they do not seize that occasion? I have taken this example because it occurs most readily to me, as professor in natural history.† The point will be made still clearer

* A very good arrangement to avoid this danger, prevails, for example, at Erlangen. Each professor of the philosophical faculty draws up a summary of the studies of his department, and a short introduction to it, to be studied. Collections of these are printed for the students.

† See "*History of Education*," vol. iii. part 1, p. 168.

by the following, which I extract from the introduction of my lectures on natural history.

In the gymnasium, I say, there is usually no preparation made for studying natural history. Let it now be imagined that students should come to the university who had not even learned *mensa* and *amo*. As little as these would be capable of profiting by lectures on Tacitus and Roman literature, would those unacquainted with the first elements of the knowledge of natural science be prepared for the higher courses on natural science.

Such should, as far as possible, make up for the omissions in their studies at the gymnasium, by lectures on natural history. These will afford them an intelligible glance into the creation; a general view of natural science. They will have penetrated into the vestibule.

If it be inquired of what use is this study, not merely to all students whatever, but to those destined for the profession to which it is related, the answer would be, in brief, as follows:

A young student of medicine will scarcely question the usefulness of the study of nature; indeed, his medical studies are, themselves, a department of the knowledge of nature. Why, then, should he not desire to be acquainted with studies so nearly related to his own as zoology, which is to introduce him to comparative anatomy, so necessary to him, as botany and mineralogy? These studies are important to the physician, not only in theory, but in practice; for he must be acquainted with the medicinal qualities of animals, plants, and minerals. And, moreover, if he has, by diligent study in natural history, trained his eyes and his understanding to a clear and thorough comprehension of animals, plants, and minerals, he has, at the same time, been preparing them to understand anatomical relations; and, above all, for acute observation of the symptoms of the sick.

To students of law, the study of nature seems much less important, professionally, than to physicians. And still, there is one point of view in which it has especial value for him. He can become acquainted, in it, with the just and loving laws of God, which are a pattern for all human laws. The whole world is governed by them, without change, and always. The law of the Lord is unchangeable. Thus invariable does it appear in astronomy, which this can, with mathematical certainty, "determine the places in the heavens, where sun, moon, and planets have stood, stand, and shall stand." It computes backward with certainty, that the eclipse of the sun foretold by Thales took place on the 17th of June of the year 603 before Christ; and Kepler computed forward, in 1627, that in 1761 the transit of Venus over the sun would take place. Thus God rules, without any variation.

And the earthly creatures, as well as the heavenly, reveal the fixedness of God's law. When the botanist* has described the species lily, by saying that its flower has a campanulate corolla in six parts, six anthers, a six-celled, three-sided capsule, &c., the definition applies not only to a German lily, but to one from Mount Carmel. And, in like manner, the careful, faithful representations of lilies in ancient pictures have also a corolla with six parts, six anthers, &c. Thus, the botanist's description applies to lilies of all countries and all times. The steadfastness of the law is clear. But an ignorant person, on hearing this, would say: All lilies, then, are alike; and, according to that, a great monotony must prevail throughout the creation. Such was the idea of the Electress who controverted Leibnitz's assertion that no leaf was exactly like another; but all her efforts to find two leaves entirely alike were quite in vain. And just as vain would it be to endeavor to find two lilies completely like each other, even if they grew on the same stem. The law of the Lord is without change; but this unchangeableness does not produce any unpleasant uniformity among the individuals of which each is a representation of the divine idea. The law of agreeable variety and free beauty is still more marked in the case of feathers. The animal creation exemplifies it still more; and most clearly of all, the human family. Here the law passes more and more out of sight, and freedom and independence supply their place to such an extent, that the supreme power of God is too often doubted and forgotten, in the life both of individuals and of the race.

Thus the laws and government of God unite things apparently irreconcilable—fixed laws and freedom. Thus they are a model for human laws; which should avoid tyrannical constraint and anarchical arbitrariness; should protect freedom, yet secure and maintain steadfast order. So lofty a model will be a light upon the path of him who devotes himself, with love and earnestness, to the study of law.

For students who intend to devote themselves to teaching, the study of nature has great value, for more than one reason.

It has already been observed how active a capacity and impulse there is in youth to examine and collect plants, minerals, and animals. In proportion as this has been recognized, has the necessity been felt of teaching natural history in the schools. As actual departments of training for the sciences, and for life, the natural sciences require also to be made elements of school education. We have seen that this demand grew to such a height, in the eighteenth century, that it became necessary to found real schools, although, at the same time, gymnasium

---

* See "*History of Education*," vol. iii. part 1, p. 173.

scholars also received instruction in natural science. Every student who proposes to offer himself for a place as teacher, either in the gymnasium or a real school, should bear this in mind.

Students in philology should also remember that a certain degree of attainment in real knowledge is absolutely necessary to any understanding of the ancients, which is to be actual, and not merely verbal. Altogether, apart from books pertaining directly to the natural sciences, such as Aristotle, Pliny, &c., some such knowledge is needed to understand the classics, which are universally and daily read, as Cicero, Virgil, Ovid, &c. Quintilian, indeed, says, that philology (*grammatice*) can not be thoroughly understood without a knowledge of music; "nor without a knowledge of the movements of the stars, can the poets be understood; for, not to go further, they often refer to the rising and setting of the constellations in defining time; nor can they be understood without a knowledge of natural philosophy; for in very many places, in almost all poems, are passages based on a profound knowledge of natural problems; as, for instance, Empedocles, among the Greeks; and Varro and Lucretius, among the Latins; who put precepts of wisdom into verse."*

If it is asked how far a knowledge of natural science is to be required of theological students, the readiest answer is, that much such knowledge is requisite for understanding the Bible.† It is well known that Luther studied natural history in connection with his translation of the Bible.

In their subsequent vocation, most theological students, when pastors, are also school-inspectors. At present, not only in cities, but in villages, many real studies are taught, especially relating to natural science. The inspecting pastor, therefore, needs a competent acquaintance with this branch of instruction, in order to judge whether the teacher instructs properly, &c. This he can only do by having himself studied natural sciences; for which, as we have seen, he finds scarcely any opportunity except at the university.

The study of nature, pursued in the right spirit and in the right manner, will, moreover, have the strongest and most wholesome influ-

---

* Compare the remarks of Erasmus on real studies. ("*History of Education*," vol. i. p. 166.) In the third edition of my Geography I have cited many passages from the classics which require information on natural subjects; see, for instance, p. 10, remark 6; p. 20, remark 120; p. 62, remark 23; p. 79, remark 36; p. 283, remark 16, &c.

† Observe the number of articles on natural science in Winer's "*Dictionary of Natural History*;" I may refer also to Bochart's "*Hierozoikon*," to Rosenmüller, &c. The application of geological hypotheses to the interpretation of Genesis is of great importance; but here only demonstrated facts should be relied on, lest the pure truth be defiled and made contemptible by fantastic human conceptions—a most dangerous misalliance.

ence upon the development of a Christian theological character. On this subject, one of the greatest English natural philosophers says:* "Another thing, then, that qualifies an experimentarian for the reception of a revealed religion, and so of Christianity, is, that an accustomance of endeavoring to give clear explications of the phenomena of nature, and discover the weakness of those solutions, that superficial wits are wont to make and acquiesce in, does insensibly work in him a great and ingenious modesty of mind. And on the score of this intellectual, as well as moral virtue, not only he will be very inclinable, both to desire and admit further information, about things which he perceives to be dark or abstruse; but he will be very unapt to take, for the adequate standard of truth, a thing so imperfectly informed, and narrowly limited, as his mere or abstracted reason. . . . And though a vulgar philosopher, . . . may presume that he understands every thing, and may be easily tempted to think that he must not hope, nor desire to learn from less able men than his first teachers; and that that can not be true, or be done, which agrees not with his philosophy; yet a sober and experienced naturalist, that knows what difficulties remain yet unsurmounted in the presumedly clear conception and explications even of things corporeal, will not, by a lazy or arrogant presumption, *imagine* that his knowledge about things supernatural is already sufficient. . . . . And this frame of mind is a very happy one for a student in revealed theology. . . . An assiduous conversation with the exquisitely framed and admirably managed works of God, brings a skillful considerer of them to discover, from time to time, many things to be feasible, or to be true, which, while he argued but upon grounds of incompetently informed reason, he judged false or unpracticable."†

To these remarks of the excellent Boyle, I will add a single observation. The capacity for objective, independent truth, such as does not depend on man, seems to have been entirely lost by many persons who have occupied themselves exclusively with purely verbal studies. There are innumerable persons who assert that there exist only strictly individual beliefs; that some have one, others another; and that this variety is an evidence of the freedom of the modern method of investigation. This unfortunate belief has caused much trouble in theolo-

---

* *Boyle's Works*, 5 vols. fol., Lond., 1744: vol. v. p. 56.

† I repeat, that these remarks are made of serious and modest consideration and investigation of *facts* in natural science; not of unreasoning, fantastic hypotheses, with no foundation whatever. These may lead astray silly laymen, and it is only when knowledge is the object that men acquainted with the subject will be followed. For this reason, visionaries have far more pupils—a larger public, than reasonable men.

gy, has opened the door to all manner of arbitrary views, and has loosened all those loving bands in which men are joined by the common recognition of eternal and holy truths. From such a wicked arbitrariness the earnest investigator of nature turns away; his observations do not entice him into error, because he only admits that his views are true when they have been proved by their agreement with the facts of nature. Before Kepler discovered his first astronomical law, that the paths of the planets are ellipses, he had determined upon another figure. As Tycho's observations did not harmonize with this, he rejected it and took the ellipse, which entirely harmonized with them. In a similar irrefragable manner do truths appear to us in crystallography; and to discover their beautiful laws, and candidly to recognize them when discovered, gives great pleasure and edification to the mineralogist.

It would be exceedingly beneficial to the young theologian, to be constrained by a knowledge of nature, to acknowledge some truth entirely independent of himself, and thus to become humbled. Under such discipline he would more nearly approach the "faith which precedes knowledge;" and would learn to approach the study of the Bible, not in presumptuous ignorance, criticising and censuring, but humbly, with holy awe for impregnable truth, fast founded, and higher than all reason.

What has been said may justify the wish, that in recommending to the students lectures by the philosophical faculty, the three other faculties may act with circumspection, and with reference to the connection—sometimes an obscure one—among different studies, and to their influence on the training of the students.

IV. Personal Relations of the Professors to Students.

From the foregoing it follows, that at present the students are regarded not as entirely free and independent men, but as youths, grown beyond school-discipline, it is true, but yet in process of development and progress toward manly self-dependence. The necessity will be recognized, of not leaving them to themselves during this dangerous process of emancipation; but of guiding it by laws and personal influence.

In this proceeding, however, paths lead off on both sides, by a tendency to do too much, and too little. Some govern too much by compulsory lectures, incessant examinations, and oversight of expenses; while others think every new student a quite free man, capable of advising for himself, and needing scarcely the most trifling guidance during his life as a student.

It is our wish, in the academical legislation, to regulate the life and studies of the students as judiciously as possible, without injuring their freedom; the best legislation must, however, interfere with a certain neutrality—with the cold heartlessness of the abstract. Misunderstandings can only be healed by paternal faithfulness on the part of the teachers toward the students. The latter are the congregations, of whom the former have the cure of souls, and for whom they must in future render an account.

Such is the sentiment expressed in the statutes of the university of Halle.* They also require of the professors unity of belief. But it is not enough, they add, for them to be pure in their teachings; they must, by an unblamable life, and serious and upright character, set a good example to the students, and not be a scandal to them; and must, by word and deed, promote piety and morality among them.

The statutes of the theological faculty of Halle go more into details under this general statement. The professors of this faculty, they enact, must maintain unanimity among themselves; must, with one accord, aid their students as if their own sons, with paternal counsel and assistance; and to this end shall consult together at the beginning of every half-year upon what lectures shall be delivered, in order to satisfy all the requirements of the students. Therefore it is necessary, they proceed, that the professors shall gain an intimate knowledge of the students. For this purpose they must, "in every week, upon a fixed day, devote an hour to the useful employment of carefully examining the progress of the students in knowledge and in life; the plan being so adjusted that each student shall come before them once in each quarter of a year. If the number of students should increase so that one hour is not sufficient, then more hours must be set apart for so indispensable a plan."

New-comers are to be questioned upon what they have studied at school or at other universities; and their mental capacity, their purposes, and their situation as to means, in order to the formation of an opinion as to what is to be particularly recommended to each one. Above all, love of God, and humility, are to be prescribed to them.†

In another place they say, that the students shall often be reminded by the professors, that in order to practical theology, elegant and

---

* The statutes are meant which were enacted in 1694, at the establishment of the university. (Koch, i. p. 466.)

† Koch, i. p. 483, &c. They recommended to the professors of theology to lay to heart an expression of St. Augustine, and to enforce it upon their students, viz.: "That they shall see, in proportion as they die to the present age; and that by as much as they live for it, they shall not see."

honorable manners and abstinence from worldly life will by no means suffice; but that it requires self-denial, which is the fruit of true conversion.*

The first impulse toward the peculiar character of the academical organization at Halle was given by Spener. As early as in 1690, before the founding of the university of Halle, he had advanced a proposal, that "at every university there should be appointed, at the public expense, a learned, wise, and pious theologian, who should not only examine the knowledge and capabilities of new-comers, but should especially give them correct ideas about theological knowledge, that they may learn how themselves to attain it, and how to study it in a proper order."†

It is evident that this reference is not to a merely scientific system of hodegetics. Spener's plan was to have only one man; for in that controversial period he might well despair of finding an entirely unanimous theological faculty to fulfill his wishes. How gratified, therefore, must he have been, when the theologians of the new university of Halle, such as Francke, Breithaupt, and Anton, united themselves with one mind to carry them into execution. They complied conscientiously with the statutes of their faculty, and even did more than the statutes required. They devoted some hours weekly to a meeting of the faculty in the house of their dean, examined new-comers, and caused each of them to give in a written account of his previous studies; and then they advised them in what direction to prosecute them, and what lectures to hear. All the theological students were obliged, every term, to advise with the professors, at a meeting of the faculty, on the lectures they had heard and were to hear. If it was found that a student was dissipated or idle, he was brought before the faculty and paternally admonished; and if this did not suffice, the case was reported to his friends.

It was also required, that the students should be in confidential communication, not only with the body of the faculty, but also with individual professors, on all matters relative to their lives and studies.

By these means the professors became thoroughly acquainted with the students; and if the faculty were applied to for testimonials relative to a stipend, they were, it is said, "able to use, in most of them, very definite expressions."

Thus do the statutes and other sources describe the religious care of the theological faculty of Halle, in the time of A. H. Francke.

Of course, such care in religious matters must have been intended

---

* Koch, i. p. 487.

† "*Francke's Institutions*," ii. p. 63.

to secure not only the fullest acquaintance with the students, but also a successful religious teaching and training of them. And now I can hear more than one reader ask, with meaning, whether I would see this plan of Francke introduced among us? The question is asked, in the conviction that its introduction would be, at least in our own times, impossible. To this opinion I must assent; and on the point, I cite Francke himself, who complains, as early as in 1709, fifteen years after the university of Halle was founded, that most of the students had lost very much of their zeal for good. He describes the coarse lives of the students, and observes, that the well-meaning care of the theological professors for the students was so little appreciated, that they decidedly objected to it, as an infringement upon their freedom as students; and that the good advice given to them produced no results. And he adds, "I can not think of this without great sorrow, and can not sufficiently wonder how it is possible that so little result has come from all our lectures and advice."*

With the best and purest intentions, a mistake had evidently been made, and a reaction was the consequence.† Instead of the prevailing wild student-life, Francke and his theological colleagues would have introduced, at one stroke, a still, pious, and almost conventual discipline. Devotional exercises were heaped upon devotional exercises. Pious emotions and excitements were encouraged in every way. Every occasion was seized for praying, preaching, exhorting, and singing. It is not to be wondered at that the student-life, based deeply on the custom of centuries and its accompanying coarse vices, diametrically opposed as it was to such a scheme as this, should have made a powerful opposition to Francke's efforts; so that he prevailed only with a quiet and meditative class of students. And it must be confessed, that he repelled not only the dissipated and wild ones, but also the pure, able, and talented.

I may thus be thought to retract the praise which I have bestowed upon the honest efforts of Francke and his friends, and their services to the students. By no means. The conscientious manner in which they performed their official duties, their true and paternal love for the students, render them rather models for all academical teachers; while their errors may, on the other hand, admonish us to proceed with circumspection, modest wisdom, and a Pauline accommodation; and to permit youth to be youth.

* *Parænetical Lectures*, iv. p. 111.

† "*History of Education*," vol. ii. p. 147. I have here referred to Luther's sound views on education, and have shown that they were decidedly preferable to Francke's, in which there already prevailed the insipid and unmanly creed of that pietism which afterward displayed itself in so many caricatured phases.

Let us return to our subject, which may be put in the form of the following question: Is legislation and strict adherence to the laws, all that the university requires? I reply, by no means. At an early period, the effort was made to control the students by personal influence. But woe to the universities if, as was the case with the ancient bursaries, goats are made gardeners; where hirelings are set over the students, who regard not their good, but their own profit. It would be better for the students to be left entirely to themselves than to fall into the hands of such men.

At Rinteln, Marburg, and Helmstädt, new students were required to put themselves under the charge of some one instructor. But this seems to have occasioned great abuses, similar to the previous ones in the bursaries. A vigorous production* of the 17th century, apparently emanating from Helmstädt, gives strange accounts of the privileges of the so-called "professor-students," that is, students who boarded at the tables of the professors; and who, as the author says, "had therefore a precedence in all things, above the convictorists" (those who ate in companies together) "and citizen-students." Among these privileges are mentioned, that they have a higher place at church and at meetings, even at the Communion; that they are to take fencing-lessons only of the fencing-master; that their disputations are printed in folio, those of others in quarto; that they may wear their swords when visiting the magnificus;† not to mention some less elegant ones. Though this author may somewhat exaggerate, still his production indicates that the sacred vocation and authority of the teacher were most vilely abused.

In the beginning of the nineteenth century, Meiners made a proposition as laughable as it was exceptionable. This was, to have boarding establishments instituted at the universities, at which "board, lodging, and attendance should be so excellent, that the young people would desire places at them for these reasons only. Persons at these should have a certain precedence, and should assert it. It would be a great recommendation if either French or English should be constantly spoken at these boarding-houses. This would free them from all invidious appearances. Parents would tell their children, and the boarders their acquaintances, that that boarding-house had been selected only on account of the language."‡

---

* "*Curious Inaugural Disputation on the Law, Privileges, and Prerogatives of the Athenian Professor-students, over the Citizen-students and Communists. . . . . By Schlingschlangschlorum.*" Athens here, as in Meyfart, must have meant an extinct German university; while Saalathen, Elbathen, &c., are designations for Jena, Halle, and Wittenberg.

† Rector. ‡ Meiners' "*Constitution, &c., of the German Universities.*" Göttingen, 1802.

Meiners printed this plan in 1802, while prorector at Göttingen. It agrees well with what he says of "a young man's success." This, according to him, "depends not merely on his capacity, knowledge, and moral excellence, but always in part, and sometimes entirely or chiefly, upon his deportment, and how he shows his bringing up."*

It is most injurious to students, whose manners are good, to be especially introduced into the social circle of the professors. Such students very often are entirely superficial, unstable, and afraid of labor; and rely for success upon some accomplishments in music, and dancing, or by a gift for uselessly passing the time away. Their instructors should rather remind such of the serious duties of their present and future vocations. To prefer such, on account of mere external show, to simple, straightforward, and able students, is most indefensible, not only with reference to those who are thus undervalued, but still more on account of those thus preferred, who can not but see, in such treatment, an approbation of their idle employments, which will, at last, leave them in lamentable ignorance and insignificance.

At a later period, Bavarian ministerial ordinances repeatedly recommended to the professors, especially deans of faculty, as much as possible, to watch over and direct the lives and studies of the students. The same requirement was made by the Prussian ministry, and especially in a rescript of 14th September, 1824. This observes that the management of the studies and of the students is, no doubt, intrusted to the academical authorities, but that this is far from being sufficient. The students often attend few lectures, or none at all; select them inappropriately, in an improper order, or attend negligently. The ministry believes that these evils can be cured, "by having at each university a number of professors to take more particular charge of the studies of individual students." And it is added, "this may be done, either by appointing for this purpose such professors as were deans of faculty when the present students commenced their course, so that at the end of their deanship they may continue in this special oversight, or by appointing, without reference to the deanship, or to any other academical or faculty office, professors specially fitted for the place, to be properly selected. In either case they will have the duty of guiding and overseeing every way the students put under their special charge, and in particular, of watching that each of them not only attends lectures, but makes a suitable selection of them, and attends them in a proper order and regularly. It would be necessary, to this end, that the professors should fully know what lectures have been

---

* Meiners' "*Constitution*," &c., p. 7.

already attended by the students put under their care; and should keep themselves assured that they are orderly and regular in attendance, that if they should fail in these particulars, they may, with paternal care, set them right. And it will likewise be necessary that no academical stipends shall be granted without their report; and that those which are given should be given only on the production of a half-yearly attestation to the recipients' studies." *

The good intentions of the ministry are too apparent in this paper to be mistaken. But no one, even moderately familiar with the usual circumstances and condition of a university, will be surprised that—by all indications at least—the plan of the ministry never went into execution. This may be concluded from a second rescript of 9th January, 1830, in which the professors of the university at Königsberg are required to assist the students in their studies with their advice. This says, "It can not be often enough repeated to the professors, that they are bound to exercise unremitting watchfulness over the industry, the learned studies, and the morals of the students; and that one advice, one admonition, given at the right time, and in the right manner, by a professor to a student, is more useful than any number of police ordinances." †

If this committee of professors, or ephorate over the students, had existed, this latter requirement would either not have been mentioned at all, or would have been, at least, expressed in another way.

Such an ephorate over the theological students at Erlangen was established in 1833. At its head was placed an excellent man, learned, upright, and intelligent, the late High Consistory Councilor Höfling, and under him four tutors (*repetenten*), one for the students of each of the four years of the course. These latter were mostly eminent men also; some of them of celebrity in the learned world. It may be imagined that though this arrangement may have been considered exceedingly improper by the idle students, yet that the industrious ones would have fallen in with it. This was far from being the case, these latter also felt themselves under constraint by it, and the idle contrived so to evade the means used for enforcing industry, as not to be reached at all. This is not the place to detail all the misadventures of this ephorate; suffice it to say, that after continuing fifteen years, it was discontinued. ‡

Thus we see that the most various efforts to gain a personal influ-

---

* Koch, ii. p. 190. † Ib., ii. p. 205.

‡ A fuller account of this ephorate will be found in the excellent biography of Höfling, by my respected friend and colleague, Prof. Nägelsbach, in vol. xxvi. of the "*Gazette of Protestantism*," Appendix to the July No., p. 9.

ence over the lives and studies of the students, have sometimes been thwarted altogether, and sometimes what was gained was imperfect in many ways, and of brief duration.

We ought not, moreover, to conceal the fact, that the students have considered all legislation for the oversight and regulation of their studies by the authorities as an attack upon their freedom as students, and have opposed it accordingly, however well meant.

They will, on the other hand, place confidence in professors who advise them truly, faithfully, and honestly, but not officially; I may say, without their official faces on. But, above all, the professor must have at heart the good of the students;* and must watch and pray that the confidence reposed in him by the students does not lead him into vanity, and an ambition to have many followers. If this should happen, he must find his reward in it only; and his influence upon the students can not be good; and for the reason that such a vain teacher will not remain open and true, but will flatter the students, in order to conciliate them, and fasten them to him.

But in this way a vain teacher makes vain scholars; who would consider any serious warning or admonition from any one else, no matter how true, well-meant, and sincere, a deep insult.

V. Small and Large Universities. Scientific Academies.

Our discussions of the various university laws, and other experiments and efforts to control and direct the lives and studies of students, will occasion many readers to imagine that one or another remark is applicable to small universities, but not to large ones; at least, what is said of the personal influence of the professors over the students. Just as there can be no watchfulness over souls, if the preacher's congregation is immoderately large, so a professor at Munich or Berlin can not attempt any personal influence upon so large a number of students; or can at most labor with those few who are especially recommended to him, or otherwise come into close contact with him.

Many persons, however, make no account whatever of any such influence. They consider the universities as institutions for the promotion of science, even to its furthest special departments; and the lectures are only of secondary importance to them. In this view, it is certainly easy to show that the purposes of a university will be better served at a large one than at a small one. They refer especially to the various important appurtenances of the larger universities; their rich

* Steffens was the model of a truly paternal friend of the students; exhibiting to them an indescribably pure goodness of heart and self sacrifice, as I can testify thankfully, from my own experience.

mineralogical and zoological collections, botanic gardens, physical apparatus, chemical laboratories, large hospitals, anatomical museums, &c. The smaller universities are contemned, because, as the proverb says, they cut their coat according to their cloth, and, having much smaller incomes, attempt only moderate things. And it is said that, by reason of these small revenues, they cannot procure the services of men of the highest grade; or, if they do accept situations, they commonly remain but a short time, the more eminent of them being invited to larger universities.

Before proceeding to a more careful comparison of the respective value of large and small universities, we must oppose the notions of the object of a university which are advanced by these advocates of large universities. Universities are by no means founded exclusively for the promotion of the sciences as such. That is the object of scientific academies; while universities are institutions for instruction. While the former consider the present aids to science only as means to be used for further attainments, as a *terminus a quo*, towards greater attainments, and are solely devoted to the extension further and further of the limits of the domain of science, and to perfect more and more fully, and establish more deeply and firmly, every particular department, the latter, the universities, have not all this for their immediate and direct object; they are, I repeat, institutions for instruction. The immediate business of the teacher is, to consider what has been already made clear and certain in his department; and to communicate this clearly and certainly to his pupils. He must not give them must, in which many impurities are still mingled, but well-worked and pure wine.

Science in itself is the object of the academician; the teaching of science, of the university teacher. This teaching is his official business; he ought not to lose sight of it. Complaints are justly made of such gymnasium teachers as lose sight of such teaching as is adapted to their pupils, and who deliver them lectures instead, idly anticipating the university. But university instructors are equally blameworthy, who lose sight of their proper occupation, and idly seek to make themselves academicians, by actual and purely scientific labors; in their chase after celebrity losing sight of their office as teachers.

One who is true to this object, however, will feel bound always to attain a more profound knowledge of his department, and to comprehend it more clearly, in order to be able to teach it more thoroughly and clearly. Upon such a conscientious endeavor a blessing will rest; and it will usually more promote scientific knowledge, than such infatuation after science and unloving neglect of pupils.

The academician requires a most extensive apparatus of books, natural objects, instruments, &c.; the newest and most abstruse. Desiring to advance further and further in his science, he must stand at the summit of it, and overlook his fellow-laborers in the earth below, in order rightly to perform his task as a member of the great republic of learning.

The university instructor, on the contrary, needs only a complete apparatus *for teaching*, of books, natural objects, instruments, &c.; an apparatus which, as to its purpose, differs much from that of the academician, and may usually be more modest and cheaper. The excessive riches of the apparatus at a great university is even a hindrance to the purpose of the instruction. The scholars are not capable of managing so much material. A light can be extinguished by too much oil, as well as by too little.

The affectionate care which the governments have of late bestowed upon the smaller universities in reference to their scientific departments, permits us to hope that these departments will gradually become capable of answering their purposes. Those at the head of them must, on their parts, apply judiciously the means granted them; must not waste them uselessly, nor seek impossibilities; nor make requisitions for their own department exclusively and without reference to the rest, and without looking to their prosperity also; which would indicate both want of fairness and of general scientific development.

Examples will make this clearer. Suppose I, as professor of mineralogy at Erlangen, had been unable to take pleasure in the collection of minerals there, having got it into my head that they were of very little value, because, for instance, they were so far behind the rich collection at Berlin; and that I was always thinking about the magnificent specimens of gold there, the hundred and five crystallized diamonds, and so many other treasures. This scientific envy would only injure my official usefulness. I ought rather to reflect thus: I receive so much a year for purchases for the collection of minerals; how can I use it to the best advantage? If I seek mostly for new and rare objects, and am ashamed that the collection should lack them, I can easily waste the whole amount upon a few newly discovered expensive specimens, which usually will have, for my pupils, a value relatively exceedingly small. As a teacher of mineralogy, I must buy what is of value to them. And, fortunately, it is precisely those which are cheapest; species which occur most frequently, being of the greatest significance in nature and in life. I should endeavor to make the collection of these as complete and good as possible; so that the pupil may have before his eyes the laws of the progression of the species, especially in a well-arranged series of distinct crystals.

In like manner, the zoologist of a small university should not aim at a menagerie like that at London; the botanist should not demand immense, magnificent hot-houses, and a special palace for the *Victoria Regina;* but should endeavor, above all, to complete the flora of his locality, as being both cheapest and the most appropriate for his instruction. Nor should the instructor in medicine be disgusted because he does not find so many singular cases as occur in the great cities and their institutions. He should, first of all, learn to manage diseases that are not rare, but most frequent—dropsy, scarlet-fever, &c.

But I may be thought, in defending the small universities, to be making a virtue of necessity. By no means.

There is no more difference between the large and small universities, either, as to those studies which are taught by words only.

There is a difficulty at the large ones, for which, at present, we see no remedy, and which arises from the large number of students. I refer to what has already been said of the necessity for dialogic instruction in all studies where actual seeing is necessary to accomplishment; and in some of which the hands must also be instructed, as in practical chemistry and surgery. This is out of the question where the number of pupils is too large; and most of all, when they are beginners, who usually are unable to help themselves, and therefore need from the teachers assistance, and continual watchfulness over the course of their acquirements.

This is the case, for instance, with students of medicine. It is extremely necessary that, at the clinical lectures, they should themselves examine and treat the sick; but this is impossible when the instructor has a large number of pupils and spectators. A pupil of a celebrated medical professor related that he was accustomed, when the professor, with his crowd of students, came into the hospital, to fix himself, in advance, near some one bed, and to be content—and to be obliged to be—with hearing his teacher's observations on that one patient. Only those close about the professor were in any better case; and most of them who followed his long circuit at a distance, received little or nothing. This was at a large university. How often, on the other hand, have I heard the praises of the friendly and conscientious care with which, at the clinical lectures of the smaller universities, the students were personally instructed, and thus prepared for their future employment!

Similar praise is bestowed upon various departments of the smaller universities. Not being over-filled, personal instruction of individuals is practicable, wherever they need it.

Lastly, I should remark, that in great cities the students usually live in a scattered manner, and are lost in the crowd of people. They fail to acquire the feeling of a university, the sense of membership of the community. Their university years do not assume, to them, any definite and peculiar character, as years, not only of learned labor, but of that serious training of the character which their collection together would promote, but which the dispersedness of a great city injures. Their teachers mostly remain at a distance from them, and so much the nearer are the temptations which offer, and even wickedly force themselves upon them.

If it is claimed that at large cities the students have opportunities of seeing and hearing works of art, it may be answered, that the students from the smaller universities go in great numbers to Berlin, Munich, Dresden, &c., to see and hear those very works, and return full of every thing which they have seen and heard.

The scientific riches of the larger universities can best be made use of by students who have prepared themselves for doing so at the smaller universities. Thus it is usual for medical students from the smaller universities, during the latter years of their student life, or even after their degree, to resort to Berlin, Vienna, &c., to become acquainted with the great institutions there; being ready to profit by them, even if they can obtain but little assistance. The same is true of those who have studied natural sciences at the smaller universities under their teachers; they are prepared to profit by collections, &c., without aid.*

In conclusion: a word on the assertion that the smaller universities contain no celebrated men; no virtuosos. This might easily be refuted by an enumeration of the crowd of eminent men who have taught at the smaller universities for centuries, from the time when Luther and Melancthon taught and labored at Wittenberg, down to our own. It is true that the eminent men are invited from the smaller to the larger universities. But they have usually acquired their reputation at the smaller; have labored there during their best and strongest years, unexhausted and efficiently. Fame usually comes late,— when they are going down hill; the invitation to the great university limps along, when they are longing for their evening rest. We often hear it remarked, that they are resting there on their laurels.

---

* I repeat what I have already said, that for students of theology, law, and philology, the larger universities have not a shadow of advantage over the smaller.

VI. Elementary Instruction in Natural Science at the University.

In the time of Melancthon, a Wittenberg mathematical teacher delivered an address of invitation to the students. In this he praised arithmetic, and urged them not to be discouraged by the difficulty of that study. Its first elements were easy; multiplication and division, it is true, required more labor, but with attention could be acquired without difficulty. There are, no doubt, more difficult portions of arithmetic; but, he adds, "I am speaking of the beginning, which will be taught to you, and useful to you." In reading this we can scarcely believe our eyes.* We shall, however, not wonder, upon becoming better acquainted with the school instruction of that period. At the gymnasia, arithmetic was either not taught at all, or as an extra study.† The university teachers, therefore, were obliged to go over what had been neglected at the schools, and teach elementary portions which are now taught in the lowest common-schools.

Let us compare with this the task of a university mathematical teacher at the present day. He only inquires, What is the business of the gymnasium as to mathematical instruction; how far do they carry their scholars? And if the answer is, To the understanding and practice of plane trigonometry; his task is, to make the *terminus ad quem* of the school, the *terminus a quo* of his own teaching, and to take his pupils from plane to spherical trigonometry, and so onward.

It is not very long since the first serious introduction of instruction in natural science into the universities; and more importance is daily attached to it. For example, my official predecessor, Court-councilor Von Schubert, was professor of natural history at large, and, at the same time, of the special departments of zoology, botany, and mineralogy. As requirements became greater, botany was first set off, and Court-councilor Koch appointed professor of botany. When I took Schubert's place I stated that, besides natural history at large, I could attend only to the special department of mineralogy; and accordingly Prof. A. Wagner was appointed my assistant to the chair of zoology. When he was transferred to Munich, a special professorship of zoology was founded, which was given to Court-councilor R. Wagner.

Any one even moderately acquainted with the progress of natural history—who has merely heard of the immense number of species collected, examined, and described, in late times, will see that one profes-

* See "*History of Education*," vol. i. p. 319. The present essay belongs with the previous portion (vol. iii. part 1, p. 130), in teaching natural history, and continues it more into detail, as to the present condition of that instruction in the universities. † Ib., p. 265.

sorship of natural history was necessarily divided among three professors.

This is the condition of the natural-historical departments in the universities, as to their scientific aims; and how completely have these become changed within the present century!

But the university teacher is concerned, not only with science, but with the teaching of it; not only with beasts, plants, and stones, but with pupils. And has there been a change here, also, within fifty years?

I answer: None whatever. As to natural history, they come to the university just as ignorant as they did fifty years ago, notwithstanding the demands of science have increased in such a great proportion. They bring just as much knowledge of natural history as the Wittenberg mathematician's scholars did of arithmetic: that is, none at all.

What *terminus a quo*, therefore, shall be selected for the instruction in natural history of the university? The no-point of complete ignorance. Elementary instruction must, therefore, be given, at any rate; just as the Wittenberg professor had to teach his students the four ground-rules.

However disagreeable this may sound, we must by no means overlook this necessity, but rather give it the more attention. We must be definite upon the beginning, progress, and purpose of natural-historical instruction at the universities. And as to the pupils, we shall not speak of those few who devote themselves entirely to natural history, but of those who pursue professional studies, especially medicine.

These, as we have seen, are, in Prussia and Bavaria, examined in zoology, botany, and mineralogy; and thus must apportion their time and labor among the three; and also, the requirements from them must be proportioned to their attainments in the same. They are also examined in physic, chemistry, and pharmacognosy; which, together with their professional studies, leave them not much time for natural history. The most valuable part of the lectures on it they hear during one short summer term; the more diligent repeating the course, as far as their professional studies will allow, during the next summer term.

Let me be permitted the following observations on this point. For teaching Latin, some sixteen terms are employed at the schools; being eight classes. And in one short term—or, at most, in two—the student is expected to acquire an unheard-of mass of knowledge of natural science, when not even the A B C of it has been taught him at school.*

* I am far from requiring that natural science shall be put on an equality with languages at the gymnasium. This would be very absurd; but the entire neglect of it, at this day, seems in-

When I was appointed professor of natural history, I set myself about considering my duties. Without confining myself strictly to the usual conception of "natural history," I determined to become, though unostentatiously, a supplementary instructor for the omissions of the gymnasium course, and to teach such studies as my pupils ought to have learned at the school: that is, mathematical and physical geography, mineralogy, botany, zoology, and lastly, anthropology. In this manner also, I became clear as to the just extent and the proper ultimate purpose of my instruction.

My lectures were intended, as I have more fully explained in another place,* to introduce youths before employed almost exclusively about words, and who knew of no organ for learning except the ear, to a department of learning entirely new to them, and prosecuted mostly by the eye. To oral explanations I added, as far as possible, the examination of minerals, plants, and animals. This was, however, only to open their eyes, as it were; for a thorough, permanent, and satisfactory acquaintance with the subjects in hand was not to be thought of; their eyes were too fast shut, and the time much too short. This practice was first commenced in the lectures on mineralogy, botany, and zoology, as connected with general natural history. The exercise of their eyes, before so neglected, and incapable of intelligent observation, was secured by examining minerals, plants, and animals, and was so managed as to proceed together with the elementary instruction in mineralogy, botany, and zoology.

Such lowest classes in natural history require a teacher who can deal with each scholar, with inexhaustible patience, and lead him to consider, in a proper order, the species in their scientific arrangement; while at the same time he goes forward in the development of his power of vison and of comprehension, and in knowledge of the subject.

In such exercises the pupil of twenty years of age has no advantage over one of ten; on the other hand, the younger has, usually, much more receptive capacity, and an apprehension of things, purer and not modified by reflection.

The teacher of these elements must have the feelings and sentiments of an elementary teacher; he must be interested as much in the development of his pupil as in his science; must be able to draw up

---

defensible. See my observations (p. 140, part 1, of vol. iii. of this work) on instruction in natural knowledge at the gymnasium. So far as such studies are introduced there, however, it is naturally the duty of the university to make changes corresponding with the amount of knowledge brought from the gymnasium by the students.

* See "*History of Education*," vol. iii. part 1, p. 168.

as correct a monograph of his scholar as of a species. Of course he must not lecture, but must teach dialogically. And after this elementary instruction, higher classes must follow.

It is the business of the scholars in elementary zoology, to go, under the direction of their teacher, if not through the whole zoological collection, yet through the most important parts of it. Its system must be made known to them, not by instruction mostly oral, such as often follows a rapid display of the animals, but must be made real by thorough examination of a scientifically arranged collection; and from this actual intuition the teacher must deduce the positive verbal definitions of the various species, genera, &c., as well as by comparing them together, a knowledge of the differences of the same.

The second class in zoology will study comparative anatomy; using, at first, Linnæus' Descriptive Zoology, and afterward Cuvier's "*Anatomie Comparée;*" the knowledge of the more important species of animals being now supposed. It is now also time to begin with organic chemistry and physiology.

The elementary instruction in mineralogy begins with a knowledge of the species by their external distinctions. Among other things, there is now necessary a knowledge of the forms and families of crystals, which can scarcely be gained at all except by the eye; and skill in recognizing them in the minerals themselves. From this elementary class different paths lead to the higher classes. The physical knowledge of the crystals leads to pure mathematical crystallography; mineralogical chemistry seems as necessary a complement to knowledge of the exteriors of minerals, as in organic chemistry, to descriptive zoology and botany. In this elementary course on mineralogy the scholar also receives the beginning of the more important departments of physical instruction, as electricity, magnetism, optics; and it is likewise a necessary preparatory school for geognosy.

Botany must also begin with the simplest acquaintance with the principal genera and species; to proceed either on the Linnæan system, or by a selection of the most distinct families of plants. Excursions and the botanic garden must be made use of at the same time. In the garden, all the species of one genus should stand together, as far as possible; and the scientific arrangement should be clearly distinguishable by the eye. A plan of the garden should also be lithographed, giving the genera as they stand on each bed. With this plan in hand, and with the names of the species on each bed, the pupil can easily make his own way, even with little aid from his teacher.

The elementary course on botany should last from planting-time till seed-time; to instruct the pupil not only in the recognition and description of the species, &c., but in the development of plants, from their sprouting until the ripening of the seed.

In higher classes, the chemistry, physiology, and geography of plants will be taught.

Elementary instruction in mineralogy, botany, and zoology should be, in my opinion, as simple as possible; and not perplexed by premature hastening into branches which belong further forward. For example, mineralogical chemistry, as I have remarked, must follow descriptive mineralogy, which relates to external characteristics. The former, without actual chemical operations, is nothing but a description of operations, a statement of analytical results—nothing but mere words. Any competent person will testify that it is out of the question to pursue a thorough course of mineralogy and one of mineralogical chemistry at the same time. A brief anecdote will show why the former must precede. A certain chemist published an analysis of zircon, which gave a constituent not before found in zircon. A second distinguished analyzer, therefore, examined a number of zircons, but could discover not an atom of this constituent. This incomprehensible enigma was very simply solved, by the fact, to wit, that the mineral analyzed by the first chemist was not zircon; he having misnamed the mineral for want of thorough mineralogical knowledge. A correct determination of the mineral must precede the analysis of it; mineralogy must precede mineralogical chemistry. In the same way the anatomist might err if he had misnamed the animal he was anatomizing, from lack of knowledge of descriptive zoology.

VII. Students' Songs.

Popular songs, which are extensively sung at any period, reveal the tendencies of the people. "Out of the abundance of the heart the mouth speaketh." Sometimes these are sad remembrances of a greater and better time past, lamentations over its transientness, longing after a better future, or joyous pleasure in the present. The unfortunate years of the French tyranny were already approaching when the Germans sang, "Life let us cherish, while yet the taper glows;" under the domination of Napoleon, was to be heard, in every street, "It can not always thus remain;" but, in 1815, the victors sang Schenkendorf's song, "How to me thy pleasures beckon, after slavery, after strife."

If we had a complete collection of the songs which the German poets have sung at different times, we should obtain profound views of the condition of the universities at those times. A chief chapter in the history of these songs includes the years of the war, 1813 to 1815.

In earlier times the students sang songs animated with the spirit of the Burschen: beer, tobacco, idleness, dueling, were celebrated in a vulgar manner; and some most obscene songs, even, were in vogue. The reverse of these indecent songs were lamentably sentimental ones, in which the singer, putting himself in the future, looks back, with sorrow, to the pleasant life of the universities, and paints the Philister-life as quite the opposite of his lost academical paradise. There were some of them which celebrated the sickness which follows a day spent in dissipation.

I am not exaggerating; the Commers-book contains my evidence. For instance, how often, among others, were numerous reckless and abandoned parodies on the psalm, *Ecce quam bonum* (Behold how good, &c.), sung.

The pitiable young men of that period had no pure and lofty ideal; no patriotism nor religion inspired them. It was only here and there that a better spirit prevailed in their songs,—where and how could it have been displayed in their lives? In the "Country's Father" they sang:

> "Life and goods
> For thee to give
> Are we all as one agreed,
> All prepared to die we're found,
> Fearing not the deadly wound,
> If the fatherland hath need."

But it must not be supposed that this stanza proceeded from the same feelings with the watchword of the war of freedom, "With God, for king and fatherland." Very distant was any such conception, in a time when there was no opportunity to die for their country except by enlisting in a standing army; a most frightful thing to a student. The display of aspiration after the patriotic purpose of this poem, then, must be circumscribed by the narrow limits of student-life, where the singers with drawn swords, and a row of hats stuck on them, thought little enough of fighting or dying for their fatherland. The *Præses* of the meeting sung:

> "Then bring him up; his head I'll decorate
> By laying sword-stroke on his pate.
> Hail to our brother! long live he,
> And hounds-foot, who insults him, be."

But we hear nothing of the *Dulce et decorum pro patria mori*, and are transferred from the atmosphere of holy and noble patriotism to the wild, unholy sphere of the Comment; to the sphere of a false honor, recognized neither by Christians nor heathens, and, least of all, by God.

With the sad year of 1806 began a new period for the universities; by the awakening, in many students, of a deep and pitiful love for their poor enslaved country. This was proved by the engagement of all the students to whom it was possible, in the war, in 1813.

At their return to the universities, in 1815, there came into vogue a new and loftier class of songs. Most of the previous student songs were disused, and their places supplied by patriotic songs by Körner, Schenkendorf, Arndt, and others. The same young men who had fought in the battles of the war of freedom, sung these songs with enthusiasm, and handed them down to subsequent generations. The influence of the Turners and of the Burschenschaft was prominent in causing this state of things.

The song-books published just after the war are very characteristic. One published by Binzer and Methfessel, in 1818, contained "ancient and modern student songs, drinking songs, patriotic songs, and songs for war and for the Turners." But it was a heterogeneous mixture. Many of the old student songs, such as "Ça ça, we've feasted," or, "Crambamboli," seem much too vulgar by the side of such lofty and heroic ones, inspired by patriotism, as "A higher sound is heard," "Sad foreboding, deadly weary," and "In a good hour are we united." The butterfly was still in the *pupa* condition. Still, some of the older songs admitted are inspired by nobler feelings, and express a noble love of country; as, for instance, "Place you, brothers, in a circle."

I need scarcely say that such men as Methfessel and Binzer would not admit any indecent songs, or even any in the least ambiguous; but they adhered too closely to university traditions in admitting songs there for many years.

In the same year, 1818, when Methfessel's book appeared, a collection was published at Berlin, entitled "*German Songs for Young and Old.*" This does not profess to be a Commers-book, and the editors were, therefore, not tempted to insert those weatherbeaten old songs; but the collection deserves mention here, because made by Turners and members of the Burschenschaft, and in great reputation among the students. It included the best popular and patriotic songs, especially such as related to the glorious war of freedom. There were also some choice religious hymns. These, indeed, could not properly be omitted; for if the motto of the Turners, "Bold, free, joyous, and pious," was true, they must naturally publish, not only, "bold, free, and joyous" songs, but "pious" ones also.

If this patriotic spirit had but continued to be more and more profoundly inwrought with Christianity! But the times were not ready for this, and therefore the young men fell into error. Sand's fearful crime, as we have seen, was a source of incalculable evils to the universities.

There next followed a period during which there was an end of innocent songs and singing; a period during which one part of the young men was absorbed in troubled melancholy and gloomy brooding over the future of the country. During this appeared, in 1819 and 1820, A. Follenius' "*Free Voices of Bold Youth.*"

These songs mark a turning-point. On one hand, they belong to the past, the period of the war of freedom; as, for instance, a number of songs by Körner, Schenkendorf, and Arndt. On the other hand, the writers, despairing of the present, turned their eyes toward a presumed better future, for whose introduction they called enthusiastically, and with a demoniac force in their poetry. There is no more despair about foreign dominion. Chivalry, empire, revolution, popular republicanism, freedom, and equality, rush confusedly about together in their enthusiastic compositions, elements most various, and even most inconsistent. Even Christianity is drawn into the elemental storm; that is, the name, for the thing itself is distorted and deformed beyond recognition.

Excellent melodies doubled the influence of these songs; their wretched convulsive perplexities were, as it were, thus gilded over.*

While this collection had a character in part only too distinct, that which succeeded it was without one. It contained songs of the most various periods, and most various and even opposite character.

After the year 1830, however, new elements are found in the song-books; radical songs, namely, by Herwegh and similar poets, marked, not by the earlier stormy poetical power, but by a profoundly bitter, and even malicious character. The confusion was increased by the addition to the previous enthusiastically patriotic songs, characterless cosmopolitan ones were added. We find Arndt's "What is the German Fatherland?" and "What do the Trumpets sound?" Körner's

"This is no war to which the Crowns are knowing,
A crusade is it—'tis a holy war," &c.

And in the same collection we find the Marseillaise! Did not these catholic-minded editors, then, know who are meant, in the Marseillaise, by the

"féroces soldats
(Qui) viennent jusque dans vos bras,
Egorger vos fils, vos compagnes—"

by the "horde d'esclaves, de traîtres," &c.? And if they did know, what is the name which their insertion of it deserves?

---

* For a correct opinion as to these songs, see the account of Karl Follenius and his friends, *ante*, pp. 111, 125, &c.

With patriotism disappeared also lofty purity of morals and piety. The ancient vulgar songs which the Burschenschaft had driven away, make their appearance again in the modern song-books, with additional ones of the same kind. The beastly indecency of the ancient ones is, however, most prominent; and becomes doubly reckless and bad.

At a very recent period have been put forth, by students' societies, song-books which adhere to Christian and to strict moral principles. In some incomprehensible way, however, have crept into these books, among songs of the most beautiful character, a few stray ones of a diametrically opposite character. It is much to be wished that this error could be cured in a new edition, and the appearance of evil removed.

FAREWELL.

A heavy responsibility rests on every writer on pedagogy; a responsibility which increases if his book has any influence on actual life.

May this work of mine, and especially the latter part of it, give pain to no reader. I have written nothing without consideration and reflection; yet I can say, with the psalmist, "Lord, who can understand his errors? Cleanse thou me from secret faults."

And I say this, even in reference to those busy years of inquiry which I passed at Breslau and Halle, after the war of freedom; especially during that wretched period which came upon the universities after Sand's unrighteous deed. And still, during the most friendly and open intercourse with loved students, I was obliged to keep silence respecting many bitter truths, which, however, if said, would only have awakened or increased ill-feeling.

I hope that that severe discipline taught me moderation and religious modesty, which will prevent me from inconsiderate haste, even in statements most interesting to my heart.

It was my repulsive and troublesome task to describe the frightful condition of the life of the students, as it appeared, especially during the seventeenth century, in the most frightful period of the history of our country. With correspondingly greater pleasure I considered the many efforts which, at the beginning of this century, and during and after the war of freedom, were made for good purposes, by the students. During the first part of this time, there prevailed an active and laborious attention to science, and in the ancient and modern classics; and the young were also deeply interested in the profound and poetical study of natural philosophy. Love of their country, however, was asleep, although afterward only too sadly awakened; Christianity wore the color of a poetical romance, its moral side being more out of sight; and the life succeeding that at the university, was thought of only unwillingly.

During the second part of this period, prevailed the powerful patriotism and strict morality kindled by the war of freedom. The romantic element, on the other hand, decreased; and Christianity appeared no longer in the character of romance, but rather suffered the *chlorosis* of a moralizing rationalism.

During about the last twenty years, the youth of the universities have passed into a third stage; I refer to the associations which have been founded under the name of Christian.

A holy courage is needed to serve and contend under that name.

> "A coward knave, who still doth stand,
> When 'Forward!' doth his chief command."

A students' association which professes that Christianity is its chief aim, has indeed aimed high. But the higher its purpose, so much the more earnest and efficient does its life become. May they always be thoughtful of the warning words:

> "Let our thoughts still watchful be,
> If our hearts for truth shall care,
> If our souls depend on Thee,
> If we *seem*, or if we *are*."

This is not said in the sense of a false pietism; it is an urgent admonition to do the truth (John iii. 21).

It should not be supposed that the previous noble aims of the youth of the universities have entirely perished, or that they are to be reckoned of a grade inferior to the magnificence of Christian enterprise. This would be altogether to misunderstand Christianity. Love of country will never be repressed, but sanctified and enlightened by Christianity. For my love of my country is the first element of love to my people; to the people among whom God has caused me to be born, to be useful and helpful to my neighbor; it is my preparatory school for eternity.

In like manner it would be a pseudo-pietistic barbarism to reject science and art; they should be purified and sanctified and made an acceptable offering to the Lord, from whom come all good gifts, and likewise all natural endowments, so far as they are good.

My love to many members of these Christian associations at the universities, upon which I heartily ask God's blessing, would not suffer me to refrain from these observations. May He preserve them, in this world of investigation, preserve them from vanity and love of life, and grant them heroic minds in the difficult age in which we live, and strengthen and establish them.

To those dear young men who preserve, in the depths of their hearts, a love to their fatherland, I would say, preserve this love, and labor with reference to the nation. But should iniquity so increase as to force us to take up arms, then fight bravely to the death for your beloved fatherland, as the German youth fought in the war of freedom. But remain ever mindful, that after this brief life, you must journey to another fatherland, a heavenly. Love not, therefore, the temporal fatherland, as if it were eternal. As you have been instructed in Christianity from your youth, you know what is requisite to attain the heavenly citizenship.

Youths who, like myself and my student companions, devote themselves especially to science, should apply themselves with such industry as Bacon requires from those who devote themselves to philosophy. A superficial study of philosophy, he says, leads from God; a thorough one, to Him. Toward Him, because it leads not only to knowledge of divine things, but to self-knowledge; to perception that our knowledge is only a fragmentary collection. Every right-minded investigator must sooner or later humbly confess, "How vast is that of which I know nothing!" Then awakes the longing, with winged speed to comprehend those secrets which the most laborious application will not enable us, within this temporal life, to comprehend. Weary of our earthly tabernacle, we long for the freedom of the children of God; and sigh, with Claudius,

"O thou land, the truthful and the real,
Thou that dost eternal be,
How I long to see thy bright ideal—
How I long for thee!"

XIII. Authorities referred to in Raumer's German Universities.

Arnoldt, Complete History of the University of Konigsberg, (*Ausführliche Historie der Königsberger Universität,*) 1746. 2 parts.

Becmann, Memoranda Relating to the University of Frankfurt. (*Memoranda Francofurtana,*) 1676.

Notices of the University of Frankfurt, (*Notitia Universitatis Francofurtanæ,*) 1707.

Bonicke, Outlines of a History of the University of Wurzburg, (*Grundriss einer Geschichte von der Universität zu Wüzburg,*) 1782. 2 parts.

Conring, H., On Academical Antiquities, (*De Antiquitatibus Academicus,*) 1739.

Dieterici, Historical and Statistical Accounts of the Prussian Universities, (*Geschichtliche und Statistische Nachrichten über die Universitäten im Preussischen Staate,*) 1836.

Eichstadt, Annals of the University of Jena, (*Annales Academiæ Jenensis,*) 1823.

Engelhardt, The University of Erlangen, from 1743 to 1843, (*Die Universität Erlangen von* 1743, *bis* 1843.)

Gadendam and others. History of the University of Erlangen, (*Historia Academiæ Fridericianæ Erlangensis,*) 1744.

Gesner, J. M., History of the University of Göttingen, (*De Academia Georgia Augusta quæ Göttingæ est,*) 1737.

Gretschel. University of Leipzig, (*Die Universität Leipzig,*) 1830.

Grohmann, Annals of the University of Wittenberg, (*Annalen der Universität Wittenberg,*) Meissen, 1801. 3 parts.

Hausser, History of the Rhenish Palatinate, (*Geschichte der Rheinischen Pfalz,*) 1845. 2 parts.

Haupt, J. L., The Landmanschaften on the Burschenschaft, (*Landsmannschaften und Burschenschaft.*)

Henke, The University of Helmstadt in the 16th Century, (*Die Universität Helmstädt im* 16 *Jahrhundert,*) 1833.

Hoffbaur, History of the University of Halle, (*Geschichte der Universität zu Halle,*) 1805.

Heumann, Library of University History, (*Bibliotheca Historica Academica.*)

Justi, Outlines of a History of the University at Marburg, (*Grundzüge einer Geschichte der Universität zu Marburg,*) 1827.

Klupfel, History and Description of the University of Tubingen, (*Geschichte und Beschreibung der Universität Tübingen,*) 1849.

Koch, The Prussian Universities, (*Die Preussischen Universitäten,*) 1839. 2 vols.

Lotichius, Oration on the Present Fatal Evils in the Universities of Germany, Delivered at the University of Rinteln, 1631, (*Oratio super fatalibus hoc Temp. Academiarum in Germania periculis, recitata in Academia Rintelensi,*) 1631.

Mederer, Annals of the University of Ingolstadt, commenced by V. Rotmarus and Joh. Engerdus, and continued by Mederer, (*Annales Ingolstadiensis Academiæ inchoaverunt V. Rotmarus et Joh. Engerdus, continuavit Mederer,*) 1782.

Meiners, History of the Establishment and Growth of the Universities, (*Geschichte der Entstehung und Entwicklung der hohen Schulen,*) 1802. 4 vols.

Meiners, Organization and Administration of the German Universities, (*Ueber Verfassung und Verwaltung Deutscher Universitäten,*) 2 vols., 1801 and 1802.

MEYFART, CHRISTIAN RECOLLECTIONS, (*Christliche Erinnerung*,) 1636. See p. 54.

MOHL, R., HISTORICAL ACCOUNT OF THE MANNERS AND CONDUCT OF THE TUBINGEN STUDENTS DURING THE 16TH CENTURY, (*Geschichtliche Nachweisungen über die Sitten und das Betragen der Tübingen Studierenden während des 16 Jahrhunderts*,) 1840.

MONUMENTS OF THE HISTORY OF THE UNIVERSITY OF PRAGUE, (*Monumenta Historica Universitätis Carolo-Ferdinandeæ Pragensis.*) Vol. 1., Part 1, 1830. Part 2, 1832.

MOTSCHMANN, LITERARY HISTORY OF ERFURT, (*Erfordia Literata.*) 3 vols., 1729—1748.

PALACKY, HISTORY OF BOHEMIA, (*Geschichte von Böhmen*,) 1842. (Part 2 of vol. 2.)

PIDERIT, HISTORY OF THE UNIVERSITY OF RINTELN, (*Geschichte der Universität Rinteln*,) 1842.

REHTMEIER, CHRONICLE OF BRUNSWICK-LUNENBURG, (*Braunschweig-Lüneburgsche Chronica.*) 1722.

ROMMEL, PHILIP, LANDGRAVE OF HESSE, (*Philipp Landgraf von Hessen*,) 1830.

SAVIGNY, HISTORY OF ROMAN LAW IN THE MIDDLE AGES, (*Geschichte des Römischen Rechts im Mittelalter*,) 3d vol., 1832. (2d ed.)

SCHLIKENRIEDER, CHRONOLOGY AND DOCUMENTS OF THE UNIVERSITY OF VIENNA, (*Chronologia Diplomatica Universitätis Vindobonensis*,) 1753. Second part by Zeisl.

SCHOTTGEN, HISTORY OF PENNALISM, (*Historie des Pennalwesens*,) 1747.

SCHREIBER, FREIBURG IN THE BREISGAU (*Freiburg im Breisgau*,) 1825.

SCHUPPIUS, BALTHAZAR, WORKS, (*Schriften.*)

SCHWAB, LIST OF RECTORS OF THE UNIVERSITY OF HEIDELBERG, FOR FOUR CENTURIES, (*Quatuor Seculorum Syllabus Rectorum qui . . . in Academia Heidelbergensi Magistratum Academicum Gesserunt*,) 1786.

TOMEK, HISTORY OF THE UNIVERSITY OF PRAGUE, (*Geschichte der Prager Universität*,) 1849.

WESSELHOFT, R., GERMAN YOUTH IN THE LATE BURSCHENSCHAFTEN AND TURNING SOCIETIES, (*Teutsche Jugend in weiland Burschenschaften und Turngemeinden*,) 1828.

WILL, HISTORY AND DESCRIPTION OF THE UNIVERSITY OF ALTORF, (*Geschichte und Beschreibung der Universität Altorf*,) 1795.

ZEISL, *See* SCHLIKENRIEDER.

INDEX

TO

RAUMER'S GERMAN UNIVERSITIES.

www.ingramcontent.com/pod-product-compliance
Lightning Source LLC
LaVergne TN
LVHW010250110826
845151LV00004B/1432

* 9 7 8 1 4 2 5 5 2 2 7 9 7 *